WHAT PEOPLE ARE

Revolutionary Keywo

Ian Parker's Keywords are an extremely useful tool for activists who want to orient themselves among the various words circulating in left discourses. With his clear and accessible prose, Parker manages to successfully combine theoretical and practical concerns, never losing sight of the goal: transforming the world through political practice.
Cinzia Arruzza, New School for Social Research, New York

Ian Parker's *Revolutionary Keywords* is an innovative and rigorous analytic for the contemporary left whose passionate discourses sometimes lose the theoretical clarity that distinguishes Marx's own writings. *Revolutionary Keywords* takes philosophical risks by unlayering the conceptual densities of such complex concepts as antagonism, normalcy, precarity, and accelerationism. In laying bare each concept, Parker provides the philosophico-historical lines of its formation and situates it within its broad social conditions. The book is a pioneering convergence of activist writings and philosophical inquiry.
Teresa L. Ebert, author of *The Task of Cultural Critique*

Revolutionary Keywords for a New Left

Revolutionary Keywords for a New Left

Ian Parker

Winchester, UK
Washington, USA

First published by Zero Books, 2017
Zero Books is an imprint of John Hunt Publishing Ltd., Laurel House, Station Approach,
Alresford, Hants, SO24 9JH, UK
office1@jhpbooks.net
www.johnhuntpublishing.com
www.zero-books.net

For distributor details and how to order please visit the 'Ordering' section on our website.

Text copyright: Ian Parker 2016

ISBN: 978 1 78535 642 1
978 1 78535 643 8 (ebook)
Library of Congress Control Number: 2016961111

A CIP catalogue record for this book is available from the British Library.

Design: Stuart Davies

Printed and bound by CPI Group (UK) Ltd, Croydon, CR0 4YY, UK

We operate a distinctive and ethical publishing philosophy in all
areas of our business, from our global network of authors to
production and worldwide distribution.

CONTENTS

Acknowledgements

Thanks to those who participated in the 'AntiCapitalist Initiative' event to launch the third edition of *Changing the Fragments* in Manchester, and in the reading group for *Dangerous Liaisons*, two places that made me begin to think seriously about new keywords, and to participants in the 'feminist revolutionary left' reading group that worked through some key texts, and thanks to comrades in different campaigns and groups, and those who responded to online first drafts of these different keywords, and thanks to Erica who read them all.

Introduction

This book is about how we turn our politics into words and into action, and why some words we use to describe what we are doing are key. These keywords in revolutionary politics have undergone some rapid change. I describe some of those changes, and fifty revolutionary keywords in the course of the book. I didn't realise how important this was until quite recently, and it is absolutely crucial to our attempt to link the many different movements that are now speaking out against exploitation and oppression.

When I first came into revolutionary politics, I couldn't understand what my 'comrades', as I learned to call them, were talking about most of the time. The words they used were unfamiliar, but bit-by-bit I learnt to use those words. In the process, I often forgot how strange they sounded to those who were outside the left, to those we wanted to win over to join our campaigns or our organisation. I would notice how strange these words were when I encountered comrades from rival groups who used the terms in slightly different ways. More so, I would be thrown into confusion when those terms were directly challenged by activists in other political movements who objected to some of our assumptions about the world that were carried along with those ways of speaking about it.

Some of the most disturbing objections were made by feminists who seemed to have their own quite different and parallel sets of terms that cut up the world in a quite different way to the one I had been schooled in. And when I say schooled, I mean how I was being taught to see the world through the networks of terms that my particular revolutionary tradition of politics used, taught through educational classes where we were taken through the Marxist classics and then, sometimes, tried to link class analysis with other kinds of progressive politics. That is, we attempted to link with the kinds of anti-racist and feminist politics that we defined as 'progressive', and in the process we also repeated what we had learnt about what was 'progressive' and what was 'reactionary', what we could tolerate and what we wanted to avoid.

I learnt virtually nothing about politics or sociology or geography from my own schooldays. I read a lot of political material later on though, and had much more time to read when I was unemployed. By that time I had joined a left organisation. Some of the material I read, a lot of it actually, consisted of internal discussion bulletins which were, I later realised, closely modelled on academic political books and articles. There were some left journals that straddled the boundary between academic and political activism, or at least they pretended to do that, and what I was learning to do was also actually how to read academic political theory. Some of the editions of writings of our political leaders published by revolutionary organisations repeated definitions of unfamiliar terms, and I eventually quite enjoyed coming across a familiar term and scanning down to the bottom of the page to find the same definition of it pasted in again for us by the editorial team.

My sense of confusion was slowly replaced by a comforting sense, that as I become part of a revolutionary tradition I could recognise how the words that held it together worked; then I could appreciate how flexibly they could be applied to new situations. In my case I had joined a group tracing a direct line back to the Russian Revolution in 1917, but it was not an orthodox straight-edge Trotskyist group. It was a bit more 'academic' than the other groups – that was the accusation levelled against it by our rivals – and more open. Detailed political-economic analyses of countries I had never heard of would be presented in line with a political language that was always reassuringly familiar. It is that very familiarity with the same old language of the left, however, that is now part of the problem we face as we try to make sense of the world and work out what we should do to change it.

What held this language in place? The easiest most obvious answer to this question would be that our Marxist vocabulary was the most accurate way of describing reality. For many years I was happy with that way of using the terms I'd learnt in the branch educational classes and by reading the left press. It was a time when there were fifty-seven varieties of Trotskyist politics, and every article was an opportunity to sharpen our analytic skills. That's what we all did, and while we shared our misunderstanding of the arguments we would correct each other's versions of reality so that they either came into line with each other, or we could at least recognise those lines that were deviating from the right one.

When I spent a little time away from my comrades and then joined up with them again a couple of years later I was able quickly to pick up the thread of the arguments again. It was a bit like spending time away from your family and then returning to it in a time tunnel. That was because the keywords they used didn't change much, even if the political situations they applied them to were very different. Then, in the 1980s there were some big changes inside some of the organisations that split and mutated and merged with each other again, some changes for the better during which some of them were really trying to make sense of feminist politics. There were some links with sexual politics with the appearance of more radical lesbian and gay movements, and then with anti-racist politics developing from independence movements and the growing confidence of minority communities here among us. Green politics began to shake things up even further, and it became clearer that those different movements were using very different terminology from us to describe their work and change the world.

These changes were happening around the world, and so the new slogans and new words and phrases we used to describe reality and intervene in it had more of an impact in some organ-isations than others. The new keywords that have emerged over the last fifty years, since the first meetings of the women's liber-ation movement in the late 1960s and then with the impact of other kinds of radical politics, caught on more quickly in groups that worked closely with what we called our 'sister organisations' in the same international political tradition in other countries. But there were analyses and debates happening in Black politics, for example, that weren't finding their way into our discussions, and we were still struggling to find a language to link the different kinds of politics that appeared on our radar.

A dramatic crisis hit some British revolutionary groups about five years ago, groups faced with accusations of sexual violence. They thought that closing in on themselves and using the old bureaucratic procedures to close down public debate would fix it. One group came in for the most attention once the press got hold of the story, but similar accusations were being made in other organisations. And although this seemed to be a local problem, something peculiar to the British far left, the international links these groups had meant that the protests about what was happening spread and input into what could be done also came from around the world.

There were purges and splits and new false starts and plenty of recrimination. You'll read about some of that in this book. One consequence of these appalling events inside the left was that many new activists coming from different revolutionary tradi-tions, including from ecological, feminist and Black politics, are often allergic to joining any kind of left group, particularly those groups that continued to operate as parties in line with how they thought the Bolshevik Party ran itself in Russia in 1917. Some groups even thought that the 'party' was so important that they immediately knew how to decide if there had been a revolution in another country. If there had not been revolutionary leadership it could not have happened; no party, no revolution.

I'd like to say that these doctrinal bits of nonsense are caricatures, and that things didn't happen like that. But the truth is that
they did. And I can well understand why a new generation of
activists steers clear of the old leaders and their bureaucratically-
run little groups. I'm often tempted to avoid them too, and to
avoid the way some groups trail after other bureaucratic politicians or trades unionists who have made a career out of left-talk
but who then click the apparatus into action to stop anything
really changing. But yet, the revolutionary left has learnt lessons
in the past, and it can do so again, and to help it learn those
lessons we have to engage with the more open groups, work with
them to develop a different kind of revolutionary practice.

Someone said to me recently that it is pointless talking to the
old far-left groups about feminism and sexuality and disability
and 'race' because they don't really care. This isn't true, that's not
the problem. I know from my continued involvement with my
old comrades, from those who have stuck with it over the years
as well as those who have recently joined left organisations, they
do care. For all of their failings, these groups have kept a revolutionary socialist tradition of struggle alive since 1917, and re-
energised that struggle after 1967. For all that they are annoying
with their manoeuvring and stale slogans, they have been at the
core of some of the most important social movements in the last
fifty years.

There is a wealth of experience connecting theory with action
that we would, I think, be foolish not to work with. The mode of
organisation of quite a few of these groups has changed, and we
do need some kind of organisation to keep going and to be collectively strong enough to overthrow this miserable political
economic system. We still need those organised groups. The
problem is that they don't get the new terms that inspire and
structure today's revolutionary movements. This book comes
from the attempts to articulate the new politics, for them as well
as for new activists.

5

In the past fifty years the 'left' has had to learn about new ways of organising itself to take on board the politics of different social movements, and that has also meant changing the way we describe what we are up against and where we are going. New activists often question taken-for-granted assumptions made by the post-1917 left, even questioning the validity of the 'left-right' spectrum in politics. This book holds to that spectrum but takes seriously the deep and difficult task of articulating socialist politics with new forms of politics from Black, feminist, queer, ecological and disability activism.

We need to key into the way people who are sick of the history of the 'left' and its bad practice around the world are now trying to develop new ways of speaking about exploitation and oppression. One problem with the transformation of language in our politics revolves around the conditions in which we work on the link between language and action. There are two ways we are under pressure to change our language. The first way causes anger and anxiety on the left, and it has the effect of isolating us even further. That pressure comes from the defeat of struggles against exploitation and oppression, the marginalisation of alternative ideas and caricatures of socialism and communism in the media. Some of the academic language used by ex-left and anti-left writers feeds that marginalisation, and the claims that we now live in some kind of post-political world, a world where the old modern politics that began at the time of the French Revolution back in 1879 are irrelevant, make things worse. That kind of pressure is intensified today in neoliberal capitalism; that is the kind of capitalism that rolls back state welfare provision and pretends to set the market free and make each individual responsible for fighting for themselves. Today's neoliberal language of individual 'freedom', fake freedom in which we are divided from each other, is poisonous for our collective struggle to make sense of how this world works and how to act to change it.

But there is another way we are under pressure to change our language that also causes anger and anxiety in the leadership of the little old left-wing sects. That second kind of pressure is something we must connect with and respond to. Every social struggle in history has forced people to rethink how they view the world, and how they describe it. When the exploited and oppressed speak about their experience and mobilise to change their conditions of life they always discover that the language of the rulers is not enough, that the dominant language shuts them out. New terms are invented, and there is a transformation of language at the very same time as politics is transformed. That is exactly what has happened with the emergence of feminism, and in the voices of Black feminists. They demand that we change our language, demand that we change, so that we can make this world a place where we can all speak and mobilise. Some of us are even speaking differently now about the relationships we have with each other as part of a system of life in which we are part of the ecology of our planet, and the language of ecosocialism helps us do that.

We can learn from those struggles, from different political perspectives, but only if we also take seriously that there are always real social forces, of the feminist movement, of the movements of the oppressed who are also too often silenced in the kind of mainstream left struggle which pretends to maintain what it thinks of as the unity of the 'working class' or 'the left' or, most often, simply their own organisation. Some organisations are closed off to this and will insist on speaking in the same way they always have, but some have opened themselves to the progressive radical pressure from social movements so that we can better take on the corrupt forces of neoliberalism.

So, this is how I put the book together. I noticed when an unfamiliar word appeared from the Black feminist movement, for example, and how my comrades struggled to make sense of it, and how they reframed it in their old political language. Then I would use that word in a way closer to how it was meant to operate, but instead of simply explaining it I would put it to work on a different topic. Then we could see better what uses it has, how it takes us forward in understanding what is going on, and creates alliances. This book is composed from an accumulating set of 'keywords' that were originally posted online. I got feedback from inside groups and from those who still shun revolutionary parties, and gathered suggestions for new terms, until I accumulated fifty of them. I hope, in the process, that somewhere along the line the old left were able to get it, or at least to get some of it. You will notice that I have not critiqued the keywords. Rather, my task was to engage constructively with them, to show how they work. That is the priority, and any constructive critique also needs to engage with how they link together. I show how they can be mapped in the essay at the end of the book, and there are pointers to critical discussion of these keywords in the further reading.

I've gone through the original postings about the fifty keywords again, and although they are set out in alphabetical order in the book, I've reworked the different definitions and applications of them so you can read the book through from the beginning to the end, or jump around and read each piece separately. These fifty little pieces in the book are the bare bones of what we need. Then I try to flesh out some more of the context, to show the context that links them together in the longer piece at the end of the book. If you are vegetarian or vegan and didn't like that metaphor of 'bones' and 'flesh' much, then you already have an idea how important language is. If you are not, then there will for sure be other bits in this book where you'll stop and think, think but wait a minute, that way of putting it carries too many bad old assumptions about the way the world works. You get the point. Language is woven into reality. How we speak and write about things makes a difference. But the real difference will come when we put these arguments into practice. Digest and enjoy.

These fifty pieces on different keywords are about different kinds of practice, but they now need to be linked together and we need to do something different alongside and inside the revolutionary groups to really make them work for us, for all of us. That's what the last longer piece is also about. I wrote it for my old comrades and for you, new comrades. I hope you like the book, and argue with it, and take seriously the overall line of argument for a new politics that connects these new revolutionary keywords so you also find more for yourself. Take it forward and do that to change the left to change the world.

Academicisation

Academicisation turns practice into abstracted knowledge. Concepts for critique, even when they are mapped out as a series of new keywords for political practice, always risk being turned into 'academic' concepts. Configuring the world in a way that the academic will understand it not only comforts the academic, academicisation also fuels the fantasy that somewhere outside deadening and self-enclosed academic discourse there is a real world which might give it life. The fantasy of some kind of real event outside the university functions as a consolation. Much academic research wants to reassure itself that it is relevant to the world outside, and so there is often a search for real events that might challenge, mobilise and thereby provide a reason for the existence of the radical academic gazing earnestly and romantically out at the world through their office window.

This problem is one consequence of the rise of the universities over the last century as places for critique, and over that time other places for conceptual-political work and for political education have been marginalised. The Workers' Educational Association (WEA) founded in the UK in 1903, for example, was a site of learning and critique that was grounded in political practice, but bit-by-bit in many cities WEA courses have been displaced by colleges and universities which at one moment provide public lectures in line with their own 'outreach' programmes and at the next close them down again because those courses are not profitable. The Plebs' League founded in 1908 was another attempt to provide independent working-class education which directly confronted the early stages of academicisation at Ruskin College in Oxford, but that college failed to prevent the university from incorporating it, and then turning out generations of trades union bureaucrats (as well as some activists who were able to stay true to the struggle).

As knowledge becomes incorporated into the university sector, whether that sector is public or private, a bureaucratisation of teaching and learning takes place, bureaucratisation which divides 'experts' employed full time from their 'students'. Those students will either be thrown into the marketplace to sell their labour power after their course – and they might also hope to sell a bit of intellectual labour power after they have learnt something – or they might aim to become little masters themselves, to become academics. A hierarchy of knowledge is thereby mapped on to other kinds of hierarchy so that men, for example, are positioned as the ones who will explain, as a form of 'mansplaining', what they know to those who can't possibly know so well (which is a stereotypically masculine mainstream academic assumption that feminist 'standpoint' approaches then threaten).

Political economy has always, of course, entailed the accumulation of intellectual capital. Students from the universities have always built up 'cultural capital', for example, when they have done work for free in the 'community', and they have then been able to cash this capital out when they get highly-paid jobs that value their 'experience'. Just as capitalism encloses natural resources so that what we collectively produce is captured and sold back to us for profit, so it encloses intellectual resources. The move by large private companies into assessment of academic work based on the Massive Open Online Courses (MOOCS) which are provided free by some universities is just the latest version of this enclosure of resources. These 'open' courses are the latest feeding ground for publishers who rely on the commodification of knowledge. This knowledge can be marketed to those inside the academic world, and to those outside it who are positioned as vicarious academics.

This leads to admiration by some activists and resentment by others, to either an unthinking valorisation of academic knowledge or an understandable suspicion that it is irrelevant. It does look irrelevant when the academics spend most of their time inside the university, and when theoretical 'concepts' merely link to each other rather than to practice. And the demand that the concepts should be written down for publication increases the risk of 'abstraction', ripping ideas out of context and turning them into a shape that fits with the university curriculum.

This is a problem for the new left that is trying to take on board feminist and postcolonial arguments, for example, and that is trying to think through how those new concepts can be articulated with revolutionary Marxism and what the new concepts actually do in politics. We have an institutional problem here bound up with the academic imperative to publish in journals or books, and that institutional problem is embedded in a political-economic problem of the abstraction and commodification of ideas. Different dimensions of oppression, of class, sex and 'race' are intensified by this academicisation, even at the same moment as spaces inside the university are occasionally seized and used by activists. And there is another trap that also needs to be worked through, which is that the flip side of the problem of radical academics being disconnected from practice is that they sometimes imagine that the solution to that disconnection is to make an immediate direct link with those they romanticise as doing the real stuff outside the university.

The problem of 'academicisation' gives us a concept, a keyword through which we can now address another quite different issue. Let's shift gear for a moment and you will see some connections with the question of 'fundamentalism'. These are the terms of debate around the concept of 'critique' that has been provoked by Islamophobic anxiety about so-called 'fundamentalism' in the real world outside the university, the university which is positioned as a 'secular' space. Then the question as to whether critique is secular goes to the heart of assumptions that most political activists in the West make when they assume that language and 'discourse', including the discourse of 'critical concepts', should be analysed, explored, unpacked. One of the arguments in the 2009 exchange *Is Critique Secular?* between Talal Asad, Wendy Brown, Judith Butler and Saba Mahmood, for example, was that the dominant model of Western 'critique' is 'semiotic'; that is, the language we use to describe the world is treated as a system of signs that we can study as if it is something separate from the world itself.

That dominant semiotic model is part of a network of assumptions about the world, language and critique that stretches way beyond the university. They are assumptions that ground the unthinking response to complaints about representations of the prophet, for example, complaints that insist on making Islam conform to this semiotic model of language. If this semiotic model is right, then offensive cartoons should be seen as no more than representations, and so Muslims should just learn to get over it. But images of the prophet, for some believers at least, are not merely abstracted representations, and analysis of them is not an academic question. They are images that are woven into the lived reality of some religious communities. In fact, the network of assumptions that grounds much academic work obscures this problem, and makes it possible for scholars to assume that the university should be separate from the world, and here we come back to the problem of academicisation.

That debate over 'critique', that 'critique of critique' shows that the problem we face is itself a question of the operation of concepts as much as it is a question of practice. The link between concepts and practice is something that needs to be worked through and worked at, putting the concepts to work and assessing what they do (just as we do with the keywords in this book). Frederick Engels once argued against what he called 'shamefaced' materialism – he was using a term he picked up when he was in Manchester in the mid-nineteenth century – as a position that was happy with a materialist account but was then agnostic ('shamefaced') about what can be done with it; Engels commented that 'the proof of the pudding is in the eating'. We should not be 'shamefaced' about using concepts to theorise what we are doing, as long as we take care not to treat them as abstract concepts to be 'critiqued' as part of an academic exercise with no consequences for those who use them in practice; we should take care not to let the university eat us.

So, a concern with 'semiotics' – signs floating free of the real world – might be useful for ideology-critique in academic research, but we need some kind of materialist approach to grasp how language and images function in the world, in our practice. The critique of 'critique' thus returns us to materialist politics. Stepping back and thinking about the limits of academicisation and of critique is a necessary part of the process of doing better academic work and using critique with, rather than against the oppressed.

Accelerationism

With accelerationism we have a diagnosis of the speeding up of contemporary life. Life under capitalism is getting faster, it seems, and we are supposed to be having more fun as well as working harder while that is happening. The question is whether there is a contradiction here that we can exploit so that the acceleration of life can be ratcheted up beyond what capitalism can bear so that we break the system, or whether 'accelerationism' as a keyword for this intensification of our exploitation is a diagnoses of something that is actually enabling the system to break us.

This acceleration of the pace of life is captured and represented in the media, sometimes in the very speed of media communication itself and sometimes in reflections on the intensity of experience and the problematic link with enjoyment. An example of the latter – the link between acceleration and enjoyment – was *The Funfair*, the first play to open the new arts centre 'HOME' in Manchester in 2015, a centre that replaced 'The Cornerhouse' as venue for non-English-language films, art exhibitions and media events. *The Funfair*, which follows the disintegrating relationship of 'Cash' and 'Kazza' in an evening at the fair, also provokes the audience to reflect on transformations that have happened in the last century, between 1932, when the play was first staged in Berlin as *Kazimir und Karoline* (set in a Munich beer garden in the aftermath of the Wall Street Crash), and 2015 in post-bank crisis Manchester and in the immediate aftermath of a general election that returned a Conservative government committed to cuts in welfare spending and flanked on the right by the anti-immigrant UKIP (United Kingdom Independence Party).

The producer of the updated relocated version of the play was explicit about the political focus of the original and of the

Manchester version, which is a focus on poverty and despair and the goading of the poor by an apparatus of 'fun', the 'funfair' itself. This is an apparatus that also highlights the gap between the poor and the new rich, those who imagine they are part of the ruling class but who are still subject to the imperatives of capital. It is a rewriting of the original play that opens up the funfair, and capitalism itself, as something that seems so futile and unfair.

The playwright of the original, Ödön von Horváth, was schooled in Budapest and Vienna before moving to Berlin, his plays attacked by the Nazis. It presents caricatures speaking media clichés and phrases, who then hear themselves speak them in the silences that mark the play so they sometimes reflect on what they have said, and so the play is about contradiction and crisis. It is about change and time; both historical time and personal responses to time which divide the characters into men like 'Cash' (Kazimir in the original) desperate after losing his job the day before and women like 'Kazza' (Karoline in the original) who hopes for a better world, who better fits the bill of what most of the Labour Party leadership candidates in 2015 (all, with the exception of Jeremy Corbyn) claimed as 'aspiration'. Above and beyond that split between stereotypical masculine despair, loss of power that leads to impotent rage, and stereotypical feminine hope – a split between the genders that is intensified as economic violence is played out as sexual violence – there is another split which 'accelerationism' has keyed into. There is a split between the idea that another world is possible, perhaps even beyond the rule of capital, and the image of the carousel, the idea that we are condemned to go round in circles, and that the speed at which we move is actually locking us in the same place.

Marx and Engels caught the logic of capitalism speeding up life in their 1848 Communist Manifesto; the phrase 'all that is solid melts into air' captured the way that the vortex of innovation and search for profit dissolves existing social relationships. The sense of exhilaration and also of uncertainty and anxiety then became the leitmotif of descriptions and critiques of so-called 'postmodern' mutations of modern society, mutations that intensified what was already there at the birth of capitalism in Europe.

The 2013 'accelerationist manifesto' (co-authored by Alex Williams and Nick Srnicek) pushes at the most optimistic edge of this movement forward to the future that capital accumulation drives us into. The argument is that the 'modern' period of world history in which we now live, and in which we can locate capitalism as the political-economic apparatus, opens up a profound shift in the way we experience time itself. Our time is then the time of progress, transition and, of course, revolution. The first stage of the accelerationist argument is that, however exhausting industrial labour is, it is also enjoyable, masochistically and hysterically enjoyable, and that that enjoyment should be harnessed by revolutionary forces, intensified to break beyond the bounds set by capitalism itself. This version of Marxist analysis concerning the contradiction between the 'forces' (which must be accelerated) and the 'relations' (which hold us back) of production is to be found, for example, in the work of the ex-Marxist theorist of 'postmodernism' Jean-François Lyotard. The second stage is taken forward by figures like Antonio Negri, and linked to a more explicit 'goodbye' to what Negri called in the title of one of his books 'Mr Socialism'. Here we accelerate beyond our horizons of socialist revolution, but it is not really clear where we end up.

Against this glorification of speed – an argument which captures and perverts the idea of a 'permanent revolution' so that the revolution is merely something that energises capitalism rather than releases us from it – there are critiques of accelerationism which use the notion to diagnose something more troubling. It is something we need accelerationism itself to put a finger on, and there are two aspects of that. The first aspect is that there is, indeed, a hope for progress that is unleashed by capitalism, but that this progress is always sabotaged; the move forward turns into a roundabout, a compulsive repetition so that we spend energy getting nowhere fast, faster and faster. There is no future. In this way the acceleration of the speed of our lives under capitalism is revealed to be rather a kind of 'frenetic stand-still'. And, the second aspect, that frenetic standstill of life under capitalism is intensified in academic theoretical work, in the fervid imaginations of those desperately urgent to find an escape from capitalism, and so desperate that they move too fast, and end up quickly recycling the same script as if it were a solution to the crisis.

A critique of the 'accelerationist manifesto' on the web-pages of the now-defunct AntiCapitalist Initiative (ACI) was the subject of some worried discussion among members of other more staid revolutionary groups keen to include the ACI in 'regroupment' discussions in 2013 (a hopeful time for the far left in the UK that some of us look back on now with some nostalgia); this seemed to be the eruption of too much new theory. Too fast, perhaps, but the later recriminations about opportunities lost, of the costs of hesitation in the revolutionary regroupment process, should now also be seen as symptomatic of broader processes in which everyone is expected to move fast, but, which, accelerationism shows, get us nowhere and, which, *The Funfair* shows, often end in miserable failure.

Agency

Agency tries to name individual and collective action, action which may be either isolated or, better, connected with change. Agency, for example, was at issue for Rohith Vemula, a Dalit student at the University of Hyderabad. His suicide on 17 January 2016 opened up a new phase of struggle by an alliance of activists protesting against the right-wing nationalist Bharatiya Janata Party (BJP) regime under Narendra Modi in power since 2014. Vemula's death and his suicide note quickly changed the coordinates of political debate in India, drawing attention once again to 'caste' as an axis of oppression that intersects with a multitude of others. And it is through the intersection with caste that some others have also again found their voice. Expressions of solidarity with Vemula in the few days after his death came from feminist, transgendered and socialist activists, as well as from academics. Each of these mobilisations was intimately linked with competing interpretations of what he meant by his suicide, and which particular aspects of Indian society were implicated. Vemula's own political act has also been configured as a puzzle about 'agency'; what this agency amounted to as his own conscious decision to blow the lid on the exclusion and oppression of Dalits in India and/or what agency is when it is embedded in a broader collective process of resistance.

'Dalit' is the self-chosen name for what used to be called 'untouchable' in India, a name popularised by, among others, Bhimrao Ramji Ambedkar, as a radical political alternative to Gandhi's generous but patronising designation of them as 'Harijan' or 'Children of God', a designation through which Gandhi ratified the caste order instead of challenging it. There are about 167 million Dalits in India, just over 16 per cent of the population, and they are now referred to in government legislation as a 'Scheduled Caste'. Legislation for the rights of a

Scheduled Caste means that the University of Hyderabad Vice-Chancellor and his cronies could yet be prosecuted over Vemula's death.

Five Dalit students were suspended from the university at the beginning of 2016, of which Vemula was one, and it appears that local BJP leaders then took the lead in ensuring that he was expelled, sleeping in the open since. The Vice-Chancellor meanwhile introduced Sanskrit and Yoga into the curriculum and attempted to change the university convocation robes to the Hindu dhoti. Vemula and his comrades in the Ambedkar Students' Association (ASA) responded with protests which included clashes with the BJP student group, and the ASA was in the process of linking its resistance against repression of Dalit students with others targeted by the Modi regime. Such was the political pressure on the university authorities, both from the BJP to clear the thing up and from student protestors at Hyderabad and across the country, that the Vice-Chancellor went on leave a week after Vemula's death, and his successor followed suit a week later.

On the right there were attempts, of course, to read the suicide note as an expression of personal distress from which the political dimension could be cleansed, and so this event could then be treated as an isolated one, a futile and incoherent appeal by a disturbed young man. BJP representatives time and again in media debate about the death tried to shift focus from what Vemula's suicide signified to what the note actually said. Because the note was about desperation and isolation, and because Vemula refused to directly point a finger at particular individuals who should be held responsible for his suicide, the university Vice-Chancellor and his political advisors have tried to make the death an individual matter. Had Vemula claimed that his death had been directly caused by the university authorities and by the BJP and its own student-wing apparatus, the suicide note would have undoubtedly been dismissed as a bitter politically-motivated recrimination at his enemies. It would have then been treated as the expression of an act that could have been just as quickly psychologised, just as much as it has been so far. Vemula could be damned either way. He can't win on his own, in life or through his death. Rather, it is the protestors with him and for him who will decide the case either way, and this will be a long game played through years of struggle.

In the weeks after the death, claims were made that Dalit students were not the only ones targeted by the University of Hyderabad, but that students from the five north-eastern Indian states were also subject to racial profiling. The event itself and the protests which followed it have thus forced into the open questions about regional, peasant and 'tribal' politics which threaten the BJP central government project to enforce Hindu nationalist ideology – 'Hindutva' – across the country. The protests against Vemula's death spread across university campuses, and were met by state violence, both by police and by the Hindu fascist Rashtriya Swayamsevak Sangh (RSS), an organisation for which Modi was once a full-time worker in Gujarat, the local testing ground for many of the BJP government's national policies since its election. It was then the 'Dalit' question that condensed a range of other social forces; crystallised, as a new social movement, this mobilisation around the Dalit functioned as the collective agency through which other voices of the oppressed might be heard, this is Dalit as a challenge to Hindutva.

The mother of a Dalit student at the Indian Institute of Technology in Bombay wrote an open letter to Vemula's family. Her son, Aniket Ambhore, committed suicide in 2014. Protests at Vemula's death called by the Ambedkar Students' Association, of which he was an active member, were quickly taken up by other student associations, including across Bombay ('Mumbai' in Delhi central government preferred parlance, one that many on the left locally refuse to adopt). There is increasing acknowledgement, and not only among the left and feminist social movements, that there is something systemic in these two events, and in many more in recent years. Suicide in India is particularly high among students, Dalits and women, and so there is already a political intersection between these three marked social categories that needs to be taken seriously, a political intersection that calls for an analysis that also takes seriously the way that the personal is political.

Individual agency in capitalist society is divided in a most peculiar way between the image of it – what we are told we can do by bourgeois ideology – and what it amounts to in practice, which is very much less. So, on the one hand, each individual is assumed to be a free agent, making decisions for themselves alone, acting independently of others. Under neoliberalism this image of the free agent becomes the ideological core of an injunction that each individual or family unit should take personal responsibility for economic decisions, education, health and welfare. Agency here boils down to doing things for oneself. On the other hand, economic inequality means that the range of choices for each individual agent is restricted to what the market-place provides, and structural oppression restricts that agency in practical terms for most people. 'Agency' itself thus operates as one of the figures of alienation, and it only turns from being a thing of illusion into a reality when the conditions which both incite it and restrict it are challenged. In practice, people then realise their 'agency' in networks of support, and it is through political struggle that they experience agency as a collective process that is much more powerful than what they have been told they should confine agency to, to their own little lives during times of business as usual.

This is why 'agency' has been one of the key terms of debate in Indian feminism, and has surfaced at the intersection of gender and religion, and played out, for example, in questions of 'choice' for and against the veil among Muslim women. The difference between the illusion of individual agency and the reality of collective agency is bound up with gender, with the difference between macho independence vaunted by capitalism, patriarchy and traditional left party organisations on the one hand, and the relational interdependence that became a key motif in the development of the women's movement. This is also why some of the most searching practical discussions about agency have come from feminism – taking action beyond mere 'behaviour' which is defined by those in power – and from socialist feminism, taking us beyond mere 'choice' that sidesteps the material conditions in which we act. The personal really becomes political when an individual acts with others to develop agency to speak of the world and to change it.

Rohith Vemula took responsibility for his own death, and it is through this personal act that his suicide has become a political event. Agency in this case, as in all cases of individual agency, was realised in conditions Vemula could not choose, but he did choose to stage his death as a protest, hanging himself with an ASA banner. The precise meaning of this as a form of 'agency' is not something that can be resolved at the level of Vemula himself – his political history and the alliances he forged indicate that he knew this – but will be worked through as a collective process for some time after the event. The protests for Vemula were thus serving not only to change the conditions which led to his death but also resignifying what he did in new political contexts in which it will come to make sense for those involved.

Animals

Animals are now at stake in the way we cut up the material world, a kind of cutting that includes us. In the dystopian parallel universe of the 2015 film *The Lobster*, compulsory coupledom is brutally enforced. As we follow the narrative of the film we learn something about the division between moral universes – of the couples and the singletons – and the difference between morality and ethics. It is a difference which revolves around the figure of the 'animal' and raises questions about what we are as human beings that enforce a vision of the world to which all of us and all other living beings must conform. In this respect, it connects with the broader domain of radical animal politics that is now, in times of industrial food production and mass-starvation, necessarily entwined with revolutionary 'ecosocialist' Marxism.

As with contemporary global politics, the viewer at many points does not know whether to laugh or cry, and many will cover their eyes toward the end of this bizarre film directed by Yorgos Lanthimos. It is not a sermon about animal rights, and has many very funny moments in what is effectively a secular critique of nasty irrational moral worldviews. 'David' (played by Colin Farrell) is newly single and so he is confined to a hotel-prison and given 45 days to find a new partner, failing which he will be transformed into an animal of his choice. He chooses a lobster. The hotel stages a series of moral scenarios to impress upon the guests the importance of being in a couple; if you are a man, for example, you will have someone to save you when you choke on your food, and if you are a woman you will have someone with you to stop you being raped. David is accompanied by a dog, his brother who failed to find a partner on an earlier visit to the hotel. The hotel (which is actually in Ireland on the Kerry coast) is a feeding ground for psychopathic disregard for others even at the very moment when each individual must, on pain of punishment, find someone to love, and this coupling is organised around the motif of 'likeness'. The only black hotel guest-inmate declares on stage, for example, that her defining characteristic is her friendly smile. David is short-sighted, and (spoiler alert and trigger warning) when he escapes into the forest he finds himself in the company of a community governed by moral rules just as severe; singletons who, outlawed and hunted down themselves, forbid relationships. Here, if it is possible, things take an even nastier turn. And it is in and against this moral community – as fiercely moral as that of the couples – that David encounters Rachel Weisz, 'short-sighted woman', who narrates the film; this encounter leads him to a horrible ethical choice.

One peculiarity of the film is that while capitalism as such is completely invisible – we don't even ever see money change hands and the only 'workers' are those who police the hotel or the city malls – patriarchy, sexual violence and the sexual division of labour is very evident throughout. And this requires some sharp cuts between what is human and what is animal, and between what is man and what is woman. When David is asked how he would define his sexuality, for example, he is told that he must choose between being straight or gay because there have been some 'difficulties' in the hotel posed by bisexuality. The moral dividing lines which govern life here are not therefore so much to protect compulsory heterosexuality but to enforce a regime of sexual difference.

The film takes us beyond the realm of 'animals' as such, even 'critical animals', to questions about how we mark ourselves off from animals, and how that separation – a separation bloodily enacted each time we eat them – is bound up with the separation of men from women, and so, inevitably under patriarchy, the power of men over women. It is this separation that links what we are with what we eat, and it links feminist critique of what we are today with eating meat, with the 'sexual politics of meat'.

Lobster is not chosen by David because it is something he likes to eat (as one French review of the film mistakenly and perhaps symptomatically portrayed it), but, David says, because it lives as long as a human, has blue blood like aristocrats and has sex all its life; lobster is defined as the animal he will become on the basis of a fantasy of likeness rather than difference.

The world of *The Lobster* – a moral-ideological complete universe composed of ideals of the couple and the individual, of human and animal and of man and woman – is the absolute reverse of what has been called, in recent 'new materialist', 'agential materialist' or 'material feminist' writing, 'Nature's Queer Performativity'. This work, most recently in the complex formulations of Karen Barad, takes forward some of the attempts from within second-wave socialist feminism to replace binary oppositions with 'hybrid', 'cyborg' forms of politics which mix humans, machines and nature. For Barad, it is 'performative' because it insists on the process by which taken-for-granted identities – of human or animal, for example – are played out and enforced through moral rules, it is 'queer' because it questions and unravels those categories of being, and it bears on 'nature' because it concerns the way the conceptual 'cuts' we make are 'materialised', made real for us as if there could be no other way the world could be.

In this world – a world which Barad treats as 'material' but also as historically materially constituted – the choices we make, individually and institutionally, entail what she calls 'constitutive exclusions' which become part of the very fabric of 'space-timemattering'. You need something as weird as the way our world is, something sharp enough to cut through the categories we take as 'real'. Barad gives us that, and helps us read the weird world of *The Lobster*, filmic representation that exaggerates and makes visible to us the moral lines of force that cut up our reality today.

The Lobster functions well as a film more in the ecosocialist tradition than in that of orthodox Marxism which aimed to master nature, to make it submit to one version of scientific rule, a version of Marxism that repeated the worst instrumental morality of capitalism – the world to be treated as means to an end – and ended up as an exploitative bureaucratic nightmare under Stalinism. The film speaks to some of us not because we are vegan; most of us are not most of the time. It is because an increasing number of activists, our comrades, are turning to veganism or vegetarianism as an ethical choice that we respect as we struggle alongside them. That choice is itself tangled with consumerism, middle-class privilege and new niche markets, but it is, they know, an ethical choice that is actively seeking to disen-tangle itself from those things. We sense, even though we may not have taken that step ourselves, that they are anticipating what it will be like to live in another ecosocialist world beyond capitalism, a world in which we are part of nature instead of alienated from it. We tread a path, between those who still write off 'animal rights' too quickly as separate from their socialist politics and those who put vegan socialist politics on the agenda as part of a broader struggle. Again, this is revolutionary politics that is not in line with moral rules – that way leads to a religious conception of animal rights which is as bad, if not worse, than the enemy it pits itself against. Ecosocialism is not about morality at all, but is about ethics in political transformation.

It is against the background of a new animal politics that we could have responded positively to Jeremy Corbyn's appointment of a vegan as shadow minister for environment, food and rural affairs in September 2015 in the British Labour Party soon after he was elected leader. The right-wing press treated the shadow minister's comment that meat should be treated like tobacco and that there should be campaigns to stop people eating it (a comment Corbyn quickly distanced himself from) as if it were a moral crusade against farmers. The warnings on cigarette packets have shifted the terrain of the debate; rather than forcing people to stop, rather than imposing a new moral regime (as some libertarians claim), the warnings and other measures to protect the health of non-smokers have opened up more space for smokers to make an ethical choice. These tobacco products are killing us; so, warnings, why not, but then why not also some other more radical measures against the companies that profit from the creation of sickness and death?

Each ethical choice connects us with others, and then it is for all of us to respond and work out what the next steps might be. Revolutionary socialist struggle is precisely about expanding the domain of ethical choice, taking us from alienated and conformist repetitive activity – eating meat because we have always done so, for example – to decisions about where we stand as human beings and what it is to be human in the world. For David in *The Lobster* (and here is a cryptic final point that will only mean something to those who have already seen the film), it will be a decision that is about what he chooses to see and what his choice to love will entail as an expansion of his many senses of being with others.

Antagonism

Antagonism is the kind of contradiction that marks the political coordinates of a culture. Bernie Sanders did threaten the Democratic-Republican stranglehold on US politics in 2016. Whether or not he intended to do this – and it turns out that he lost his nerve at the last moment – this was the effect of his grass-roots campaign inside the Democratic Party that rebelled against Hillary Clinton, and which put the term 'socialism' back in circulation again. However, to break that stranglehold it was also necessary to mobilise outside the Democratic Party, and that meant making some strange alliances that opened things up by working at an 'antagonism' at the heart of the debate which connected with class antagonism and, in practice, with the voices of the oppressed who are still struggling to be heard. Before the spectre of communism, it is the spectre of 'antagonism' that frightens liberals and anyone who wants business as usual, who wants the old to and fro between the two main parties which are both loyal to capital.

This has everything to do with antagonism as a keyword for the anti-capitalist movement, and it is a name for a polarisation of politics that is also disturbing for many from the old Marxist tradition who would prefer a predictable sequence of thesis-antithesis-synthesis, a steady unrolling of the dialectic which is supposed to move us forward through history. Antagonism is messier than that, and never-ending, opening rather than closing down what we expect next. It is the centrepiece of contemporary European radical thought, articulated in slightly different ways by the radical academics Alain Badiou and Slavoj Žižek. Each theorist to various extents acknowledges their theoretical debt to the German philosopher Hegel, to emphasise the 'negative' moment of the dialectic, and so antagonism could be thought of as one of the names of contradiction. This kind of contradiction operates not only directly through class struggle, however, but runs through the social, dividing those with power from those impelled to challenge it.

Those moments when the challenge breaks out into the open and disturbs taken-for-granted assumptions about the terms of political debate are moments of antagonism. For Badiou, those moments are moments of an 'event' in politics which forces an ethical choice which divides those faithful to the event from those who betray it. For Žižek, those are times of an 'act' which disturbs the symbolic coordinates which govern our lives and throws up new ways of interpreting and changing the world. For both Badiou and Žižek they are moments when we touch the 'real', a real which Marxists have sometimes conceptualised as the real bedrock of the political-economic structure which is usually covered over by ideology.

The debates inside the Democratic Party and outside it which were centred on the figure of Bernie Sanders began to shake the symbolic coordinates of US politics in 2016; the key question was then how anti-capitalists – by which we mean a contradictory alliance of 'democratic socialists', 'independents' and revolutionary Marxists – could make of this movement something more drive deeper into something we could call antagonism.

This contradictory alliance brought into play some forces that disturbed the old politics, including old left politics. We must take seriously, for example, the challenge posed by 'independents' who are not all signed up to the left, far from it. This includes the mobilisation of independents that was being undertaken by successors to the New Alliance Party (NAP), a formation that has always disturbed the US far left. Now, in the form of the 'independent voting movement' headed by Jacqueline Salit, a veteran of the NAP, a variety of different independent or 'third party' groups across the States were assembled to fight Democrat-Republican rule. This is the NAP that was active in the 'Reform Party', an initiative which in the past allied with Ross

Perot and which linked with Pat Buchanan and even then with Donald Trump! Does this mean the old NAP activists are on the right, or is there a deeper paradox they are working at which turns right tactics into left politics, a deeper paradox that opens up something of antagonism? Maybe.

There was one big difference between Bernie Sanders and Donald Trump which was how 'loyal' they are and what they are loyal to, this even after Bernie capitulated and endorsed Hillary Clinton for the Democratic nomination. Bernie Sanders was speaking the language of good and reasonable politics, and this is what the reassuring phrase 'democratic socialism' meant in his campaign; the 'democratic' part of the phrase is significant here, and it signalled where his loyalties lay. This was also signalled in the first abysmal reactions of Sanders campaign supporters to the challenge by Black Lives Matter, a reaction which prioritised reason over anger, and we could see it in Sanders' hopeless 'balanced' response to the question of Palestine which effectively sided with the Israeli security agenda. This home-spun unthreatening alternative was given voice by celebrities like Dick Van Dyke, a side of Sanders which ran alongside something a little more edgy which was given voice by Pussy Riot's Nadia Tolokonnikova. It is that edgy side of Sanders we liked.

But when it comes down to it, what this meant was that when Sanders was defeated by Clinton inside the Democratic Party he rolled over and handed over all of the votes from the left that he had been accumulating with all good faith, handed them over to Clinton. He wouldn't stand as an independent and break the consensus, the assumption that one of the two main parties must rule.

Donald Trump, on the other hand, spoke the language of conflict, a language that was laced with hatred, poisonous to the left, to the working class and to the oppressed. Trump is dangerous, will be an extremely dangerous force as President, but we should notice exactly how and why he is dangerous, and what contradictions lie in that danger. There are, for sure, dangers for any progressive agenda, but there are also dangers for the consensus, dangers which, even despite Trump (who is more concerned with his own personal success than political change), also lay the conditions for a real antagonism to appear. Trump, if he had been defeated inside the Republican Party, would have broken from the party and would most likely have stood as an independent. Trump was clearly not loyal to the Republicans, and it was that unpredictable disturbing aspect of his campaign that the independent voting movement keyed into and used. To take antagonism to the left, Sanders, and the movement he built, needed to be disloyal to the Democrats just as Trump would have been disloyal to the Republican Party.

It is in this context, in the context of taking seriously what 'antagonism' could do to really shake things up, that calls by US revolutionary Marxists to support the Bernie Sanders campaign inside the Democratic Party by building a movement outside the party was absolutely right. Only that could have opened the way for Sanders to be taken beyond himself, beyond the ideological coordinates that the left is used to, to a politics that touches the real. The Trump presidency is a nightmare, true, but not because he broke the consensus. Now he is so dangerous precisely because he will adapt to it and garner support from the Republicans who will help him implement his policies more 'efficiently'.

Appropriation

The word 'appropriation' is often used to describe how culture is stolen from others, but it also includes taking back representations of us and our creative activity. This much is clear in the Ladybird books case. The UK Christmas bestseller for 2015 was the retro-Ladybird guide *The Husband*. This joke-book works through appropriation of feminist discourse about men and the appropriation of a genre of writing for children. Unlike some of the radical books for children produced after the Russian Revolution by followers of the 'Suprematist' art movement led by Kazimir Malevich, for example, this book is for adults, with children in the background as the pretext for the joke to work. This Ladybird book also conceals another story of 'appropriation' which throws light on the way the process of taking someone else's voice and speaking for another is tangled up in questions of representation that are political questions about creative activity treated as private property. The privilege certain categories of people have to represent others makes appropriation a potent keyword for those who have been denied the right to speak for themselves, and it also works as a keyword for the revolutionary left when those political questions of representation are embedded in power and resistance.

Today in popular media representations of the left and feminist politics, 'appropriation' is often treated as an amusing cluster of concepts which include, we are often told 'cultural appropriation', objections to the privilege that some people have when they can speak for others, and the sometimes impossible attempt to trace back representations of people to those who are supposed to be the original natural source of those representations. In this tabloid press framing of the issue, the motif of 'appropriation' is treated as a joke, a joke about hypersensitive minorities who demand that everyone else 'check their privilege'

before they dare to open their mouths. Questions of representation in politics in this way thus become reduced to a series of
interpersonal grudges and power-plays. This also becomes a
feeding ground for the so-called 'alt-right' objecting to 'political
correctness', given free rein under Trump, and waging war on so-
called 'Social Justice Warriors'. However, we do need to take this
notion of 'appropriation' very seriously and treat it as what it
really is, a complaint against commodification, the turning of
human creativity and of people themselves into commodities.

There are clearly issues of political judgement in relation to
representation and power that need to be addressed. Questions
of sexuality, gender and 'race' are often defined by those with
power, and one way of combating that power is to insist that
those who are on the sharp end should have the right to speak
first and to articulate who they are rather than have their identity
articulated by others. Some of those dimensions are difficult to
resolve by simply saying that those without power should be the
ones who speak and those who have privilege should shut up.
The role of children in society is a case in point. When they are
very young they cannot speak. There is a question here about the
way that those who complain are positioned as victims and
treated like children, and that treatment speaks volumes about
the way that children are themselves seen as not yet fully human.
A socialist politics of childhood under capitalism tackles this
question of how children should be accorded rights, rights that
they cannot directly exercise but which they learn to take on as
their own. In this process, children have to overcome how they
are represented, and how they are represented to themselves.

Take for instance the case of Ladybird books which were
initially marketed in the 1960s for children to educate them to
know their place and to identify as 'Peter' or 'Jane', as a well-
behaved good boy or girl. This is a case of appropriation in its
literal sense. This is how it functions for revolutionary Marxists
who oppose this wretched political economic system that turns

our creative capacities into things to be bought and sold. Art student Miriam Elia appropriated the Ladybird format in 2014 for her little book *We Go to the Gallery*, and she sold the short-run of 1000 copies to friends and supporters for twenty pounds apiece. The book itself was about 'appropriation', and the joke was that Peter and Jane and their mother at the art gallery are confronted with all kinds of stupid art works accorded value by virtue of their price. The children's comments and questions reveal how empty these images are. Art under capitalism is, after all, all about appropriation, and the creative activity of the artist is one of the things that is really reduced to a 'thing', an object that will realise a profit in the art market.

This process of appropriation then entails other kinds of enclosure of creative activity that become linked with and reproduce colonialism, as when creative products from different colonised cultures are turned into artworks, into commodities. It is that kind of appropriation that is at the heart of serious complaints against it, not the absurd stories peddled by the bourgeois press about non-Italian people eating pizza. The tabloid press mocks those who do complain about those little acts of cultural appropriation precisely because they, the press, are in the business of harvesting and marketing images of other people.

When Penguin books, the giant publishing corporation which now owns Ladybird, found out about Miriam Elia's project and her critique of the art market, they threatened her with legal action and made her pulp the remaining copies of the book. They appropriated the appropriator, but in a reactionary way, in a way that is exactly the opposite of what we revolutionaries aim for. This is corporate appropriation rather than democratic collective appropriation. It is of a piece with the kinds of 'appropriation' we challenge in anti-racist and feminist politics. Miriam has fought back with some fantastic sarcastic responses that appropriate once again what has been stolen from her. One day we will appropriate the appropriators of our creative labour when we collectivise and share in the objects of our labour, and so create the conditions in which cultural appropriation will flourish in horizontal networks rather than vertical ones, in relations of equality and respect rather than in relations governed by the market. But in the meantime, the question of 'appropriation' reminds us what we are up against, reminds us how pernicious capitalism is.

A quick immediate libertarian response to complaints about 'appropriation' has been to wish away the problem and simply say that no one owns culture and therefore we should simply do away with the gatekeepers. These libertarians are outraged by what they read of the activities of anti-racists, feminists and the left, and part of the problem here is that they are reacting against what they read, a series of representations speaking for the publishing industry which magnifies and distorts the real issues. This libertarian response is misplaced. As we have seen, it is not true that 'no one' owns culture. Some people do own it, literally. Cultural products are enclosed and jealously protected, and that enclosure and protection is part of a general process that is at the foundation of capitalism. The problem is not that cultural products are representations of people but that those cultural products become private property and then also necessarily become bound up with relations of power. That is why many objections to cultural appropriation are objections to the way that representations of subject peoples turn those peoples into objects to be exploited as part of the enclosed cultural material that can be bought and sold, turned into exchange value.

Yes, it is true that colonised cultures and those subject to power under capitalism and patriarchy are 'appropriated', and we are with them as they struggle to give voice to their own experience of what it is to live under racist and sexist rule. We learn from them and in the process we learn to treat 'appropriation' as such as a problem that is part of the reification of our lives. And we can then, as we learn from those extreme end points of reification, also reflect better on how we are increasingly made to treat our own lives as objects, even to treat our bodies and brains as objects which we are only then allowed to connect with through bizarre quasi-scientific representations of them; representations of bodies in the dehumanising advertising and pornography industries, and representations of brains in the attempts to detect and then tell us what we are really thinking.

To add insult to injury, Penguin followed up its threat to sue Miriam by appropriating her brilliant idea and producing the 'Husband' book that minted it for the company at Christmas (recuperating Miriam as well, publishing under their own imprint *We Go to the Gallery*). Appropriation is one name for an insidious process by which bits of our bodies and our brains are turned into things and turned against us. That really is no joke. This enclosure and appropriation of our very selves under capitalism is destructive of us all. We need to deal with the roots of the problem together, all of us together. And, to make that possible, we need to acknowledge that representation of ourselves and, crucially, those who are configured ideologically as 'other' to us, is bound up with power. This is power we make visible through enabling resistance, the resistance of those who seek, with us, to collectively appropriate the appropriators.

Campism

Campism entails dividing the world into good and bad, allying with some dubious regimes to do that and, in the process, excluding the left. It is tempting to assume that the enemy of your enemy is your friend, but this is a very dangerous mistake to make, both in the realm of friendships and in the sphere of world politics. No less in the case of internal disagreements among anti-capitalists as to how to make sense of the balance of forces and how best to fight back. What is sometimes called 'campism' makes exactly this mistake, and in the course of this leap to make new friends we can end up in the grip of some old enemies. It is this campism that is driving a wedge into the left, and leading some of our comrades into the arms of Putin and Assad, and just as surely it is this campism that is fuelling some of the bizarre distortions of left strategy we once called 'No Platform'. No Platforming expresses the revulsion of society against ideas that seek to destroy it, ideas that would, if put into practice, lead to intimidation, violence and eventually elimination of fellow human beings. One of the problems with campism is that it bit-by-bit, through its alliances with our enemies, treats other comrades as enemies too. One of the barbaric logics of campism, not its only logic but one we should beware of, is that it leads to attempts to No Platform those who are resisting capitalism rather than those who are intent on making it more brutal, turning it into barbarism.

Campism exploded into the anti-imperialist left after 2014 over Ukraine, with the argument that if you are against imperialism this must mean that you support those powers that are also rivals to the West. So, the argument goes, you should object to the West's military intervention, but keep quiet about, or even quietly celebrate Russia's own intervention. It also includes the use of smears and lies directed at those that some on the broad feminist and anti-racist left disagree with on some issues, smears and lies that end up with a refusal to share a platform with them and with attempts to stop the other point of view from even being discussed. We should be clear here that there is actually a big difference between these two responses to severe disagreement, two ways of showing the depth of disagreement, and pointing to the dangers that lie in their wake. The first response is to refuse to share a platform with particular speakers or with representatives of certain organisations that have said reactionary things or have behaved in a despicable way. Refusal to share a platform is one way of creating a link with comrades and rallying them to also object. An example of this response would include the refusal to rent rooms to these individuals or organisations, as happened during the 2013 sexual abuse crisis that hit the Socialist Workers Party in Britain. This response was not 'No Platform', but a legitimate practical objection to what that group was up to in an attempt to make its members see sense, as is refusing to buy *Socialist Worker*.

An entirely different response is to attempt to implement 'No Platform', that is, to prevent someone speaking. It is this 'No Platform' that is being resurrected, it seems, by those intent on turning the politics of the left into a monstrous parody of dialectical discussion of strategy, and turning 'No Platform' into a zombie politics that will eat the left and its allies. The issue blew up at the Left Forum event in New York in May 2016 over the decision to invite Slavoj Žižek to speak. The protests against Žižek were led by Taryn Fivek on the basis that Žižek had repeatedly made racist comments in the course of his analysis of the predicament of the refugees arriving in Europe. It seems that there were also some little but significant mistakes in the way the Left Forum organisers handled communication over whether or not to include Žižek in the first place, but once he had been invited the question slid quickly from being one about invitation to one in which Fivek and her group effectively called for 'No

Platform'.

What makes matters worse, as Fivek pointed out in her inter-vention, was that it seems Žižek had been paid to attend. This was unlike many other participants, something which sends an unfortunate if unintended message about the complicity of Left Forum in the ideas they were hosting. Some small publishing groups responded by standing against this 'illness on the left', saying they 'stand with Žižek', itself a bad response to a bad situation. Fivek herself ironically, perhaps, but tellingly launched a new project called 'No Platform' which was designed to give a voice to disenfranchised voters across the US. This is a particular political project that flowed from Fivek's leadership of FIST, which is the youth wing of the Workers World Party, a group that has its origins way back in a split from the Trotskyist Fourth International and which has made support for Black Lives Matter into one of its brand selling points. There are no innocent parties here, and it is not stretching the point a little to say that Black Lives Matter was being hitched by Fivek and her pals to a 'campist' position. Just as in the late 1950s, when her group saw Maoist China as its friend and endorsed the Soviet Invasion of Hungary, so it now supports North Korea and lines up the world accordingly in terms of friends and enemies. And, like many other campists who ally with Putin or Assad, it begins to see those on the left who disagree with these battle-lines as enemies rather than friends. If there are any 'false flags' in left politics, then Fivek's attack on Žižek was one of those; it was a good opportunity, sure, but there was another agenda, the unspoken agenda of campism turning into No Platform inside the left.

One way of approaching this question is to remember the fateful mistake many Eurocommunists in the 1970s made when they were besotted with the work of Antonio Gramsci. For them, the battle for 'hegemony' consisted of a series of alliances across the political field. What they overlooked was the fact that Gramsci saw this hegemonic struggle, the battle for ideas, as taking place inside the workers' movement, not with the 'progressive' right. Now the lesson of campism turning into No Platform is a new twist on this mistake. Now we have to be clear that there is a difference between our own debates, the battles of ideas that we together engage in among ourselves, and the very unusual strategy of 'No Platform' that we all together implement against the real deadly enemies of the left.

Revolutionary Marxist 'No Platform' has a history in anti-racist and anti-fascist practice, and what was meant by that term as part of a strategy to deal with the fascist National Front in Britain in the 1970s is very different from what is being done now to people we would, on other issues, have a lot in common with, people who are our allies, not our all-time foes. Our No Platform is part of a struggle against fascism in which, as Trotsky once put it, we should be willing to come to an agreement with 'the devil and his grandmother' to oppose it. Our comrades in different rival groups on the left are not devils and we should be seeking agreement with them whenever possible. Even when, and precisely when they are themselves getting drawn into some unfortunate and dangerous alliances of their own.

Campism is not merely the marking out of territory, about setting up a pitch and defending it against rival revolutionary groups with a different analysis of the balance of forces and also, perhaps, a different agenda. It is much more than that when it appears here among us. It is the insinuation into the left, feminist, anti-racist and anti-capitalist movements of a strategy, campism, and then No Platform, that once was and still should be directed at those who really seek to destroy us. We still do need to mobilise together to implement, alongside all those repelled by poisonous ideas, something we once called 'No Platform'. We want to destroy capitalism and patriarchy and the wretched racist practices that divide us from each other, and we do that together. But 'No Platform' has no place inside our movement, and when that idea creeps into comradely debate to poison us we should reject it. Campism is the first glimmering of a mistake that calls upon this idea, and through a dangerous logic campism can turn debate among us from dialectical working-through of political strategy into something that links part of the left with the right and then ends up wanting to silence the rest of the left in the process. That's why we should contain and discuss campist politics now, and even when some of us have tactically adopted a campist position, be clear that it is our own politics that is in command, and not the agenda and logic of campism itself.

Cis

The term 'cis' draws critical attention to the way we often enforce divisions between one side – that's where we think we are – and that of the others. The keyword 'Cis' appeared on the sexology radar in the late 1990s in Germany, and then in feminist activism in the early 2000s globally, and it now has implications for revolutionary politics way beyond how we talk about the link between gender and the body, and how some people identify with that link. Technically, cis in chemistry refers to groups of atoms appearing 'on the same side' of part of a molecule, and so it describes a physical correspondence in the material world between objects and their naturally assigned place. As we know, things in the material world often shift place and mutate, sometimes into their opposite, just as they do, of course, in the social world, and so the carry-over of cis from chemistry into gender both marks, questions and subverts what we take to be 'natural'.

The use of the term 'cisgender' is just the start of this progressive unravelling of how we are fixed in place by ideological systems that pretend to tell us what our real nature as human beings is. And while 'cisgender' refers specifically to those whose gender identity is supposedly on the 'same side' as their naturally-assigned sex, we can extend its use to question how peoples of a certain culture come to be certain about who they are because they assume that their cultural identity lies naturally on the 'same side' as their 'nation' or 'race'. Taking on board the word 'cis' as a description of assumptions that cisgendered people make about themselves as being fundamentally different from those who are 'trans' – those whose identity does not correspond with the body they were told they were born into – is not necessarily an accusation, but, as some activists have recognised, acknowledges what many of us take for granted. The problem is not what identity is as such but the fact that it is taken-for-granted, assumed to be the immutable ground from which we and everyone else should speak. Those who are frightened by the word 'cis' are very often hostile to those who use it, and they often angrily deny its use, saying they are against the cis/trans binary, an objection that rather misses the point of the cis critique of binary oppositions in the first place; there is a defensiveness here that looks very much like some forms of racism.

Anti-Semitism is a case in point, and the mobilisation of anti-Semitism in Ukraine illustrates something of the peculiar hostility of those who would like to feel that they are on the 'same side' as what they imagine to be their own kind, and how dangerous they can be when that identity of individual self, geographical space and racial group is disrupted. Ukraine as borderland is then turned into a nation defined by blood. This is where anti-Semitism that has operated inside the implicit coordinates of nationalist history seems to erupt again, anti-Semitism that is sometimes ignored as part of the pretence that a new order has put it in the past, sometimes condoned by the state in order to discredit opponents, and sometimes deliberately fuelled to divide friends of the state from its enemies. It seems to come out of nowhere, but actually it was already at work to define not only what the identity of the anti-Semite is, but also used as a lesson, a false ideological lesson about how important fixed and visible identity is as such.

For anti-Semites, Jews disturb the coordinates of national identity, they are not 'cis'; they are not on the 'same side', and anti-Semitic ideology often points to their nature as ambiguous, that it is not easy to define what a Jew is from what they look like or even from what they do, and, worse still, their allegiance to the nation state is ambiguous. That is an accusation that surfaces in the anti-Semitic complaint that Jews are 'rootless cosmopolitans', and this 'cosmopolitanism' was one of the code-words for anti-Semitism in the Soviet Union just before the death of Stalin. This 'cosmopolitan' label, of course, is an accusation that any self-respecting revolutionary versed in dialectics would understand as a compliment to those who are 'internationalist'; we are not of a nation and none of us are really cis in that sense. We are on the 'other side', believing that another world is possible, beyond local culture, nation and 'race'.

The Maidan protests in 2013–2014 against the attempts of Russia under Putin, contemporary site and one exemplar of cis, to block the separation of Ukraine from its natural geographical motherland, a historically-assigned identity which some Putinites would like to see as lying in the realm of their own Greater Russia, already saw the re-emergence of anti-Semitism. Fascist organisations used the protests to define what the Ukrainian struggle for sovereignty should really be about, and the hard struggle of the Ukrainian and Russian left at the Maidan was to articulate not only the demands for autonomous democratic self-government against Russia but also to resist the pull to a hard-line nationalism that would pit those on 'the same side' against those on the other. This became a struggle that would pit those who had built into their politics an idea that it was crucial that there should be one true side that made you who you were against those most dangerous enemy forces that would dissolve the difference between sides, those enemy forces they named 'Jews' in a revival of fantastic conspiracy theories of history, Jews who functioned as the 'cisfunction' in Ukrainian politics. The internationalist left refused this identitarian cis politics, and still does, developing forms of 'Ukraine solidarity' that are in solidarity with the Ukraine as a multiplicity of identities, identities that must, as a function of the historical struggle of the Ukraine as a nation under the years of Tsarism, Nazi occupation and Stalinist rule, include the Jews.

And, as if in a mirror where one identity stares in hatred at another identity that it will set itself against and that will also confirm it as model for what it imagines its identity should look

45

like, campists around the world rush to complain about Ukrainian anti-Semitism – which is a real threat – and thereby cover for Putin, cover over the anti-Semitism of Great Russia. Campism – the claim that you are this and so this is who your friends are – in this context is cis. Putin's nationalist supporters in Donetsk and Luhansk are also virulently anti-Semitic, for the very existence of difficult-to-identity Jews of uncertain allegiance disrupt what their own dear-held idea of a nation state is. Conspiracy theories flourish on 'this side', with roots back from Putin to Stalin, and function just as surely to make out that inter-nationalist 'cosmopolitan' politics are the real threat; Putin funds fascists across Europe to further these ideas. In Crimea, not incidentally, the Tatars also serve the 'cisfunction', a people who have lived in the region for many years but who have been subjected to mass-transportation of populations and so still carry uncanny and unpleasant reminders for the Russian nationalists of an enemy within that disturbs the boundaries between what is inside the nation-state and what is outside it. The Tatars are also here reminders of the existence of the real hidden enemy for nationalists of all stripes, of the Jews.

Jews are being instrumentalised in the competing conspiracy theories about Ukraine and Russia on both sides that attempt to fix the identity of the anti-Semite. And, it should also be pointed out that the identity of Jews is fixed in place by nationalist and incipient cis politics around the world. We should have great respect for those like Shami Chakrabarti who investigated the issue inside the British Labour Party, and who take anti-Semitism seriously. And we should have contempt for those who instru-mentalise it and engage in reactionary attacks on those seeking to end the conditions which created it; fundamentalist Christian Zionists in the United States or apologists for the racist Israeli cis-state, for example. The ideological stakes of anti-Semitism are brutally material everywhere, whether it is in Ukraine or Russia, or in the stupid reactionary fantasies of those on the left in the

West who think they have finally discovered what makes the world tick and who the real hidden enemy is. One of the opposition terms to this identitarian cis politics is 'trans', which for us revolutionaries here is transnational, international solidarity with the Jews; solidarity with all who declare their identities for themselves to define who they are, and with all those who transcend the boundaries between those on 'the same side', including the others in Ukraine and beyond, and those of us who declare ourselves to be 'other' and who fight for another world for all.

Discourse

Study and intervention into 'discourse' is concerned with patterns of language grounded in power and history. Much more than language is at stake in the challenges to corruption in the South African parliament and the attempts to cover things over again, for example. This 'much more than language' is what the French historian and philosopher Michel Foucault aimed to capture with the term 'discourse'.

Now it is clear that the official state discourse of 'transformation' promised by the African National Congress (ANC) in the 1950s has been corrupted and subordinated to another discourse of 'economic freedom', and the discourse of economic freedom has now been seized and turned against the ANC in power by a Marxist-Leninist-Fanonian breakaway group with seats in parliament called the 'Economic Freedom Fighters' (EFF). The EFF led by Julius Malema, formerly head of the ANC Youth League, interrupted President Jacob Zuma's State of the Nation address to parliament on 12 February 2015 by politely asking, as they have repeatedly over the past months, when Zuma will 'pay back the money' (that is the 13.7 million pounds he has spent on his luxury estate near Nkandla in the hills of KwaZulu-Natal). The ANC had already anticipated this interruption of the President's discourse with a botched attempt to switch off mobile phone signals from the chamber before he spoke, and then the South African Broadcasting Corporation obligingly kept the camera on the speaker of the house while armed police removed the EFF.

Discourse, power, resistance, and more discourse were tangled together and unravelled in terms that Marxists (and Leninists) will already recognise – an irony of history for the ANC as a party in which the South African Communist Party plays a key role as ideological force and disciplined militant core

– and that supporters of Frantz Fanon, a Lenin of Africa, have something to say about, but these events also make Foucault very relevant here today.

Foucault himself broke from the French Communist Party in 1953 (for a combination of reasons which included the Party's homophobia and Soviet anti-Semitism), and was, from early on in his work, attuned to the way that language is intimately linked with power. The link with power is the first aspect of discourse Foucault works at. The language we use to do politics in our questioning and debating is structured, organised in broader systems of meaning that we can't completely predict and control. The language of Marxism, for example, is enmeshed in the history of the Stalinist bureaucracy in the Soviet Union (and closer to home in Southern Africa in Zimbabwe under Mugabe, a figure that the EFF explicitly supports even if the favour is not returned). That enmeshment of Marxism with oppression is something only collective action that puts democratic principles of transformation and freedom to the forefront will be able to untangle.

Foucault showed how discourses of the 'normal' and 'abnormal' operate within 'dividing practices'. In discourse linked to practice the good folk are divided from the bad, and these social divisions are maintained. His description of the way the modern prison system works by categorising and observing the minute behaviour of each prisoner is also a broader description of modern systems of power: Discourse and practice is combined in each CCTV camera and every lie detector, in the immigration agencies and on Facebook. Discourse in practice, linked with power, is then at work in the definitions of terms we use in political debate.

The attempt to bring about 'transformation' as a state project dearly beloved of the ANC then turned from being a word that had a revolutionary meaning in the enactment of the Freedom Charter in the 1990s into a bureaucratic code-word. It became part of the ANC's management strategy. As a component of a state apparatus which is economically corrupt the term in a discourse of 'transformation' becomes a site of contest, a site of struggle over what it means to speak of transformation and what different agendas transformation plays into. So, on the one hand, there is a radical history of the term in the transition from apartheid, a drive to change the racial composition of educational institutions, for instance, and even to connect this social transformation with gender equality. At the very same moment 'transformation committees' are forced to operate in institutions that are being privatised, subject to a market logic in which 'freedom' takes on a very different meaning, and in a context in which even the once-radical 'Gender Commission' has been neutralised. Then the imperative to 'innovate', in vacuous appeals for 'curriculum transformation' for example, confuse one political agenda with another so it is no longer clear even to those who obey what it is they are actually transforming or why. They are then lost in the discourse of transformation, which today amounts to neoliberalism.

Discourse for Foucault has a second aspect just as important as power, which is subjectivity. When particular discourses, of 'freedom' say, are organised across a society or even globally, and are linked in some places with those of 'transformation', they hook into the speakers who use those discourses. The language connects with and reinforces, and sometimes disrupts, how speakers and listeners, readers and writers understand themselves in what is being said or read. So, when the EFF battled in parliament for its right to wear its trademark red boiler suits and construction helmets (or, in some contexts, red berets) it was for the right to be in their discourse of 'economic freedom' as workers, to mobilise themselves as workers against the corrupt leadership of the bosses, of the ANC. Their discourse includes subjectivity, a sense of who they are in that struggle, and provides a point of identification for their supporters, so their supporters do not need to wear a red beret to feel themselves part of the freedom discourse (though it helps). The twist for Foucault in his history of confession in Western culture – that is, confession of what you feel inside that runs from the Catholic confessional to the psychoanalyst's couch – is that nowadays you are increasingly expected to speak of yourself, of your subjectivity, in order to be heard and taken seriously within a discourse. (In South Africa that confessional aspect has been drummed home through the 'Truth and Reconciliation Commission' which was underpinned by a form of therapeutic discourse.)

The third aspect of discourse is resistance. Where there is power there is resistance, Foucault said, more than once. A discourse can be combated by a 'counter-discourse', where the term 'black', for example, is reclaimed so that it speaks no longer of denigration but of pride. Foucault is one of the patron saints of queer politics precisely because that politics refuses to make a necessary link between identity in discourse – such as the discourse of the good little girl or that of the macho breadwinner – and subjectivity. Queer politics is resistance to dominant discourses of gender and sexuality; it is defined by what you do, not what you are. Resistance was central to Foucault's description of the architecture and practice of the prison, a history that was first inspired by his participation in the prisoner's movement. So, criss-crossing with the discursive transformation of 'transformation', as the ANC ditches the Freedom Charter for neoliberal economic reforms, comes a form of resistance from the EFF. The term 'freedom' was and is crucial to liberal and then neoliberal economics but it is now thrown back in the face of the capitalist state in South Africa. The EFF interrupted Zuma at the moment he spoke the significant words 'Freedom Charter' early on into his speech: it was as if they knew he must say those words and as if it was a signal to act which was charged with meaning.

Does that mean the EFF were well-worked out revolutionary socialists, or lumpen elements resisting just because they really want a bigger slice of the pie? It is true that Malema has said he will rejoin the ANC if Zuma goes, and he faces calls to pay back kickbacks and back-taxes himself (which we recognise as discourses to discredit him when they emerge in the press as claims that he owes a gardener and domestic worker money, for instance). The EFF faced internal revolt as they repeated discourses of discipline against their opponents, discourses they at other times resist. Debate on the left about the EFF included whether they are really fascist, characterisations that risk reinforcing discourses about resistance in South Africa that are themselves racialised. Discourse eats all those who use it, but we have no choice. Including Foucault, whose innovative link between discourse, power, subjectivity and resistance has itself been questioned for buying into a neoliberal conception of what politics is. That Foucault is everywhere is itself, perhaps, a sign that his analysis plays into modern discourse. But he is also with us revolutionary Marxists, questioning every attempt to tie politics down or to tame it with a well-meant but often conservative discourse of fundamental fixed elements of 'human nature'. Foucault was for transformation and freedom, and so he subjected the discourse to detailed critical analysis to help us break free of it.

Ecosocialism

Ecosocialism is one way of connecting our humanity with our nature, to protect both. It is international in scope, and provides a detailed focus on specific conflicts, such as the one that erupted in Syria. The uprising in Syria against the Assad regime was conditioned by two intersecting global forces. That intersection has consequences today for the solidarity we build with the Syrian people, and for the kinds of political perspectives that can break their isolation, that can connect them with forms of resistance that must, if they are to finally succeed, link revolutionary socialism with ecology. Syria is just one of many crises facing humanity that points to the importance of transforming our own internationalist politics, reconfiguring our strategies for change and the aims of our movement around the keyword 'ecosocialism'.

The first global force is governmental and explicitly political: neoliberalism, which today repeatedly deconstructs and reconstructs different regions and nation states around the world to make them more easily amenable to capital accumulation. In Syria, just as in every other country subject to the neoliberal shock doctrine, there is a combination of the privatisation of collective state production, health and welfare services, the stripping away of social support so that each individual or community is isolated and forced to take responsibility for the chaos that ensues, and the imposition of a strong state apparatus that prevents any form of collective resistance to defend services or to link individuals and communities. Syria can only be understood in this global neoliberal context.

Inside Syria, the neoliberal privatisation of state assets was speeded up by Assad soon after he came to power in 2000, and encouraged by intergovernmental agencies wanting to ensure the integration of the Syrian economy into the world market, a privatisation that had disastrous consequences for local communities and which met with some important early protests and even the beginnings of mass resistance. The world market was keen to inspire and protect the neoliberalising regime as one of its own kind. In 2006, for example, the Syrian regime became the fourth-largest recipient of foreign capital, as well as of Arab Gulf states' investments. This was one of the origins of discontent with the regime, but a strategy of divide and rule, the sectarian pitting of different Islamic faith communities against each other to ensure the dominance of the minority Alawis around Assad, was accompanied by increasing repression against progressive groups that attempted to work across those confessional boundaries.

The second global force is ostensibly 'natural' but also just as tightly connected with the actions of human beings driven by the accumulation of capital and the correlative exploitation and destruction of natural resources. A severe drought between 2007 and 2010, exacerbated by climate change, impacted on millions of small farmers and led to mass unemployment and emigration into the cities. This particular manifestation of climate change, the construction of canals and dams to divert water and the withdrawal of resources that would otherwise maintain aquifers in communities, was clearly human-made. Syrian state and commercial interests made short-term managerial goals and the extraction of profit take priority over human and environmental needs.

The Assad regime's brutal suppression of the uprising that began in the city of Deraa in March 2011 was quickly followed by a cynical strategy of releasing fascists from the prisons, fascists who mobilised under different banners and who would become a most virulent threat to the progressive forces in the form of 'Islamic State' (IS). The uprising and the repression are not at their heart about 'Islamism' at all, but about the way that the regime and then IS appropriates the term and fills it with their

54

own meaning, fills it with meaning in such a way as to ensure, on each side, that Syria will continue to follow a most vicious neoliberal path.

On the side of the Assad regime, that means using poison gas and other measures against civilian populations to terrorise them into abandoning the struggle for a democratic collective welfare state, a return to and, of course, improvement on the welfare policies that characterised the regime before Assad's neoliberal turn in the context of the ecological crisis. For many of those involved in the early demonstrations in Deraa, those reformist hopes underpinned the most minimal demands of the opposition movement. And, on the part of the regime, it also meant calling in Putin who, in pursuit of his own Islamophobic agenda in Chechnya and the Caucasus, and with an opportunity to drum home the new strength of Russia against a weakened United States, was more than willing to use indiscriminate air-strikes against different opposition groups, and, note, not so much against the areas controlled by Islamic State.

On the side of Islamic State, a brutal force that Assad was willing to do business with, the control and exploitation of the oil fields requires a system of capital control no less elaborate and neoliberal, one that combines intense repression of any group that threatens private property with a series of negotiations and deals that also effectively embeds IS in the global market. The fascists that have seized rebel areas, and ensured that there is no progressive collective threat to Assad, thereby function as a mirror of what still exists as a regime in Damascus, both competing with it and keeping it in place.

The combination of global forces that led to the crisis in the first place then feeds back into the crisis at both levels, at the level of human misery, the destruction of life, and at the level of environmental degradation, the destruction of nature. The death toll in Syria since 2011 has already surpassed a quarter of a million, over ten per cent of the population killed or injured, a flow of refugees trying to escape and find a place of safety in the Western states that have, themselves, also been engaging in airstrikes in order to buttress the Assad regime. This is also an intensification of the ecological crisis in which it is increasingly difficult to maintain even the most basic social and welfare services, not to mention systems of production and consumption. The air-strikes have led not only to the displacement of populations on a massive scale, but also the release from building rubble of metals, polychlorinated biphenyls and asbestos. The bombing, including by the West, has led to the destruction of oil-field installations and the spread of pollution, with the displaced populations now suffering from increased cancers and other diseases usually confined, and hidden, inside the industrial complexes.

Among the small organised progressive forces in Syria, the Revolutionary Left Current has always made it clear that the struggle to maintain opposition to the regime must, in some senses, be 'intersectional'; it links a series of different struggles. That is, it knows that it must work across the boundaries between and across the relationships that link the different confessional groups, that link the Syrians and the Kurds, and that link the fate of men and women fighting for their own liberation. And it is clear that this intersection of different forms of politics, the only signs of hope in an impossible situation, must also include an intersection between what human beings can do working together and ecological struggle, culture and nature.

Ecology is not a luxury in Syria, not merely a next step to take after the overthrow of the Assad regime, after the destruction of Islamic State fascism and after the construction of a socialist republic which will one day, working together with the rest of the Arab world, end capitalism in the region. It is not an optional and desirable additional factor in the struggle for freedom there any more than the liberation of women is. Ecology in Syria, as in every other part of the world, is now intrinsically and necessarily linked to every reactionary and progressive political movement, and it is only through ecosocialism that we can tackle the destruction of nature and the destruction of life, and the intimate link between the two. It is through ecosocialist politics that we can understand better the roots, the stakes and the progressive outcome of the struggle in Syria, and through ecosocialism that we will eventually survive the horrors of the war and build something better that will ensure this disaster never happens again.

Empire

Empire today is the diffusion and organisation of power as global and local. It is global and local and sexual, concerned with the intensification of power, as we can see from the case of 'Roosh V'. The Roosh V 'Return of Kings' meetings planned worldwide for Saturday 6 February 2016 were cancelled, but the despicable 'pick up artist' behind them was still going strong. It is clear now that this was a stunt, but the mobilisation against it was the right response. Roosh V might have been sobbing crocodile tears that he was forced to backtrack for the moment by feminists, but is even so still gloating in meetings of the US 'alt-right' at the publicity he has received so far. The meetings were organised as 'Tribal Gatherings'. As a global event they draw attention to Roosh V – US-based Daryush Valizadeh – in particular, and the recent rise of 'Pick Up Artists' (PUA) in general – those men who sell and buy strategies to bed women – operating as a phenomenon conditioned by a peculiar dialectic. This is a virulent reactionary dialectic of nationality and perverted inter-nationalism that some activists in the alter-globalisation and occupy movements will recognise as being that described by Michael Hardt and Antonio Negri in their 2000 book *Empire*. How so?

Empire provided an analysis of contemporary forms of power, and it shifts emphasis from traditional Marxist categories of class, the capitalist state and imperialism, to local 'assemblages' through which what Hardt and Negri call 'multitude' is kept in check. A Marxist account of working-class resistance to capital is of that resistance being conditioned by the economic forms that create it; there was no 'proletariat' in ancient Rome, for example, and it would not make sense to see in the Spartacus uprising the early origins of proletarian revolution. Capitalism creates its own gravediggers, and the revolution will thus lay the basis for those forces themselves to disappear once they have done their work. The 'multitude', on the other hand, is sometimes represented by Hardt and Negri as pre-existing Empire, as if it was always there bubbling up against it as a creative dynamic force. The concept 'Empire' also shifts emphasis from traditional feminist categories of patriarchy and the family, preferring instead to analyse new forms of 'immaterial' and 'affective labour'. This shift is problematic. We disagree with it, but let's work with it and see what can be made of it.

What the analysis of Empire does do, even as it sets itself against a 'totalising' account of capitalist and patriarchal order, is to piece together a historical account of how different forms of power operate to muffle, stifle and crush the life out of the multiplicity of forms of life that together mobilise against oppression and exploitation, forms of life we envisage as coexisting in a future post-capitalist society. That is, 'Empire' is the name for what we each from our different struggles encounter, and as we name it we are then able to configure it as a common enemy just as we configure ourselves in solidarity with each other. That was precisely the brief success of the 'Occupy' movement and the politics of the 'ninety-nine per cent'.

Now we see the logic of this notion of empire elaborated by Roosh V and the PUA movement. They provide a lesson about contemporary power for us in a different kind of way; what we have seen in Roosh V and the Tribal Gatherings has been a weird kind of 'intersectionality' in reverse, a kind of political response to progressive social movements that recognises the importance of gathering together different reactionary forces in order to produce a social block that can drive back the gains made in recent years by feminist, LGBTQ+ and anti-racist activists. Roosh V and his PUA followers crystallise the logic of Empire, showing us that it is necessarily more centralised than Hardt and Negri made it out to be, and that we need to integrate into it again an account of gender, sexuality and 'race'.

Much of the attention directed at the planned Roosh V meetings was directed at his argument that rape should be legalised, an argument that is actually straight out the neoliberal individualist textbook, even to the extent of claiming that if rape is made legal in private spaces then women themselves will be 'empowered' to protect themselves, instead of relying on what Roosh V calls the 'daddy state'. This argument should be set alongside his claim that 'all public rape allegations are false'. So, driving sexuality into the privacy of the home – something that the institution of the family under patriarchy has always entailed – is a strategy that goes hand-in-hand with the call for any kind of public resistance to be shut up.

Roosh V himself is quite open about this, and part of the declared aim of his 'neo-masculinist' movement is to reinstitute patriarchy. Men were told to meet up on 6 February 2016 and check out with their fellow men that they were at the right spot by asking the code question 'Where's the pet shop?' (The correct answer was 'the pet shop is here'.) They were also told not to bring their girlfriends, and to be clear that this was a meeting for heterosexual men only. The dimension of gender organised explicitly around the motif of 'patriarchy' is thus embedded in a broader understanding of the relationship between gender and sexual politics.

And there is another dimension to this that is not often remarked on, which is that this 'Pick Up Artist' movement is a sexist phenomenon which is closely bound up with racism. One of the dangers of the Tribal Gatherings was precisely that they would draw in and mobilise fascist sympathisers. In fact, the Roosh V PUA movement is, as it articulates its critique of feminism and broadens out that critique to other progressive social movements, one of the faces today of incipient fascism. Notice, for example, how Roosh V, in his video calling for the 6 February 2016 'International Tribal Meeting', comments that these gatherings are designed also to prepare men for 'times of emergency' when these men will be able to 'reach out to men' they can trust. He notes that he has been hearing from men in 'European countries' that are being 'invaded by afro-islamists' that this is a time of threat. And so, the dimension of gender and sexuality is also articulated with 'race'. In fact, 'race' is a key motif in the PUA movement, and Roosh V has plenty to say about the sexiness of women of different 'races' in what he refers to as the 'totem pole of attractiveness' and the speed with which they will respond to 'pick up' lines.

One of Roosh V's other recent activities was to engage in 'fat shaming', his argument being that the increase in weight by women worldwide was reducing the field of attractive partners for heterosexual men like Roosh V (and his followers), and that the obesity epidemic needed to be stopped. This particular twist on normative sexism was challenged on a television show, and one of the blog responses to that is indicative of the chain of different reactionary political positions that are being created. The blogger, who was broadly sympathetic to Roosh V, complained that the host of the TV show included fat women of colour in a celebration of diversity of body size. The rise of 'fatness' has had another effect, the blogger complained, which is that 'racial difference appears to diminish'. The key point, and this is a point which these two participants (the blogger and Roosh V) agree on, was that racial differences should be made more visible and that those differences should be acted on; acted on at a local level as the PUA assesses the racial characteristics of the women he targets, and acted on at a global level as the 'Tribal Gatherings' prepare men for the times of emergency during which their countries may be invaded by 'afro-islamists'.

The Roosh V phenomenon is sexist and racist, it mixes in a number of other reactionary political movements, and as it does that it condenses different dimensions of 'Empire'. It is as if Roosh V knows it from the inside, and as he articulates his knowledge, fleshes it out and acts on it, we must learn from what is happening here too. Despite the attempt by Hardt and Negri to shift attention from the United States as a 'centre' of imperial domination which then repeats the colonial and racist history of some nations 'picking up' others, what Roosh V shows us is that power is organised, that it does have a centre, and that at times of crisis this power becomes even more brutal, ideologically and materially. Feminist, anti-racist and socialist responses to Roosh V and the PUA have also had to be organised, and in that organisation of the 'multitude' in all its diversity we also learn something about Empire so that it can one day be brought to an end.

Eurocommunism

Eurocommunism was one of the reform strategies inside the Stalinist Communist Parties around the world in the 1970s that failed, but it still lives on. The failure of the Syriza leadership to mobilise the Greek people against the troika (the European Commission, the European Central Bank and the International Monetary Fund) in 2015 led to self-critiques by comrades working inside Syriza, reflections on the possibilities and limits of working through parliamentary institutions in alliance with those who want reforms rather than revolution. The possibilities, as with the Corbyn leadership of the Labour Party in Britain, are precisely that mobilisation with reformists inside the institutions also opens more space for mobilisation outside. The limits in the recent self-critiques have been given the name 'left-Europeanism', the present-day manifestation of 'Eurocommunism' which emerged during and as part of the disintegration of the Stalinist Communist Parties in the 1970s. These two sides of the same coin – an opening to revolutionary mobilisation and a reformist capitulation to capital – highlight the contradictory character of Eurocommunism itself, and it is important to remember that, bad though it was, it was not all bad.

Yes, it was bad. Eurocommunism was a symptom of the crisis of Stalinist politics. The Communist Parties around the world, which had been launched into a series of alliances with different reformist and bourgeois parties depending on what suited the diplomatic interests of Moscow, followed the centrifugal logic of that strategy. Allegiance to 'socialism in one country' in the USSR was replaced with allegiance to the local national context, with the 'British Road to Socialism' as programme of the Communist Party of Great Britain (CPGB), for example, increasingly adapting to the politics of the different forces it hoped to ally with. In fact, the centrifugal process, which eventually led to a break with

Moscow (and so to the final disintegration of what was left of the Third International), entailed a shift to the right, away from revolution to reformism. 'Eurocommunism' was neither communist nor European; all around the world the same process was happening, whether it was in Britain or Spain, South Africa or Japan.

The 'Eurocommunist' strategy, which was viewed as a betrayal by the old Stalinists in the party, was actually following through the line to its logical conclusion; eventually in Britain seeking an alliance with the left-wing of the Conservative Party (mimicking the hopes for a 'historic compromise' with the Christian Democrats proposed by the Italian Communist Party). In this respect, Eurocommunism always continued the Stalinist tradition of adapting to nationalism, to the national peculiarities of each context that amounted to wanting to work within the existing institutions in each country, and that is why some of the sharpest critiques, those made by Ernest Mandel, for example, referred to it, in the subtitle of his 1978 book *From Stalinism and Eurocommunism*, as the 'bitter fruits' of 'socialism in one country'.

The theoretical justification for what was happening was patched together as the process intensified, with the hope that what the Italian communist Antonio Gramsci called a 'war of position', one which emphasised building new alliances and seizing ground from the capitalist state, could complement the old 'war of manoeuvre' taking on the state in a full-frontal assault to replace it with soviet power. The search in the CPGB theoretical journal *Marxism Today* for new theoretical underpinnings for old reformist strategies included two strands: 'discourse' theory (particularly in the work of Ernesto Laclau and Chantal Mouffe, theory which was influential among some of those involved with Syriza in Greece and Podemos in Spain); and 'cultural studies', especially in the work of Stuart Hall on 'Thatcherism', a recoil from the supposed horrors of 'economic determinism' associated with old Marxism and an engagement, instead, with other kinds of politics.

That second strand still exists, if now very small and barely existing outside networks of ex-CPGB and fellow-traveller academics, around the so-called 'Kilburn Manifesto', though there is still more energy spent on trying to bury the old Stalinist past (which is repeatedly painted as being the same as a revolutionary approach) than actually elaborating an alternative beyond repeating reformist 'policy' ideas. Commentary on the 2015 UK general election fiasco from within this tradition also seems to replace economic determinism with psychoanalysis (a theoretical resource for Ernesto Laclau and Chantal Mouffe as well as for Stuart Hall).

The problem was mainly that the Eurocommunist embrace of 'new' ideas (from feminist politics, anti-racism and postcolonialism, among others) already took as its starting point the false assumption that revolutionary politics was 'old' and that in one way or another it must necessarily be tainted by Stalinism. An assessment by the CIA in 1985 which was later made available online was that Eurocommunism had already failed, but that doesn't at all mean that the story is over, and we still need to ask what, from our own revolutionary standpoint, was in it that we still need to take seriously and what we can reclaim.

First, the critique of traditional left organisation by socialist feminists that was used to fuel the Eurocommunist revolt inside the CPGB drew attention to the importance of relations of power beyond the capitalist state, relations of power in the family, for example, that then enabled that state power to maintain itself. There was, of course, a critique of Stalinism in that new politics, but it was a critique which was actually developed in the book *Beyond the Fragments* by feminists from three revolutionary organisations: International Socialists (now the SWP), Big Flame (now defunct) and the International Marxist Group (at that time the British Section of the Fourth International).

Second, the development of postcolonial and anti-racist

critique, which was particularly important in the work of Stuart Hall, was repeating and reconnecting with classical Marxist arguments that had been lost with the rise of Stalinism. The influence of 'socialism in one country' had consequences not only for the way that the Soviet Union presented itself as the highpoint of civilization, as a socialist state that needed to be defended by its loyal supporters whatever the cost, whatever lies needed to be told, but also consequences for the reintroduction inside Marxism of the idea that there were 'stages of development' and that some cultures were lesser than others.

Third, the false opposition that was set up between 'old' undemocratic revolutionary socialism and 'new' more democratic forms of organisation in Eurocommunist discourse made it seem as if the 'party' as such was bad and structureless networks were good. It then made sense to fold up the party into the 'Democratic Left' in the early 1990s, and then to fold that up as well. This was all presented as if there had never been arguments inside the communist movement about 'democracy', as if the Bolshevik Party itself had not included different factions arguing about strategy, as if the first crime against the revolution in Russia by Stalin and his supporters was not precisely to close down internal party discussion. The 'new' debates also forced a clarification by the Fourth International in 1985 of what 'dictatorship of the proletariat' meant as an extension of democracy rather than a suppression of it.

The danger at every point in the evolution and disintegration of the Communist Parties was that the revolutionary left would simply react instead of responding, would react by complaining of the shift toward more explicitly reformist politics instead of responding to the genuine interest in feminist, anti-racist and democratic politics that was being used by the Eurocommunists to try and make sense of their past. Reacting instead of responding always made it seem as if the revolutionary left actually wanted to return to a democratic centralist party guided by one correct analysis of the economy and contemptuous of the intersection between class and other forms of oppression.

And now, with the revival of new broad movements for social change, there is a trap. The trap is that we make it seem as if, because we already know what is wrong with reformism, we should refuse to participate in the debates that are happening among the new forces drawn into politics for the first time. The sectarian left already have their answers sharpened and ready, and those reactions by the bizarre authoritarians of the self-styled 'CPGB (Provisional Central Committee)' spawned by this history, reactions to anti-racist feminism and to attempts to make left organisations more democratic (reactions that include lashing out at the idea that there should be 'safe spaces' for debate inside the left of Labour British political party Left Unity, for example) serve to confirm all that the Eurocommunists said about revolutionaries as they tried to distance themselves from their own past. Instead we have to show that we too were always looking for alternatives, and that we welcomed the internal decomposition of Stalinism; not because of what 'reforms' might be possible inside the apparatus but because of what mobilisation of revolutionary ideas and practice it would provoke outside, revolutionary ideas and practice that we can and must connect with and learn from.

Event

To speak of an 'event' is a way of conceptualising the eruption of the unexpected to transform politics. When we name significant political events we draw them into political discourse, and in that way we give them a life which extends beyond the one moment when they occurred. The keyword 'event', marked out as a particular term attached to politics, and popularised among academics by the philosopher Alain Badiou, raises at least two questions about how we speak about movements and parties like Podemos and Syriza. The first concerns the theoretical discourse of event, and the second concerns events that have not yet happened.

The first question concerns a theoretical discourse about *Being and Event* from Badiou in, for example, his 1988 book of that title. For Badiou, an 'event' calls for a repeated evocation of it and of what has changed, including what has changed for those subject to it, which he termed 'fidelity' to the event. The scope of this theoretical discourse can be seen in the way that Badiou describes such 'events' as occurring not only in the field of politics, but also in the fields of science, art and love (where Badiou's own fidelity to psychoanalytic discourse is adapted and modified). There is discussion among Badiou's followers as to whether the Russian October 1917 Revolution, or the Paris May 1968 protests, or the Greek January 2015 election of Syriza, count as an event. Badiou himself asked whether the election of Syriza might have led to a 'rupture'. But more important than that is the frame of the discussion, so that what is described is always already interpreted within its own theoretical discourse, even where, in the case of the election of Syriza for example, we know that there are performative consequences of the description for what might have happened next.

There is a danger that this theoretical discourse about 'event' is enclosed in an academic discourse. We need to notice straightaway that Badiou himself, who graduated from the Union des communistes de France marxiste-léniniste to the École Normale Supérieure, is an unusual academic, involved for some years as an activist in L'Organisation Politique for example, but is an academic nonetheless. His involvement with politics, which is that of 'being' an academic who is writing about 'events', is one that still entails, therefore, an involvement that reaches out through the window and tries to embrace what is going on outside. The 'problematic' of this theoretical discourse – that is, the constellation of issues that this discourse organises itself around – is precisely how to connect 'being' with an 'event'. This theoretical discourse wants to interpret the world by changing it (which seems Marxist enough), but (and this 'but' introduces an element of uncertainty into its Marxist ambition) it wants to change the world through the frame of a theoretical discourse.

This is also the problematic of Podemos in Spain, but with a difference. It is the problematic of Podemos because that project was precisely that of academics in 'political science' around Pablo Iglesias Turrión from inside the Universidad Complutense de Madrid. They reached out the window to connect with the Indignados and, despite Pablo Iglesias' own political history as former member of the Unión de Juventudes Comunistas de España (the youth wing of the Spanish Communist Party), that movement was understood by them, and by many of the partici-pants themselves, to be a form of 'anti-politics'. Iglesias' own academic work includes research and writing in the fields of political and social theory and in psychoanalysis, and it is engagement with theoretical debate that led the Complutense group to organise their own academic discourse as one which sought to intervene at the level of politics itself; that is, they draw upon the 'post-Marxist' discourse theory of Ernesto Laclau and Chantal Mouffe described in their 1985 book *Hegemony and Socialist Strategy*, for example, in order to reconfigure the

Indignados movement as what Laclau and Mouffe would recognise as a form of 'radical populism'.

This political-theoretical strategy entailed sidelining the post-Trotskyist Izquierda Anticapitalista, which had played a key role in building Podemos while insisting upon the properly political aspects of the Indignados movement. Izquierda Anticapitalista were themselves so keen to remain involved in Podemos as a party that now prohibits dual-membership that they dissolved their own organisation in 2015 so that they could continue participating, as an 'Anticapitalistas' movement with the Iglesias group in command. Changing the world through the frame of a theoretical discourse is the same problematic as that of the search for and celebration of an 'event' that might also change the 'being' of Badiou and his academic followers who aim to find an event outside the university. The difference is that Podemos has so far succeeded in implanting its discourse in the wider political field. They have succeeded in making their 'anti-political' discourse resonate with an 'anti-political' suspicion of the anti-austerity movement. That very success may be its undoing, and the attempt to maintain its position in lead poll-position led Podemos to propose policies that take what may be a fatal step from 'populism' to 'commonsense'.

The danger then is two-fold, for along with the theoretical framing of politics which hopes for an event to occur there is the emergence of something in politics that is not an event as such. Rather, it is something that appears in the place of the event which then all too easily seduces and reassures the academics. Might we see the rapid growth of Podemos in this light, and the shift of position of its architect in a movement that, against the hopes of its members, turned itself into a political party, with a 'Secretary-General', and with a representative function in the European Parliament? And from that position, from the position of someone who was an academic and who is now a 'politician', the world looks a little different, looks perhaps less like a world where events might take place and more like a world that is waiting for policies to be promised in a general election.

There is closely connected to this question a second question, which is about how we relate to events which have not yet occurred. In 2015 the election in Greece of Syriza as an event or not was still uncertain, but this election did play a role as precursor to the possible victory of Podemos in Spain. This transnational dimension of Podemos is what gives it significance beyond Spain (and, by the same token, it was the transnational dimension of the momentary victory of Syriza before its capitulation to the troika that gave it significance). It gave it significance as something that could for a moment at least stand in for an event, so that something that really counts as an event might happen in the future. The philosopher Immanuel Kant once remarked that the 1879 French Revolution (which he celebrated) was of moment not so much for those who actually participated in it but for the enthusiasm it produced among its supporters across Europe.

Something of that was once true in the case of Syriza which had a double-function for Podemos, and this begins to help us answer the question as to how we relate to events that have not happened yet. As could be seen in the massive Podemos demonstrations against austerity and in solidarity with Syriza that took place in Madrid immediately after the Greek election, whatever deal the finance minister Yanis Varoufakis (who was never actually a member of Syriza) struck with the troika, the election of Syriza was the promise of the election of Podemos in Spain. At the same time, Syriza was desperately buying time, waiting for the election of Podemos, waiting for something to happen elsewhere in Europe that would finally, retroactively, make it possible to say that the election of one, and then so of both, would be a combined event. Even as the space between the two elections opened up, the space for either election to operate as event was also closing down. While we were waiting in the space between the elections in Greece and Spain we were also working to keep the space open for them to operate together as an event.

And so, here in the alternative to an event that had not yet happened, and as an alternative to the hope for an event outside its own theoretical discourse, there was a task of solidarity by those of us who Badiou and his followers gaze upon hopefully waiting for something to happen that they can then interpret. Our task of solidarity was a political task, and it is eventful, composed of a series of activities that linked us with Greece and Spain. Our task was also to turn enthusiasm for radical change that was flowing backwards and forwards across Europe into a broader international response to the global crisis of capitalism. For just as Greek revolutionaries needed their Spanish comrades, and vice versa, so support for what might be called an event needed to be extended in order to also break open fortress Europe.

Fascism

Fascism is barbarism as the last resort of capital to protect itself. Revolutionaries are usually very careful about using the term 'fascism' out of context, and they are careful because it is too easy to throw it around as a term of abuse, applying it to things that are reactionary or just plain bad. Then the definition of fascism loses its precise meaning, which is dangerous because, when the real threat of fascism appears, we can be accused of crying wolf. Then fascists can also avoid the accusation, willing to play up their differences with other fascist movements and so pretend that they are different, that they have been misunderstood. The term has mutated, however, not only because it has become a banal word, evacuated of meaning at times when revolutionary struggle is on the defensive and the ruling ideologies are so strong, but also because fascism itself mutates every time it appears, appears in different shapes that we need to track and respond to when we turn to this keyword to describe what is happening.

Judging people against an ideal body image, arguing in favour of certain kinds of food, refusing to buy particular clothes, are among the most ridiculous popular uses of the term 'fascist'. It not that politics as such is absent from any of these domains, even when the term is also used by the right, and fascists have certainly had something to say about each of these things in their attempt to impose segregation and order. More seriously, the murderous attacks by Islamic State (IS) have been described by some revolutionaries as 'jihadist barbarism' rather than fascism, but perhaps now we need to be more precise and call things as they are, insist on our own analysis of IS. We need to do this, among other reasons, in order not to slip into just as lazy caricatures of 'jihad' so beloved of the bourgeois press.

There is a little relativist trap that Marxists are prone to fall into when they are wary of using the term 'fascism' outside the context of so-called advanced capitalist states. The historical experience of fascism for the left in Germany, Italy and Spain makes it seem like it should be applied only in those political-economic conditions. And so when IS, Al-Shabaab ('the youth') or Boko Haram ('western education is forbidden') appear outside the West, the trap is that these apparently less advanced or developed conditions seem to require their own separate analysis that does not conform to Western categories. One problem here is that we overlook a key tenet of the development of Marxist analysis itself which is that the world economy has become an increasingly interdependent global entity. The uneven development of each and every part of the world is now combined with the others, and Western imperialism that suffered at its heart the barbarism of fascism extends its economic and political rule everywhere.

Fascism mobilises 'tradition' for sure, just as it did in the heartlands of Europe, and just as it threatened to do in the United States when there was the prospect of a large enough labour movement to frighten the bourgeoisie. The capitalist class that benefits from this economic world order will resort to anything to defend its interests. However, this class in the West, its political parties and its States – the bodies of armed men that protect its private property – rather like democracy. They like it because democratic values have efficiently persuaded generations of workers to believe that they too could be rich, that there is the possibility of 'class transition' and a trickle-down of wealth. At the same time, the ruling class will tolerate dictatorship abroad in the uncivilised 'third world' (which serves too to reassure the West of its superiority), and even at home if it is necessary. Fascism is an extreme solution, desperate and brutal, not only for those it is directed at – the workers and the oppressed – but also for those who apply it (for it is inconvenient, restrictive, and unfortunately necessary for the bourgeoisie). Better if it can be

74

kept at a distance, which is why Western states and their allies will unleash it reluctantly when they are at a loss for any other kind of solution.

Fascism is unleashed as a response to a crisis in which capitalism itself is imperilled, as the gay anarcho-communist Daniel Guerin argued in his book *Fascism and Big Business*, a classic study from 1939 which has always been part of the best revolutionary socialist literature on the topic. Not only did fascism directly and immediately save capitalism in Europe from working-class revolution in the 1920s and 1930s, but, as Guerin points out, it also increased profits massively for the large companies. This was not only because of the use of slave-labour in the camps, the reduction of the proletariat to the most abject conditions, to the less-than-human objects, commodities, which they had always been viewed as by their masters, but also because any resistance to exploitation had been broken with the destruction of the labour unions. In Germany (and, to an extent also in Italy and Spain) fascism succeeded after the left had failed – a failure that was bound up with the disastrous tactics of the Communist Parties under the control of Stalin – and the 'solution' to the continuing crisis of capitalism that would also deal a death-blow to the communists was at hand.

Already in the context of early globalising capitalism, it was not only the German, Italian and Spanish bourgeoisie who benefitted from fascism, but big business in other capitalist countries, including in the United States; Ford, General Motors and IBM (the company responsible for the numbering system tattooed on to the concentration camp prisoners) participated actively and made a financial killing from fascism in Europe. And the destruction of revolutionary resistance to capitalist rule in Afghanistan, Saudi Arabia and then the rest of the Arab world made a killing for capitalism in what Gilbert Achcar has termed, in the title of his 2006 book, *The Clash of Barbarisms*. It found a way of unleashing forces that would protect private property and enable a fresh start, reconstruction as part of contemporary 'disaster capitalism' or 'shock capitalism' outside the imperialist centres.

This is why fascists of every stripe are explicitly unleashed against the prospect of a revolutionary overthrow of capitalism, and this is why an essential part of their propaganda is to attack 'communism'. The Nazis, for example, targeted the 'Bolshevik-Jewish' conspiracy as the main threat, and Jews were demonised and then slaughtered in the camps precisely because they were supposedly pulling the strings during the Russian Revolution and then in the impending revolution in Germany. The naming of Jews as the enemy behind the scenes fulfilled an ideological function for the Nazis, a function that was not so necessary to other fascist movements, but was a consequence of the deep-ingrained anti-Semitism in German history. 'National Socialist' fascism in Germany, then, as with every other variety of fascism, was a populist alternative to revolutionary socialism, and was able to patch together available prejudices to construct a machinery of mass-murder.

What Nazism shared with every other variety of fascism was the transformation of the terms of popular political debate – the ideological dimension in which revolutionaries elaborate their argument against capitalism to build a communist movement – so that in place of an internal contradiction there is conjured up an external threat. In place of class struggle, and in place of any other division between exploited and exploiters, between oppressed and oppressors, a struggle in which we are able to see that the enemy is at home, fascism is able to enforce an ideological consensus that the enemy is something foreign to be rooted out and destroyed. When it is identified, rooted out and destroyed this will thereby guarantee the organic and natural unity of the body politic. This is why fascism always resorts to naturalistic and quasi-medical metaphors to describe how it is cleansing the body politic of the disease of communism. The good health of the nation is ideologically looped around the health of each good citizen and back again, in the spectacle of pure-blood heritage mass rallies against the threat from outside.

The exact content of fascism is therefore secondary to its form and to its function in capitalist society, in any particular capitalist society or in the destruction and reconstruction of capitalist society anywhere in the world. This is why under some aspects it indeed looks as if Nazism – the form that fascism took in Germany – built on its Christian heritage (Martin Luther's hatred of popular revolt combined with polemics against 'the Jews and their lies' was useful for these purposes) and at the same time many Nazis themselves were more taken with a Pagan return to supposedly authentic Nordic or Greek roots. The claim to one or the other, or the search for other cultural origins of Nazism misses the point, as does the claim that fascism is necessarily explicitly anti-woman or anti-gay (as the recent incorporation of gay rights in the homonationalist discourse of the Front National in France makes clear). Each kind of fascism pukes up its own particular kind of 'undigested barbarism' from the past of its own culture and irrational hatred of others, hatred of impurities in its vision of an organic unity that will ensure the health of nation and the economy; irrational hatred that is combined with mysticism and mystification takes its own particular distinctive form in different places and different times.

So, there was fascism, of course, in Japan, where Shinto was the glue for an ultra-nationalist movement that aimed to eliminate the left (a project of containment and persecution that continued during the anti-communist witch-hunt under the US occupation after the Second World War). And there is fascism in Israel, where ultra-Zionists direct their attacks on the left as traitors to the nation who stand up for Palestinians (and Albert Einstein, for example, warned against the danger of fascism in Israel back in the 1930s). There is fascism in Russia, a new great Russia under Putin after the final failure of a regime that pretended to be communist, and the revival of anti-Semitism is a vicious tool to weld the nation together into one organic unity. And there is fascism in Greece, waiting in the wings, at one moment suppressed and at the next unleashed, waiting to be used by the capitalist class at home and, if necessary, to be encouraged in Europe proper (again reluctantly, with agonising hand-wringing and in such a way as to also confirm the idea that there was always an underlying barbarism of the Greeks which finally explains why they were so untrustworthy).

And there is fascism in the Arab world, now in Syria, where the Assad regime released the most deadly anti-communist fighters from its prisons in order to destroy the opposition, a version of the 'clash of barbarisms' where one deadly solution is still being applied to stabilise the political order. In the case of Syria, as elsewhere, the real threat of fascism – now in the shape of IS – comes after the failure of the left. This time it is failure not as a result of internal divisions or an incorrect programme, but as a result of brute force, murderous assaults on those who defended the Kurds in the north-east of the country.

This is not really 'Islamofascism' any more than the Nazis were 'Christofascists' or 'paganofascists' or that Golden Dawn in Greece now are 'hellenofascists'. It is barbaric, but not because it is 'jihadist'. IS is designed to destroy any left alternative, to terrorise the opposition, to protect private property, and to mobilise hatred of difference, to enforce an organic unity of the community and enable the reconstruction of capitalism. It is a shock to the system that will save the system; it is fascist as such, and we need to name it in order to understand how it works, how it appeals to those without other kinds of hope for a better world, name it as part of the struggle to defeat it.

Feminisation

Feminisation replaces feminist critiques of gender-power and patriarchy with a celebration of flexibility, starting with that of women. Feminisation is an ideological motif that is deployed to mark out who is to be admired for showing these stereotypical 'feminine' traits. Remember Yanis Varoufakis? Yanis Varoufakis, Greece's so-called 'erratic Marxist' Finance Minister, was represented in line with a number of different stereotypes as part of the ideological response to, and sometimes even also defence of Syriza. Among these stereotypical representations was one briefly debated on a little Facebook thread, whether he was being 'feminised' by the media. This argument was kicked off by the objections to Varoufakis agreeing to a photo-shoot for *Paris Match* which showed him posing with his wife in his lovely apartment in the shadow of the Parthenon while trying to sell a deal which, it was hoped, would fool the Germans and mollify the Greeks.

The question seemed to revolve around whether he was a tough guy standing up for Greece, a real man shoulder to shoulder with his comrades, or whether he was giving way and would be a passive partner with the troika and so lead his country-folk to humiliating surrender. The stakes for Syriza were high, and the struggle inside the party was about buying time while enabling the Greek people to mobilise for the real showdown. That endgame, which seemed to entail a choice between macho resistance and feminine submission, was a distraction from the political-economic issues in the streets and strike-committees. But it is an ideological distraction that did show us something of the way that capitalism pits winners against losers and men and against women, and it drew attention to 'feminisation' as a significant process in which the workforce and then national identities are being reconfigured today.

This 'feminisation' should not be confused with feminism, and the only connection between the two is the idea that women are more intuitive and caring of others – qualities that have histori-cally been used to treat women as lesser than men while pretending to make them more lovely – which was mobilised by some feminists is now harnessed to the needs of contemporary capitalism. That is, some forms of feminism which emphasised the biological and 'maternal' character of women, sometimes tactically, have been recuperated, neutralised and absorbed by capitalism, as Nancy Fraser argues in her 2013 book *Fortunes of Feminism*. This is the case most dramatically in the service sector, which has rapidly expanded in the past fifty years in what is sometimes, after the work of the Belgian Marxist economist Ernest Mandel, called 'late capitalism'. The rise of the service sector – including hotel, restaurant and shop-work, as well as all kinds of call-centre and consumer support – which now forms the highest proportion of the economy in most countries, including in the 'developing' world, saw the re-entry into the workforce of women on a massive scale. The early years of capitalism in Europe had actually involved women as workers – something lost to historical memory with the enclosure of women as homemakers in the nuclear family – and the globalisation of capitalism now calls upon women as workers worldwide.

Women in the service sector are especially valuable employees because they bring stereotypical 'feminine' values to the workplace and to interaction with customers, and this involves more intense forms of exploitation and alienation. The feminist sociologist Arlie Hochschild described, in her 1983 book *The Managed Heart*, how airline stewardesses, for example, have to be not only efficient workers but also to be super-attentive to the needs of travellers. This 'emotional labour' is draining. All the more so because the stewardesses have to engage in what Hochschild called 'deep acting' in which they display their emotions to others, not able easily to guard a private space away from the workplace. It is difficult to remember that this work, this interaction with the customer, is not all there is to life when emotional energy is poured into being very nice. This feminisation of interaction with customers then spins into a broader feminisation inside organisations, and now not only in the service sector, as there are demands to comply and to mean it, to be very nice to managers and to show some depth of emotional commitment to the organisation. This is then the context in which managerial advice is given to help women (and men who must also learn from women in this process of feminisation) to cope and help workers present 'a positive face' to their customers and employers.

This feminisation of capitalism, the re-entry of women into the workforce, their exploitation and then the transformations of the process of capital accumulation which entail the management of emotion as well as behaviour, also has repercussions for the way the oppressed are treated and represented. Racism, for example, has drawn on a range of contradictory strategies to pathologise the oppressed, sometimes treating Black men as hyper-masculine, as an animalistic threat to civilization, which is assumed to be something closer to feminine sensibilities, and sometimes feminising races and nations who are treated as if they are childlike, like women, and so not yet up to the standards of modern rational society. This is lose-lose for the oppressed in the game of stereotypical masculinity versus femininity, and the trap of feminisation is set for them. Resistance to imperialism can then be characterised as macho protest, as refusing to comply with the rules of the game, or, at the very same time, the 'other' of the West can be rendered as less than masculine, feminised, which was the argument made by Edward Said in his depiction of strategies of 'orientalism', which is clearly relevant to the way that Greece was treated as traitor to the European ideal and, by implication, closer to the orient. It is in this sense that we might say that Varoufakis himself was being 'feminised'.

One response to the recruitment of women's stereotypical

qualities and capacity for care in the service sector is to connect that care to solidarity and so to deliberately make the link once again between feminisation and feminism, though this time in such a way as to reframe those qualities as strengths rather than weaknesses. This has been the way for some Marxist traditions learning from feminism and redefining their politics so that collective mobilisation connects with everyday life, so that 'big politics' connects with the everyday political tasks and with how men and women relate to each other. This is Marxist feminism that takes seriously the slogan 'the personal is the political', and it is in that context that there have been discussions inside some revolutionary organisations, for example, about 'feminising the organisation'.

Another response, which complements this attempt to revalue the contribution of women in radical politics, is to unravel masculine stereotypes and so open the space for a different, perhaps queerer way of working through questions of power. This unravelling of stereotypes in politics by exaggerating them and mocking them sometimes backfires but is still worth a go. This was the way in some of the interventions to support Syriza negotiating with the troika, inside Greece and inside Germany. This unravelling applies to national and gender stereotypes. Rumours from Athens immediately after the election of Syriza in January 2015 included that a popular chant among some demonstrators in support of the new government was 'Halloumi, Souvlakis, Yanis Varoufakis', though the nearest slender evidence for this actually has 'bread' instead of halloumi (which is actually Cypriot). Meanwhile, German solidarity with Syriza was sometimes more implicit, self-mocking and targeted the image of Varoufakis, not as feminised as such but rather as the other side of feminisation, as a hyper-masculine leather-jacketed motorbiking threat. Either way, feminisation reinforces rather than unravels gender binaries, and is a mixed blessing for the left.

Globalisation

Globalisation today is mainly about colonial rule enforcing imperial versions of universality. Even, it seems, in the academic work of one of its critics. Noam Chomsky, for example, is an energetic presence on the left, adding his voice to many protests against injustice around the world. He can be relied upon to sign open letters and to speak on political platforms devoted to progressive campaigns. He stands four-square against imperialism, and in this respect he is a valuable player in the anti-globalisation movement that claims that another world is possible, another world to capitalist globalisation, one in which there are genuine bonds of international solidarity. In this capacity as activist, he is known to be some kind of anarchist, though it is not always clear to those who invite him to speak what that means. And, as an added ingredient to his well-earned authority, of status that he brings to many campaigns, Chomsky is also known to be a respected academic, a distinguished researcher in the field of linguistics, of the study and theory of how language works. But, in fact, although Chomsky works on linguistics as a professor at the Massachusetts Institute of Technology (MIT), and even though he has plenty to say about the use of propaganda as a key part of imperialist power, he has nothing to say about the link between language and politics. That gap, that refusal to say anything about the link between his academic and political work, enables us to see something important about the role of 'globalisation' today, how it works, and how it relies on forms of expertise that marginalise people around the world.

Chris Knight's 2016 book *Decoding Chomsky* examines the gap between linguistics and politics, and spells out some of the consequences, expanding arguments that have already been rehearsed by Knight in journal articles and in video presentations in recent years. Knight is in a strong position to make this argument, a respected academic stalwart of the 'Radical Anthropology Group' and long-standing activist who put his political work on the line against the academic institution. Past editor of the magazine of the tiny Trotskyist group 'Chartist' and then a leader of the 'Chartist minority tendency', he has continued linking theoretical critique with radical activism, flirting with a number of different groups since. His book on Chomsky is a thoroughly researched impassioned critique of the separation between academic knowledge and radical politics, but it fares less well in dealing with an equally problematic aspect of Chomsky's work which replicates and reinforces that separation; that is, the separation between the global and the local, between globalisation and indigenous knowledge. One would expect that Knight as a trained anthropologist would be a bit more canny about this, and be able to home in on the way that Chomsky ends up trumpeting Western science in the field of linguistics, over how different language groups actually speak.

This is a vitally important question for any genuinely internationalist revolutionary movement that has learnt from the history of colonialism and imperialism and that reflects for a moment on how the Western left is implicated in that history. Globalisation today is a process of insidious control that continues the dynamic of market expansion that Marx noticed back in the first volume of *Capital* in 1867; capitalism forces local cultures around the world to adapt to the market, and to the dominant ideological parameters of what it is to be a good economically active citizen as specified and managed by the old imperial centres, in Europe and then the United States, and in the new imperial states, such as Russia and China that mimic the old powers in order to push capitalist growth. That process of globalisation today entails its own peculiar forms of 'recuperation' of local economies so that what is 'indigenous' does not pose a threat to industrialisation but is harnessed to it. And so it is, for example, with the phenomenon of 'glocalisation' which is able to get niche markets to work in the service of what is, at its base, a commodified standardised world culture governed by and feeding the super-rich.

Chomsky himself is deeply contradictory on this score. At the one moment he hails indigenous struggles as the cutting edge of popular resistance against globalisation, and, at the next, he explicitly proclaims himself to be in favour of globalisation. Knight's book does help make sense of that paradox, but there are limits to his critique. Before we return to that blind-spot in Knight's account, let's look at some of the paradoxes he does neatly identify in Chomsky's work that throw more light on this particular problem of globalisation.

Knight's argument is that Chomsky's work on a universal grammar funded by the Pentagon – and there is no doubt about this, Chomsky is quite open in citing military support for his revolutionary work on syntax – is systematically sealed off from Chomsky's own anti-war activity. The theoretical and practical stakes of this are high; the linguistic work on universal syntactical structures was part of the Pentagon project to develop a basic machine language that would enable the development of a human-machine interface with weapons technology. That is, the Pentagon knows better something about the connection between theory and practice than Chomsky. Knight claims that this is a choice made by Chomsky that repeats the choice that the French philosopher René Descartes made in separating mind from body back in 1637. That separation was made in the context of what Descartes was learning about the suppression by the Catholic Church of Galileo's work, and Descartes drew the conclusion that it was prudent to speak about the body in such a way as to keep it well out of the domain of theology.

No wonder, then, that Chomsky takes Descartes as one of his intellectual heroes. And when Chomsky is asked about the connection between his theories of abstract global grammar and his political work, he says that he doesn't make the connection – he claims that his mind works like a computer with two separate buffers – and he scorns the contribution of anyone who is not an 'expert' to his intellectual field. The weird separation, between Chomsky's linguistics and his politics, also has dramatic consequences for each sphere of work. On the one hand, the linguistics is abstracted and theoretical, having no connection with actual spoken languages. Chomsky is against anthropological research of that kind. And, on the other hand, the critique is antithetical to any kind of connection between the personal and the political, or to feminist 'standpoint' theories which ask how and why certain kinds of knowledge are produced.

Language is at the heart of recent transformations in left politics, but as language intimately connected with practice. That understanding of language is precisely the reverse of the way that Chomsky plays it. This is why Chomsky has, on those rare occasions when he has strayed into debate with so-called 'post-structuralist' theorists of knowledge and power like Michel Foucault, resorted to claims about science and human nature that end up reifying both, treating both as unchanging bedrock of reality, a reality that is rooted in a particular conception of the world that makes it seem as if the West tells the truth and it is the job of the rest of the world to catch up.

A bizarre twist toward the end of Knight's book *Decoding Chomsky* is when the same universalist motif is wheeled out, repeating arguments he is best-known for in anthropology from his 1995 book *Blood Relations: Menstruation and the Origins of Culture*. This is all the more bizarre because claims from anthropology are used by him to tell us what biological imperatives underpinned matriarchal societies at the dawn of human history. This biological argument is a brave attempt to provide the evolutionary theory of language development that Chomsky assiduously avoids, but it falls into the trap of taking what Western anthropologists think they have discovered about indigenous cultures, piecing it together as an academic theory and then selling it back to the world as global knowledge.

Knight's book pits itself against Chomsky but reiterates the underlying ideological motif of globalisation: the language, knowledge and practice of the West will rule, and the local will be understood and managed in line with that. Revolutionary socialists are not against globalisation as such, of course, but our internationalism is for the globalisation of another world of struggle and solidarity which brings together the diverse strengths of each culture, of each local culture as, in some senses, simultaneously indigenous and dislocated, in its place and moving beyond it. That means speaking out against the globalisation of our languages, either in the attempt to make them conform to a standard Western conception of what language is or in the attempt to reduce them to biologically wired-in relationships between women and men. That means reclaiming the space for diverse indigenous struggles and ways of being which are in line with some of the more really radical anthropological research that also connects with politics and turns against abstracted academic models of who we are and could be.

Homonationalism

Homonationalism is one way that sexual politics is incorporated into capitalist state agendas. This keyword for a new left comes from Black feminist and queer analysis and from interventions into the way that lesbian and gay subcultures are recruited to reinforce the imperialist state. An analysis of 'homonationalism' deepens our understanding of the way Islamophobia operates today and also of the ideological stakes of the slogan 'Je suis Charlie' plastered all over the Radio France Internationale website after the January 2015 fascist terrorist attack on *Charlie Hebdo*, and in many other places. Homonationalism is a way of grasping the intersection between racism, sexism, heterosexism and the nation state.

An early account by Jasbir Puar in her 2007 book *Terrorist Assemblages* argued that liberal tolerance of lesbians and gays has mutated into something more dangerous. Grudging acceptance of sexual minorities, on condition that they are invisible and obedient to heterosexual institutions, is now replaced with active attempts to recognise, celebrate and include a range of queer subcultures. But this active inclusion comes on condition that they show allegiance to the state, a state that is adapting itself to redefine who its friends and who its real enemies are. Puar and other writers developed this analysis of homonationalism to argue that hostility to Islam is one of the conditions for queer-friendly imperialism, and that it not only reinforces each Western state but also underpins relations between states, supporting Israel, for example, in its claim to be an oasis of tolerance for lesbians and gays surrounded by a barbaric and backward Arab world; such 'pinkwashing' of Israel is intimately linked to Islamophobia.

In the wake of the attack, and what was presented in the mainstream media as a successful and victorious conclusion of the response by the French security forces, there were warnings that this victorious atmosphere should not spin into reaction against Islam. The problem is that Islamophobia is not a reaction to what has happened but the very context for the events. Many of the *Charlie Hebdo* cartoons crystallised some of the most potent and pernicious ideological elements of homonationalist Islamophobia. This is not to say that some of their cartoons were not also poking fun at other religions or politicians, were progressive even, and not to say that some of the cartoons weren't also funny, a pressure-valve release for frustrations of the sometimes humourless left. There was an understandable temptation to join in and chant 'Je suis Charlie', a fake collective response to the attacks which was effectively colluding with liberals who have contempt for the left, or for anyone and everyone who really believes in something and will fight for it.

What should be noticed about the worst examples of the cartoons, though, was that they homed in on the supposed difference between the open sexually-liberated and tolerant reader – one fantasy that the homonationalist likes to have about themselves – and their intolerant and sexually-restricted targets, images underpinned by a series of lurid fantasies about what Muslims can't bear about what lies underneath their robes and veils. This 'satire' is not directed at the powerful but at the weak, at those who are already subject to racist and sexist abuse, at the excluded and oppressed. Worse, this vicious glorification of the privilege of those who are included in the homonational state pathologises those who will not laugh with it. One classic cover image from the magazine, for example, circulates to show how *Charlie Hebdo* believed, in the words of the headline, that 'love is stronger than hate' ('L'amour plus fort que la haine'), and it shows two men kissing (a cartoonist and a Muslim) with the joke being, of course, that this is exactly what a Muslim can't stand. There is momentary satisfaction and relief that they don't really enjoy like us, reassurance that we, unlike them, know how to enjoy (and then we are like the cartoonist who will take a bet on love).

Homonationalism today has a number of different aspects which it glues together, and which we see at work in the claim 'Nous sommes tous Charlie', more than being in solidarity with *Charlie Hebdo* we are also willing, each and all of us, to be who they were. There is an enforcement of identity of those allied with the state and security forces that protect our liberty to free speech and love against hate, the state fantasised as homogeneous, and, at the same time, closure of the identity of each kind of sexuality, of homosexuals alongside heterosexuals mobilised as a kind of global homostate for love and against hate (an identity, as if it were self-identical, wherever it is in the world). Those two aspects come together in the pinkwashing of Israel and in the anti-Semitic assumption that the Israeli state speaks for all the Jews, homonationalist logic in which all of us are this and all of them are that. This combination of the two aspects can be seen in the bizarre decision of President Hollande to phone Prime Minister Netanyahu to tell him four hostages had been killed in the assault on the kosher supermarket in Vincennes. Hollande's victory rally in Paris then brought together Chancellor Angela Merkel and the then Prime Minister David Cameron, Cameron who was keen to insist that the holy institution of marriage was such a marvellous thing, that it should not be denied to lesbians and gay men.

The first demonstrations in Paris after the attacks were in solidarity with the murdered cartoonists, with a strong left component in these mobilisations independent of the French state, and the Nouveau Parti anticapitaliste, for example, also made it clear that the protest must also be against the increasing Islamophobic climate of opinion. Already, however, the Front National intuitively understood something about homonationalism, and Marine Le Pen shortly before the attack appointed a leading gay rights campaigner Sébastien Chenu as her cultural adviser.

This is the ideological battleground. On the one side stands French state-sponsored identity politics that operates alongside state terrorism at home against Muslim communities and abroad alongside the other Western homonationalist states. On the other side there are protests against Islamophobia that also include lesbian and gay activists who sometimes use their identity tactically to claim rights and sometimes refuse to play the game of the state (just as many Muslims have done in the past). These activists in groups such as 'Palestinian Queers for Boycott, Divestment and Sanctions' made it clear that homonationalism is actually a bitter betrayal of lesbians and gays, co-opting them after their past struggles, and requiring identity and loyalty that they never demanded. To mobilise today for conditions in which the freedom of each is the condition for the freedom of all requires that we refuse to say 'Je suis Charlie', and instead find new combinations of identity that are diverse and overlapping, that use analyses of the closed worlds of homonationalism precisely to take the next step, to replace them with authentic open internationalism.

Identification

Identification describes how we are drawn into becoming like and becoming trapped in images of others. The band Laibach played again in Manchester on Good Friday 2015 to an audience of old punks, rockers and some younger emo-types, different subcultural identities drawn like moths to a flame. The question was whether this would disturb and unravel those identities or simply confirm them. The political project of Laibach was once upon a time part of the Neue Slowenische Kunst (NSK) intervention into decaying Stalinism in Yugoslavia, an intervention that drew a strict line of separation between 'identity' and 'identification' as a keyword in a quite different kind of politics.

Identity is precisely what the Tito regime revelled in, anti-fascist identity of the League of Communists and of socialist self-management pitted against the West and against the Soviet Union, and identity of Yugoslavia forging itself out of the different republics in the federation. This identity is of something each citizen aspires to become, undivided and unitary, the identity of each good citizen in one state. This conception of identity, of the prison of the self that is defined by membership of a particular category of being, was dismantled by NSK, with Laibach as 'politicians' of NSK State in Time as the vanguard force.

Identification, in contrast, is a more fluid and unstable process by which an audience, of a band or of advertising or of political propaganda, is sucked into a contradictory series of ideal types. In supposedly 'post-Marxist' post-structuralist theories of the type that informed the Podemos project in Spain, for example, the self-contained 'identity' of the working class is assumed to be out of date, in line with an argument made by the late Ernesto Laclau (Argentinian theorist of populism and ex left-Peronist) and Chantal Mouffe. Instead, politics is directed to competing 'identifications' with a variety of different agendas (of the people against the 'caste', of the nation against the corrupt few, or even still, why not, of the workers against the bosses). Against fixed forms of self are mutating alliances that call for a different kind of politics canny with images, appealing to something in the human subject that operates outside consciousness, and is not restricted to a self-identical grid of old 'class consciousness'. Whether we like it or not, we need to attend to this 'identification' as something that names a politics that operates with, and sometimes in competition with, Marxism.

One of the peculiarities of the left opposition in Slovenia was the influence not only of punk, which kick-started the protests against the regime in the 1970s, but of so-called 'post-structuralist' theories that included those used by Laclau (who was responsible for the first book-length publications of Slavoj Žižek, one-time ally of Laibach and NSK, into English). Those theories combined a particular notion of language as an ever-mutating and self-deconstructing system of 'signifiers' with a notion of the self as something whose 'identity' is split and uncertain. In fact the term 'self' is still too sure of what it is, and is here replaced by 'subjectivity', a subjectivity as divided and distributed between different forms of discourse (of the working class, of woman, of patriot, and so on); subjectivity in this critical work is as described by psychoanalysis (in particular the subversion and reorganisation of psychoanalysis in the work of Jacques Lacan).

Psychoanalysis provided a weapon for NSK and Laibach to reconfigure identity as identification, and to intervene in politics through art and music projects in order to subvert the dominant discourses and produce new forms of discourse. And, by the same token, that psychoanalytic understanding of identification of an audience with desirable images and leaders, identification which operates at an unconscious level tied to enjoyment, itself became a powerful discourse inside Slovenia and then beyond. This is a psychoanalytic discourse that today circulates in the academic world, but also in some sectors of popular culture, including in Žižek's work (which is a combination of Lacanian psychoanalysis, Hegelian philosophy and quasi-Marxist interpretation).

Laibach was born in the industrial coal-mining city of Trbovlje in Slovenia in 1980, and quickly banned by the Yugoslav regime for using as its name the German term for Ljubljana, capital of what was then the North-Western-most republic. Never appearing in public out of uniform, Laibach provoked anxiety, posing a question to the audience, 'What do you want?' which they would not themselves provide an answer for. Žižek's defence of Laibach and NSK in the 1980s argued that they were not fascist, as the Yugoslav authorities claimed, but that they operated like psychoanalysts, drawing the audience into a kind of 'transference' (in which the patient re-experiences past significant relationships) where the audience themselves must decide what they want. In that process, what is activated and questioned, mobilised and unravelled, is precisely 'identification' (identification with leaders wearing uniforms who promise a secure and powerful identity, for example, top of the list of targets for Laibach).

This kind of 'identification' comes from the language of psychoanalysis circulating among the opposition in Slovenia from the 1980s, and was then taken further as a political weapon in what was termed 'overidentification'. There have been squabbles over overidentification between supporters of Žižek and NSK as to who borrowed the notion from whom. Members of Laibach and NSK did attend Žižek's lectures as fine-art students in Ljubljana, but the practice of overidentification was perhaps first present in NSK's interventions to be later theorised by Žižek (who once used to cite Laibach as key example). Overidentification pushes always already unstable identifications with power to breaking point, and it breaks the link between power and truth, breaks the power of a regime to define what is taken to be true (a process that raises the spectre of post-structuralist relativism for some Marxists).

For example, the design wing of NSK effectively sabotaged Yugoslav 'youth day' in the 1980s after winning the competition for a poster which the judges declared symbolised the struggle of socialist youth but which was then revealed to be based on a 1930s Nazi poster. Their 'overidentification' with the discourse of the state took the ideology of the regime more seriously than it liked, and revealed its obscene hidden underside. The very name 'Laibach' and performing in uniform were also forms of such 'overidentification' with the state. After the formation of NSK State in Time in the early 1990s (an apparatus with passports and more citizens than the Vatican state), neo-Nazi skinhead fans of Laibach were faced with a contradictory injunction, to enjoy military uniforms emblazoned with a black cross (which NSK borrowed from Russian-Revolution period Suprematist Kazimir Malevich) and to subscribe to a 'global state' which operated for anyone who wanted to become a citizen regardless of geographical territory. Fascists and anti-fascists used to fight at Laibach concerts in a battle over territory and signifiers.

Competing identifications, using them to break them, were still at work in the Laibach concert to launch their 2014 album *Spectre*. *Spectre* is an album and the name of a new party, the outcome of a political process and break with their parent organisation following the NSK 2010 Citizens' Congress, a party that you can join (but that, they remind you, you cannot then leave, though the party can leave you). Automated computer-voiced demands on the audience to 'dance' and 'clap' were of a piece with the old politics. (The previous time they played in Manchester was to perform the soundtrack to the 2012 crowd-sourced film *Iron Sky* about Nazis on the moon.) In 2015 the politics was a little more overtly progressive, with a celebration of the Occupy movement and of 'The Whistleblowers'. There were reminders of the old days during the encore when they played 'Tanz Mit Laibach', but this was 'identification' that was less oriented to critique, transformation and the future than to some kind of nostalgia for the old NSK-Laibach axis.

The point is not whether Laibach (and NSK) are correct or not, whether they offer a politics to be admired and followed. It is precisely the reverse. The point is that they did, in one context at one time, provide alternative forms of identification that tactically levered open the ideology of a regime. Now, when we dance with Laibach, however, we do not so much 'identify' with them as 'overidentify' so we know better, while we enjoy the music, the imagery and the political message, that we will not ever really follow them. And we learn some lessons from their interventions, and from the spawning of a psychoanalytic discourse of identification in contemporary politics, that we have to take seriously new forms of subjectivity that are running alongside, if not displacing, our old powerful but still true revolutionary Marxism.

Identity

Identity is a source of self-confidence that also risks fixing the essence of who we are into unchangeable categories. Identity is a weapon against power, and the oppressed makes this so either by discovering a name for their experience or by seizing a name used against them to turn it against the enemy. This is why the turn to 'identity politics' announced by the Combahee River Collective in 1977 was so important. Notwithstanding third-wave queer feminist critique, this turn was crucial to the development of the women's movement and of Black feminism. Identity discovered or seized by the powerless is hard won, but also carries with it the bitter traces of the times of silence, hatred and often enforced self-hatred of victims, and no more so than when those speaking their own history of the violence wrought against them are survivors of child sexual abuse.

That double-history is one of historical time – of children disbelieved and made passive, that is, of oppression running alongside and reinforcing that of women in the family – and of personal time in which the survivor gathers the courage and resources to speak of what happened to them and who they are. It is a personal question that is also a political one, and this is why political organisations that are both socialist and feminist have put campaigns against child abuse on their agenda for change.

This is a burning question at a time when sexual violence on the left is so visible, and when some groups in transition from the left to 'anti-establishment' politics are keen to disparage what they call the 'victim lobby' response to 'paedo panic'. Such groups overlook the key difference between a victim organising themselves to speak against power and someone with power speaking as if they too were a victim, which is a key difference between progressive and reactionary uses of 'identity'.

In fact, paedophilia has long been a battleground of identity, with attempts by paedophiles declaring their identity then trying to ally with the left in campaigns against age of consent laws in the 1970s (which succeeded in getting support from leading intellectuals, including the historian Michel Foucault, existentialist philosopher Simone de Beauvoir and the Catholic Lacanian child psychoanalyst Françoise Dolto).

One attempt to open a 'debate' about this 'identity' in the left in 2015 included a link to a 2006 *Guardian* newspaper interview. In this case the pseudonymous individual who sent appeals for a 'debate' about the issue to members of different left organisations was clear that he was 'non-abusing', that he had never acted on his desires. There was a deliberate and bizarre attempt to shift the question from the domain of the law to that of identity. The *Guardian* interview describes an experience of what the interviewee calls his 'morally abominable desires', and the 'triggering incidents' in his own childhood of being abused which were discovered, he says, during his psychoanalytic treatment with the then head of the Portman Clinic (a British National Health Service forensic psychotherapy service specialising in 'sexual perversion'). The analyst was an International Psychoanalytical Association (IPA) psychoanalyst who supposedly told his patient after two and a half years that he should sleep with a woman, at which point he surmised that he had been 'cured'. Except, what seems to have remained is a need to speak about a category of identity which is based on what is named as a 'sexual orientation'.

One of the bones of contention between the IPA and traditions of psychoanalysis after Jacques Lacan has been over the goal of strengthening the ego, and hence of personal identity, in the IPA tradition, or the subversion of the ego in the Lacanian. There have been some quite different ways of puzzling about memories of child sexual abuse using Lacanian ideas which were written for the left but which did not attempt to configure left politics in line with what happened. Those explorations draw attention to the role of the 'guilt of the abused', a form of self-hatred which usually reinforces their silence and isolation. In contrast, in this particular case something was driving a declaration of identity and a compulsion to speak about it.

The difference of clinical orientation has sometimes led to the assumption that the Lacanian option is therefore more politically subversive, which is belied by the reactionary stance of some Lacanians and the progressive activity of some IPA analysts, including this psychoanalyst (political participation in the struggle against apartheid is noted by his 'cured' patient). In fact, the extrapolation of personal therapy into politics is part of the problem here, and what may have been arrived at as a source of consolation and strength – memories, narratives, ideas about the development of the self – inside the therapy is not something that then operates in the same way outside it. There are issues here above and beyond the damage that would be caused to the left if it was drawn into some kind of dialogue about that kind of experience.

There is a double-effect of a discourse of perversion as a pathology which here is tangled up with the identity of a 'paedophile' still compelled to speak from within a category assigned to him. The first is the cutting out of the social fabric of a type, the perverted paedophile as one about whom psychiatric knowledge has much to say in terms of their character and development and predisposition to offend, but little to say about the sexualisation of gendered power relations under capitalism. The second is the compulsion to speak about the self within the terms supplied by psychiatry and psychoanalysis so that there is a contribution to that knowledge – the incitement to speak about the pathological self is exactly what the 'psy' wants so that it can know more – but also with the effect that the individual believes that they are supplying valuable information.

The link between the two aspects of the double-effect –

between psychiatric knowledge of perversion and self-knowledge of the identity it assigns – is the turning of social relations into separate things, reification in which they circulate as commodities and circulate in the discourse of the clinic, both inside the clinic itself and in the culture which needs the clinic as a separate space to 'cure' and adapt people to society. These paedophiles are then things that speak, and if they speak, they also speak the language of power, seizing and, as it were, perverting the claim for rights to speak that were made by the oppressed.

It should be clear that support for these particular 'survivors' of child sexual abuse should not be taken up within the discourse of rights such that someone who identifies as a 'paedophile' (even if it is as someone who has never committed an offence) can present themselves as a 'survivor' who must also be supported, as if they must be supported as one of the 'oppressed' battling 'dehumanised references' to what they are. That would not be a 'contribution' to 'an open and inclusive debate', and instead of being in 'solidarity with demonised groups' it would be dangerous to those who really are abused and oppressed.

What this kind of plea for the recognition of identity overlooks is the way the discourse itself operates within relations of power. Someone making this kind of appeal is, on the one hand, disconnected from those social relations, compelled to speak about identity, and, on the other hand, also repeating the psychiatric categories that psychoanalysis could have disturbed, could have broken him from. If he was really 'cured', then surely we would expect that he would not remain so attached to those terms within which he was categorised and expected to speak.

So, our response to appeals of this kind to open a debate should be to continue the analysis by stepping back from those terms, by insisting that he give up on the attempt to use them to structure the political movements he wants to participate in. This response is in line with warnings made by Black feminists against those who, in the sphere of academic debate, want to speak of their 'whiteness' and thus colonise the voices of those who have been tracing its contours as a form of resistance.

Identity is double-edged, and this is why even those who claim it also suggest that it should be used only strategically, and that is why they worry about how it often becomes a kind of commodity. This is a danger for the oppressed themselves speaking against power, but it is an even bigger danger for the oppressed when it is claimed and spoken by those with power.

Intersectionality

Intersectionality is one way of working with the layout of many forms of oppression. The 2013 crisis over sexual violence inside the British-based Socialist Workers Party (SWP) provoked an attempt by some of those involved to try to explain what happened then and since in some of the new organisations that emerged from the crisis, in terms of 'intersectionality'. And then something very peculiar happened, this new keyword, intersectionality, itself became the target, treated by some old leftists as the reason for all their woes. It's a tangled story in which intersectionality was twisted and turned into something quite unrecognisable to the Black feminists who developed it in order to grasp the connection between different forms of oppression. So, what is intersectionality, why does it help us make sense of what happened, and how was it distorted to suit the agenda of the organisations it had been applied to?

The term was developed as an alternative to accounts of 'multiple' oppression in which the combined identities of different groups – workers, women, Black people, and so on – could be accumulated and counted up to determine who was most oppressed, who was at the bottom of some kind of overall hierarchy. Even the attempts to take seriously the combined effects of different kinds of oppression did not themselves intend to involve those kind of divide and rule mechanisms, and there were serious radical attempts to take different kinds of 'identities' on board in progressive politics. Even so, the reduction to separate 'identities' posed problems for those trying to build alliances, interconnections between those oppressed by reason of their class, race, gender or sexuality. Salma Hayek's comment that 'You can't be more bottom of the ladder than Mexican, half-Arab and a woman over 40 in Hollywood' illustrates where some of the problems with an approach based on the multiplication of identities leads.

The key step away from identity towards intersectionality was taken by the Black feminist US legal theorist Kimberlé Crenshaw in 1989. The key case that provoked this step comes from a working-class struggle where a group of five Black women sued their employer, General Motors, for discrimination. They were told that they could make a complaint on grounds of race discrimination or sex discrimination, but any kind of legal case based on the particular combined effects of two or more forms of oppression would be thrown out of court. Crenshaw came up with a commonsensical term from the metaphor of what in the US is called an 'intersection', or road crossing, where there are different streams of traffic, and where there might at times be a collision between cars in which it is difficult to work out from the marks of the cars on the tarmac exactly which direction each of them were coming from. The case of the five women against General Motors could then, quite appropriately, be understood in terms of a car crash metaphor. The metaphor is actually a bit more complicated than it first appears, and it certainly avoids a reduction to the fixed 'identity' of the cars or drivers involved. The problem lies not in each of the cars or streams of traffic but at the intersection as such. This is why the term has also been embraced by some US revolutionary socialists, for it better does justice to the struggles of Black working-class women mobilising themselves across identities and against the attempt by the legal system to divide them from each other.

One of the side effects of the crisis in the SWP – a side effect that might actually turn out to be one of the best main effects – was that women leaving the organisation realised that the phenomenon of sexual violence raised questions of feminism. Then, in some of the organisations that developed later, the debates in feminism were also about the many different kinds of oppression that had been sidelined under the bigger heading 'working class' (something which mostly meant compensating working-class men for their lack of power under capitalism, something which is itself an intersectional issue). Gender, sexuality and race quickly came on to the agenda, and as these were debated and worked through the SWP rubbed its hands with glee as some of the conflicts at the intersection came out into the open. Some unwise comments about the representation of a Black woman in an art installation led to what was termed the 'kinky split' in one rival group, for example, but instead of asking what was going on here and how intersectionality could make sense of it, the old male left piled in to blame intersectionality itself. The term was being twisted from being a keyword to help us describe the way in which different forms of power intersect and create new, quite different problems that the left needs to respond to, and can only respond to if it takes debates in feminism seriously. It was twisted to make it seem that if we all stopped talking about 'intersectionality' then everything would go back to the way it was and everything would be fine. Some hope, bad lesson.

It didn't help that some liberal feminist accounts of intersectionality muddled the old multiple oppression and identity arguments and ran them all together. Some of those in old left traditions (that actually have their origins in the SWP many years ago) now moving toward libertarianism eagerly took the opportunity to spitefully confuse things by claiming that the approach was really 'sectional' and 'sectarian'. When the University of London Union refused a room booking for the annual SWP Marxism event, the ULU statement was quickly condemned by other left groups who have long been suspicious of feminism, and they detected the malign influence of 'intersectional feminists'. That brings us full circle; back to the very problem that intersectionality was grappling with. The old male left that sees feminism as an enemy of class struggle, rather than as an integral part of the history of feminism in alliance with revolutionary Marxism, turns intersectionality back into identity. Now it is the 'intersectional feminists' who are the enemy, treated as if they are a particular group that we have to avoid to stay pure.

That purity of Marxism disconnected from other kinds of political struggle is exactly what intersectionality questions. It questions identity politics and then questions Marxism which sometimes configures itself as a form of identity politics obsessed with prioritising and idealising the working-class vanguard (and, of course, privileging the leadership of the party that will speak for and direct the working-class vanguard). It also questions the turning of Marxism into some kind of cover-all quasi-religious system that will explain anything and everything, including 'diversions' from the one true path. Marxism is not a form of identity and it does not explain all history everywhere. Intersectionality is a way of grasping not only the historically-constituted nature of apparently little struggles under capitalism but poses some big questions about what we are up against and where we are going. There are some really good lessons there too.

Islamophobia

With Islamophobia, we see an orientalist twist on old racism to confirm the value of modern capitalist civilization. An electoral court ruling in 2015 against Lutfur Rahman in the London borough of Tower Hamlets threw into relief how the British establishment uses and fuels Islamophobia today. The liberal white press pretended to be against the 'racialisation' of politics, but the claim that Rahman ran a corrupt 'dictatorship' in the East End of London stank of Islamophobia, which is now one of the most potent ideological motifs, a key word in contemporary Western racism.

Much was made of the company Rahman kept, drawing attention to allies in his defence campaign after the court verdict, and it is true that he did shift political allegiances rather opportunistically in the previous few years. But this is the case for any politician whose horizons are limited by electoral politics and the possibilities of using the local state apparatus to bring about progressive policy changes. If there was a problem with Lutfur Rahman, something which differentiated his strategy from that of revolutionary Marxists, for example, it was that he was forced to pick and choose alliances which would enable him to get into one of the seats of power. Putting that complaint against him aside, we need to understand why Tower Hamlets was marked out, treated to special measures by the British state, and how quite different standards than those applied to other bourgeois politicians were used to discredit this particular council.

Tower Hamlets council under Rahman as mayor had been breaking from the austerity consensus, making it clear that it opposed the reviled 'bedroom tax' (a vicious attack on poor people in social housing imposed by the Tory government which targets those on welfare benefits), and the council has used resources to support families affected by the tax. This went alongside quite explicit resistance to the government scrapping of educational maintenance grants for poorer students going into further education, and transfer of resources to make up the shortfall for students from the borough. Limited though this break had been, and it was largely limited to local budget reallocations, even that break was too much for the British state and private mass media. One easy way of discrediting this kind of resistance was to demonise the community which seemed to provide Rahman's electoral base.

The court case was brought by four local 'petitioners', two of whom were from the Labour Party, those in it who are keen to get rid of anything to the left which would build real opposition to the government's austerity agenda, so keen that they were willing here to ally with the secretary of the local United Kingdom Independence Party (UKIP) to do it. The judgement of the court did not treat the Tower Hamlets' 'Muslim community' by the same standards they would use for the 'secular and largely agnostic metropolitan elite'. Yes, this community was like every other religious community, bound to its leaders by 'loyalty and obedience', but in this case the spectre of 'apostasy' was thrown into the mix, and this is where the judgement chimed with fear of Islam as something more dangerous than other religions. Little evidence was provided of this spiritual influence, but the judge decided that this influence was the 'real meaning' of the Imam's interventions.

This race card used against Tower Hamlets played on what the mainstream media tells us about Muslims in the inner cities. The popular commonsensical line that there must be antipathy between the new immigrant communities, in this case from Bangladesh, and the older East End Jewish community, was neatly skewered by a Green Party commentator on the case who drew attention to historical parallels between the experiences of the two communities. The kind of community mobilisation that Rahman's 'Tower Hamlets First' party engaged in – this is where it went beyond the limits of electoral politics and became a real threat to the state – repeated the strategies of minority communities over the last century. The new council had actually been supportive of the Jewish community as an immigrant community that preceded it in the borough, allocating money for restoration of the East London Synagogue, for example.

Likewise, Rahman mobilised the local population against the fascist English Defence League, making it clear that the council stood with the LGBTQ+ community in Tower Hamlets against fascist attacks, he had been photographed with his arms round drag queens, and had protested against closure of a Shoreditch LGBTQ+ pub. A BBC television documentary filmed a customer of another gay bar in the borough that had been saved from closure by Rahman's intervention, but did not include the footage in its broadcast, presumably because it did not fit the line of the programme which was hostile to the Tower Hamlets council.

This particular singling out of Islam as an enemy within was actually also a repetition of older British colonial strategies of divide and rule, pathologising those over whom it rules. The charge of 'spiritual influence' was actually last wheeled out in the nineteenth century against Catholic clergy in Ireland who were urging parishioners to vote for home rule. The old accusations of 'spiritual influence' made by British colonialism in Ireland also served then to pathologise and infantilise the natives, turning them into childlike victims of their priests. In this respect, 'spiritual influence' is part of the package of the 'orientalist' ideology described by the Palestinian scholar Edward Said in which subject peoples are treated as if they are less than human, that is, less than European middle-class white men and rather more like women and children.

There are, of course, two linked elements in this ideology, for every childlike faith community susceptible to 'influence' is seen as subject to the barbaric manipulation of leaders. Some kind of feminisation of the followers runs alongside the hyper-masculinisation of their dangerous leaders. Early British 'Islamophobia', as we might now term it, homed in on its first 'Mad Mullah' resisting the Empire in Somaliland a century ago, and this motif has been wielded whenever necessary against Muslims ever since. It turns anti-colonial political resistance into something else, into religious conflict, and today also into some kind of abnormal psychology.

There is a risk now that accusations of 'Islamophobia' play the same game, turning politics into a battle of 'influence' in which one side – Islam – is reduced to the level of naïve victim at the mercy of a brutal leader, while the other side – those who seek to demonise Islam – are treated as individuals with some weird kind of phobia. 'Islamophobia' names hostility to Islam and, like 'homophobia', also pathologises those it names (and also treats those who suffer from it as having a sickness, individualises it). Reactionary Christian commentators have noticed the parallel, complaining that the 'phobe' part of the accusation is part of what they see as a 'totalitarian' attempt to discredit their own suspicion of both Islamic and LGBTQ+ political activity.

In this sense the motifs of 'influence' and 'phobia' operate as mirrors of each other in a discourse that turns politics into psychopathology, and so we need to grasp how the one – 'spiritual influence' – was used by the electoral court and bourgeois media to demonise Rahman and Tower Hamlets council, while the other – 'Islamophobia' – was used by anti-racists to name ideological hostility to a community, in the case of Tower Hamlets one that dared to defy central government. Yes, it is possible that some of those who were celebrating the outcome of the court case really are 'phobic' about Islam, but what is crucial here is that this Islamophobia is functioning now to racialise British politics; religious discourse is being used as a weapon by the right and the state.

Forms of political identification by communities under attack have shifted over the years in Britain, with 'Black' as signifier once claimed by communities under attack now turning Asian youth movements into 'Black, Asian and Minority Ethic' (BAME) communities subject to Islamophobia; they are bureaucratised and racialised, often within religious discourse. It is not enough to bewail that shift. We need to analyse and respond to it. We need to distinguish between mobilisation of faith communities against injustice, something that has a history going back at least to the development of the British Labour Party in the Methodist chapels, and the appeal to religion to poison politics and turn it into something else.

Islamophobia must be understood as a political response, a reactionary response, to the mobilisation of a community which makes it seem as if that mobilisation cannot be understood in any other way than as subject to 'spiritual influence'. That is why the problem of the 'phobia' seems to mirror the problem of the 'influence', and that is why defending Tower Hamlets against this attack by the British state was necessary to break that mirror relation while combating and eventually ending the ideological function of Islamophobia, understanding it for what it is, the racialisation of political resistance.

Justice

For us, justice is about authentic democratic rights for each to define what counts for all. We learn about what it means as a general concept from particular struggles around the world. For example, a remarkable political experiment is taking place in Afrin, Cizire and Kobane, three autonomous cantons that make up Rojava held by the Kurds in the north of Syria on the border with Turkey. It repeats in some ways the best practices of the Zapatistas in Chiapas, Mexico twenty years ago. The communes in Rojava are drawing a balance sheet, in theory linked with practice of the successes and failures of various attempts to replace the capitalist state with 'soviets', a democratic form that marked the Russian revolution a hundred years ago and which have characterised many anti-capitalist movements since. Each time the 'commune' or 'soviet' form has emerged in the course of popular resistance it has had to engage with new social movements that bring different demands and forms of organisation to revolutionary struggle. Rojava is engaging with some of the most radical social movements, explicitly learning from them, and in this way is filling the term 'justice' with new content.

The complaints across the political spectrum about so-called 'Social Justice Warriors' (SJW) – a popular motif in current trans-class post-politics – about those who seem to shift from complaint to complaint about different aspects of symbolic oppression while, in the process, emptying 'justice' of any positive content, also takes on a new light. Those who complain bitterly about SJW are also unwittingly recycling the discourse of the so-called 'alt-right' in the United States which targets what it sees as 'political incorrectness' in order to justify its own grotesque insulting social media posts. The real problem with justice in SJW for those who are still on the left, however, is not what they argue against but what they fail to argue for. Rojava is a positive example of how different 'justice' looks in the abstract to what it looks like in practice.

Justice in the revolutionary Marxist political tradition has always been contradictory, with different readings of Marx finding some arguments for justice as central to the strategy and aims of communism and some indications that this 'justice' is in itself empty, is given meaning by the context and balance of forces at any particular historical moment. Developments in so-called 'post-Marxism' in the wake of the crisis in Stalinism and the emergence of Eurocommunism saw 'justice' along with other kindred terms like 'democracy' as being 'empty signifiers'. These signifiers do not mean anything as such, but they stand in for what Ernesto Laclau and Chantal Mouffe referred to as the impossible fullness or unity of society; they function as terms that sum up what we imagine we are fighting for as a world free from injustice and violence, even though we may each have quite different notions of what those terms that will heal the divisions and lack in politics really amount to.

Social justice in Rojava, mainly led by the Kurdish Democratic Union Party (PYD), is being given a new meaning, for example, in political statements made by Abdullah Öcalan, who is still in a Turkish jail, and being loyally implemented by his followers. 'Justice' now in Rojava is closely linked to 'democracy', to what Öcalan calls 'democratic confederalism'. There are critical questions we need to keep open in this new democratic space through which the Movement for a Democratic Society (TEV-DEM) mobilises people to participate in neighbourhood assemblies and city and regional councils. These questions concern the nature of the political apparatus with Öcalan still at the top of the Kurdish Workers Party (PKK) that can decide that democratic, pluralist, ecological and feminist politics should define how Rojava operates at this particular moment. Öcalan's turn to what he argues should be a popular trans-class movement in Rojava is possible at the moment because of the destruction of much of the economic infrastructure and the absence of a strong capitalist class apparatus. We should remember that democratic conditions have not always obtained either in Rojava or in Öcalan's own political party, a party over which he has in the past maintained strict control.

Today Öcalan declares that social hierarchy began with the domination of women by men, and therefore it is necessary to deal with the question of patriarchy in social movements and inside revolutionary organisations. One of the targets of Öcalan's new feminist politics is what he calls the problem of 'killing the dominant male'. The implantation of this line in practice now means that the Women's Protection Units (YPJ) have been at the forefront of the military struggle against Islamic State as well as defending the autonomous areas of Rojava against the Syrian and Turkish state forces. There are quotas that ensure participation by women at all organisational levels in Rojava, and concerted attempts to include women and men from the Arab, Assyrian-Syriac, Armenian, Circassian and Chechen communities. This participation makes the feminist politics in the communes and councils a pluralist multi-ethnic politics attentive to difference, and this has been crucial to the military and political defence of the multicultural society that Islamic State aims to destroy in their fascist attacks on what they call 'the grey zone'.

Öcalan has been inspired, while languishing in prison, by libertarian politics that combines ecology with socialism and this has also led to a rethinking of how the Kurdish struggle might be carried out in such a way as to weaken the power of the state, instead, as in some national independence movements, of strengthening it. Öcalan now argues that the drive to form a Kurdish state has had destructive consequences for Kurds in Syria and Turkey, as well as in Iraq and Iran. There has been a shift of focus in Kurdish politics under Öcalan, from the direct aim of achieving statehood to an attempt to develop a post-nationalist framework characterised as a 'democratic, ecological, gender-liberated society' set against capitalism and totalitari-anism in the region. This has inspired feminist activists outside Rojava. And there are lessons from what is happening in Rojava for how we organise elsewhere.

Some political movements on the revolutionary left in Britain have been quicker than others to rally in solidarity with Rojava, and those who have been quickest have been those, like the liber-tarian group Plan C based in Manchester and in a couple of other British cities, who have emerged out of the crisis of sexual violence in the left here and who have drawn explicitly feminist conclusions from that crisis that also connects with contemporary anarchist politics inspired by Rojava. They have concluded, for example, that the organisational forms of revolutionary politics need to be reworked and that political interventions need to be rapidly reconfigured to each specific situation, keying into the changes of consciousness around different aspects of exploitation and oppression. In this way, Plan C fills terms like 'justice' and 'democracy' with different content depending on the occasion and comes up with surprising new initiatives and slogans tailored to each opportunity for tactical intervention. Rojava is just such a tactical intervention for them. And the organisation makes an ideal fit with the phenomenon in this case. Plan C is a well-run group, with a pluralistic fluid circle of 'friends of Plan C' and friends of friends that surrounds a tightly-organised core with international links (and a quite high membership turnover). Those who join are attracted by the open revolutionary ethos of the group, while those who leave complain that the rapid shifts of line are made by a central leadership. As a group that works with the contradictions of revolutionary struggle and organi-sation, Plan C is one group that represents the cutting edge of left feminist politics, but the same questions about top-down revolu-tionary leadership apply to it as apply to Öcalan.

The Kurdish struggle has always been a contradictory movement, suffering at some historical moments and benefitting at others from the coincidence of imperialist interests in the region. There has always been an intense debate in the revolutionary left, for example, over how to square support for the Kurdish independence movement with the manoeuvres of the leadership under Barzani in the Kurdish enclave in Iraq, a leadership that has been very willing to accept material and logistical support from the United States military intelligence agencies. And the foreign policy agenda of Israel has always included the 'periphery doctrine', at moments prioritising support for the Kurds as a diplomatic lever against the Arab communities inside Israel or against Arab states immediately adjoining it. This has been one reason why liberal Zionists have been happy to support calls to defend the Kurds and to argue in a quite empty way for 'justice' for them in the region. There has even been praise for Rojava from the British conservative newspaper *Financial Times*.

Nevertheless, Rojava shows us what is possible when a grass-roots movement that draws on the strength of women directly inspired by feminist politics begins to take power, and the way that an ecological sensibility can energise a new way of thinking about the nature of alternative democratic political structures. It also must make us examine closely, in the context of active solidarity with Rojava, how this has been possible because a new line came down from the political leadership of the PYD, and we have to be ready to defend this grass-roots mobilisation against any future attempts to limit it or even twist the line in other directions. This is a good line, one we must support and which we must build into our own politics of justice outside Rojava.

Multitude

Multitude names the collective creative processes of global resistance to power. The International Organization for Migration announced in a press release on 22 December 2015 that with 4,141 migrants or refugees landing in Greece the day before, it could now confirm that over a million 'irregular migrants and refugees' arrived in Europe in 2015, mostly from Syria, Africa and South Asia. This was the highest migration into Europe since World War II as measured by the IOM 'Displacement Tracking Matrix – Flow Monitoring System'. This 'migration flow' is actually not the highest in the world; the biggest 'migration corridor' is still Mexico to the United States, and the Russian Federation is second on the list of both migration destinations and emigration locations. However, 2015 was, for Europe at least, a time for *Multitude*, the massive mobile population theorised and celebrated by Michael Hardt and Antonio Negri in 2004 in their book with that title (a follow-up to their 2000 book *Empire*), a keyword for those looking to alternative or supplementary social actors to the old static working class. It was also a testing time for those anxious to defend the 'European legacy', Europe as the supposed birthplace and heritage of democratic political struggle which should be protected from the incursion of pre-revolutionary hordes.

You can imagine the response of the bourgeois press to this. There is tabloid hysteria about the need to 'stem the flow of refugees', the need to 'control the stream' and ensure that those who are accepted respect 'the Western European way of life' because 'that is the price to be paid for European hospitality'. The centre-right broadsheets note that these refugees 'are possessed by a dream', and discuss 'drawing up of an all-European plan' to deal with them, insisting that through 'clear rules and regulations', they 'must accept the destination allocated to them by the

European authorities'. There is some hand-wringing about how this flow of refugees is the 'price we pay for a globalised economy', and musing about 'a new kind of international and military intervention' that will avoid the problems caused so far. And, of course, the newspapers blame the victims and especially those who have dared to resist brutal regimes propped up by the West, including calls for 'international pressure on Saudi Arabia' and other Arab states to accept refugees because they have made the situation worse 'by supporting the anti-Assad rebels'. We know these ideological games all-too well. Note well these claims. We will refer to them again in a moment.

This is what the notion of 'multitude' aims to break from. Instead of speaking about these mobile networks flowing across old national boundaries from the standpoint of power, multitude speaks from within and alongside this new creative force which is breaking from fixed-location capitalist production, anticipating now the freedom of association that Marxists have always dreamt of. *Multitude* was the second in the Hardt and Negri trilogy; the first was *Empire* and the third *Commonwealth*. *Empire*, published in 2000, described a regime of power that spread beyond existing territorial boundaries, operating as if it were universal and outside history, regulating every aspect of human life and how we understand nature, and, though 'bathed in blood', presents itself as 'dedicated to peace'. *Commonwealth*, published in 2009, is about the reclaiming of the 'commons' and of human happiness; against the enclosure of property and then of individual selves separated from nature and from one another under classical capitalism. That book argues for collective struggle, as what Hardt and Negri call 'revolutionary parallelism' in which there is an intersection of the relatively autonomous domains of class, race and gender. *Multitude* from 2004 thus names the force which is the 'living alternative that grows within Empire' and which enables the attainment of collective common wealth governed by love, something which is a material and spiritual force. *Multitude* shifts attention – in line with the Italian autonomist Marxist tradition, second-wave feminism and anti-racist politics – from 'structure' as operating independent of people's will to what is called in *Commonwealth* 'the standpoint of bodies'.

Liberal critiques of *Multitude* complained that it was a 'neo-Marxist extravaganza', a 'postmodern pastiche' which was too Marxist and 'not sufficiently specific to be of use to policymakers or activists'. It is true, it is not at all specific, and the style is as important as the argument; it is about redemption and, as Hardt and Negri themselves say, about 'the becoming divine of humanity'. For Naomi Klein, on the back cover of the book, it was 'inspiring', but for some this was part of the problem, operating as a 'last-ditch salvationist movement' for the 'born again' enthusiasts for 'networks' in the tradition of the seventeenth century Dutch philosopher Spinoza rather than Karl Marx. And actually it was inspiring enough to be very useful to many activists who embraced the description of Empire in the first book and then saw in multitude the free-flowing creative force that would resist it.

Negri himself insists that he is a Marxist – it is 'poverty and wealth' that make the world go round, 'poverty more so', he says – and that he has never been an anarchist, which is the way that some 'Marxists' have labelled him when they react to the emphasis on the creative self-generative aspects of multitude; unlike classical Marxism this redemptive force is not created by capital but precedes and will outlive it – hence Negri's comment that 'poverty' is perhaps more important than wealth. Some critics then attack multitude as a notion that is the worst of Spinoza as an alternative to Marx and, even worse, indebted to the French philosopher Gilles Deleuze's celebration of desire as always already at work rather than arising as a function of 'lack', and as leading to 'the illusory vision of multitude ruling itself'. That last complaint is the one levelled by Slavoj Žižek, for whom 'lack' is an ineliminable ontological category – a philosophical category concerned with the underlying nature of things – that he draws from psychoanalysis and for whom the kind of self-governing collective activity that revolutionary Marxists have always aimed for must be an illusion because, his masters Hegel and Lacan tell him, you cannot think or act without a 'master'.

Actually, multitude really is the antithesis of Žižek's politics, and we can see in Hardt and Negri's account not only another take on revolutionary Marxist politics, but also an analysis which reveals some serious limitations in Žižek's own response to the refugee and migrant crisis in Europe. Žižek has been an important force in left-academic debate, and has inspired a new generation of younger social theorists, impressing on them the importance of taking Marx seriously (albeit to be read alongside Hegel and Lacan). But Žižek is not a Marxist, and this is nowhere clearer than when he is writing about politics as such rather than about political or social or psychoanalytic or philosophical academic 'theory'. He is great at critique, he makes us think, but he offers little for revolutionary practice, and, leaving aside the malign influence of his reading of psychoanalysis on his sexual politics, some of what he writes about practice is downright reactionary.

The 'only path to true unity', according to Žižek writing in 2013, is 'a Master'; people want to be passive and so 'they need a good elite', and that's why, he says, just as the French needed Charles de Gaulle to lead the resistance and make a historic decision to do so even against the majority of the French people, 'what we need today is a Thatcher of the left'. And now, in response to the refugee and migrant crisis, we need, Žižek declares, to notice that there is 'something enigmatically utopian' in the refugees' demand that they arrive at their dream-destination of Norway. They are beset by a fantasy that being in Norway will solve their problems, unable to appreciate that, even for people living in Norway, 'there is no Norway' in the sense of full freedom and provision of welfare for all. And so on, with every one of the phrases we cited above in the second paragraph of this piece as being from the bourgeois press actually coming from Žižek's own article!

Žižek's motif of the 'non-existence' of Norway in the title of his widely-circulated opinion-piece is a little in-joke for Lacanians who like to say that 'The' woman does not exist, for she is a fantasy formation. But, worse, what he does here is to speak from the standpoint of a 'we' that is 'Europe' and wants 'them' to face 'the hard truth' that there is no Norway, this after having interpreted for us the fantasy that drives 'them'. This actually goes against some of the other theoretical arguments he himself has made about 'universalism' and 'particularism', and, as has been pointed out, the 'particularism' – a specific located response to enforce the identity of a community against the universal – is 'entirely on the part of Europe'; a Marxist response should be that if there is no Norway, we should build it ourselves. To do that, we need to be part of the multitude, and that is the challenge of revolutionary politics Hardt and Negri pose for us.

One of the more bureaucratic critiques of *Multitude* – by a party leader (of the SWP, in this case) who is understandably threatened by the idea that their party of 'the Leninist type' could be seen as 'creating a new elite' – concludes that 'Of course Marxists should not put up barriers to working with people influenced by Hardt and Negri's ideas', but should be clear that this is a fundamental attack on the idea of the working class. We should be less grudging than that, more open to the transformation of the terrain of political struggle today and more welcoming of the new globalisation that 'multitude' tries to name; this notion, for all its limitations, re-energises our internationalist legacy, the limits of Eurocentrism, and also, crucially, traverses the borders between fortress Europe, which Žižek effectively defends, and the rest of the world.

Neoliberalism

Neoliberalism is the intensification of individuality and competitiveness and power. It is a big deal in higher education today. For capitalism to maintain its grip, it needs not only to drive a mass of the population into poverty but also to educate the population to believe that poverty is their own individual problem rather than a function of this miserable economic system. Attacks on trades union organisation in the universities should be understood against that context. The destruction of trades unions in the higher education sector is part and parcel of the neoliberal agenda of the three main political parties in Britain, with 'reforms' being pushed through by the Conservatives now, and in alliance with the Liberal Democrats in the last government, having been instituted by the Labour Party a decade back.

The case of Damien and Jenny Markey at Bolton University illustrates this process very well, and also shows how neoliberalism which trumpets the 'freedom' of the individual in the marketplace relies, as capitalism always does, on an apparatus to strike fear into those who resist it. Neoliberalism is not 'soft' power, replacing old-style repression with friendly persuasion, even if it does harness women's labour to 'feminise' the workplace and bring emotional pressure to bear on workers to play the game, the bosses' game. Neoliberalism, as the classic experiment in Chile from 1973 under Pinochet proved, requires brute force and increasing secrecy, because making people shut up about what they know is a way of enforcing obedience.

Stories in the press in 2015 that George Holmes, Bolton University's vice-chancellor, was given near on a million pound loan by the university to buy a house, and was paid for travel to Lake Windermere where he moors his private yacht, led the university authorities to find a culprit whistle-blower, which, very conveniently for the university, was Damien Markey, secretary of the local University and College Union (UCU). The *Times Higher Education Supplement*, which was one of the newspapers which broke the story, made it clear that Markey was not their source, as did the *Bolton News*. Damien was pulled out of an internal review in the university and immediately taken into a disciplinary hearing, accused by a manager who had been appointed to the role that very morning of leaking information to the press and then he was sacked. As for Jenny Markey, also an employee of the university and Unison union member, her crime was to be Damien's wife, obviously guilty, and so also sacked a few days later.

For sure, these two union members are now on the breadline; from having two full-time earners in the household to look after their three children, the Markeys are on welfare benefits, but this punishment is designed to serve as a message to anyone else who might speak out, who might speak about the public secret of grotesque disparity of salaries in the universities, of which vice-chancellor Holmes is just one example. That is why the May 2015 demonstration in Bolton protesting against the sacking of the Markeys was such an important show of resistance. Many lecturers and support staff in Bolton who support Damien and Jenny were afraid to attend, but many did come out that day. There were speakers outside Bolton Town Hall from nearby Salford, where the university is also clamping down on the trades unions.

The UCU was forced to take this protest seriously with more than a petition, and regional full-time organisers were present at the protest, conveying messages of goodwill from the union leadership. That was something better than the UCU response to some of the other local disputes in recent years. Joint union action is what could have taken the collective response to the Markeys beyond the immediate charitable support to keep them going until Bolton University was beaten back and reinstated them.

While the demonstrators marched through Bolton, students at

the University of Manchester occupied a building in the Business School, days later succeeding in smuggling in thirty more students and food supplies past the university security staff. The local UCU issued a statement of support for the occupation. The demands of the students, organised as 'Free Education MCR', included free education, against the use of security legislation to demonise Muslim students, workers' rights in the university – of lecturers and support staff – and accountability. This last demand, for accountability, runs crashing up against the undemocratic management structures of the university sector.

In Bolton University that lack of democratic accountability enabled the vice-chancellor to spend, spend, spend, and in the University of Manchester the student occupation was explicitly set against the prospect of the appointment of Peter Mandelson as next Chancellor of the University. Mandelson commissioned the 'Browne review' for the Labour government which recommended the introduction of student fees, which Labour then happily implemented, which the Liberal Democrats promised to repeal but then went along with as a price for being in coalition in the last government, and which the Conservatives are increasing beyond the means of most working-class students. Finally, in the elections for Chancellor, Mandelson was defeated, and the radical poet Lemn Sissay elected instead. Mandelson was given the consolation prize of Chancellorship of Manchester Metropolitan University, an institution that does not elect for the post, and so he was spared another humiliation. The Markeys, meanwhile, were paid off to keep quiet, a bitter end to the dispute which they had little choice to accept.

The transformation of capitalism into 'neoliberalism' is not merely a return to the old classical liberal political economy of the nineteenth century; it is return to the days before the days of the welfare state, but with a twist, which is that each individual is targeted so that they come to believe themselves to be responsible, or must find other individuals to blame. One of the first analysts to coin the term 'neoliberalism' was the historian and philosopher Michel Foucault, who described it as a process by which we are 'individualised' to the extent where the idea of 'society' itself appears absurd. And there is a crucial double-aspect to this shift to neoliberalism, which is that it is not merely a return to old liberal economics with a twist, but that, alongside economic compulsion, there is a political project to educate people to accept their subjection. Neoliberalism is a lesson in austerity that is being implemented in the universities to silence radical lecturers and support staff and to teach students how to be obedient 'good citizens'.

It is no coincidence that the announcement of the failure of the Markeys' appeal against dismissal came the day the Conservatives triumphed in the general election. The Conservatives under David Cameron and then Theresa May, no longer held back by the hand-wringing agonising of their erstwhile Liberal Democrat coalition partners, are intent on pressing ahead with neoliberal 'reforms', stripping back the welfare state while ensuring that higher education is an education for the masses about what they cannot and should not dare to change. But the lesson of these protests is also that collective resistance is still alive, and that new forms of rebellion against neoliberal capitalism today continue a tradition of Marxist critique and rebellion against old classical liberal capitalism in the North West, and beyond.

Normalcy

Normalcy is the enforcement of what is assumed to be 'normal' under capitalism, which necessarily involves forcing everyone to be fit for capital accumulation. The theory and practice of the radical disability movement poses a challenge to capitalism, and to the way that anti-capitalists organise themselves. The key problem here is 'organisation', which too-often perpetuates oppression through mechanisms of divide and rule so that those labelled 'disabled' are seen as the problem when they demand to participate in society or in political action to change it. And one key word from within the radical disability movement which draws attention to that labelling and pathologisation of those disabled by capitalism is 'normalcy'.

Capitalism feeds on the normal and it 'normalises' the way we behave and think. In the sphere of production capitalism organises normal bodies whose behaviour can be most easily observed and efficiently fitted into the assembly line; efficiency and speed of production rely on these normal bodies to make the process as cheap as possible. In the sphere of consumption capitalism organises itself to target different markets which must be predictable enough to enable the realisation of surplus value when a sale is made; each specialist market is then defined by norms around which designer products can be sold most profitably.

This organisation of production and consumption itself rests on two things which 'normalcy' as a practical critique of what is assumed to be 'normal' unravels. One is the material layout of institutions like factories, shopping malls and schools, the institutional spaces we move around and which are designed to 'enable' us to journey through them so that we can produce, consume and learn our place within the social order as good producers and consumers. The other is the body through which we appear to others as separate human beings and through which there is an embodiment of the possibilities and limitations of the institutions in which we learn how we fit and move or how we don't fit or are blocked.

These bodies don't just move around institutional spaces as if the factory, mall or school is a kind of 'environment', as if the body is something separate from the space to which it then needs to be adapted. Instead, the 'normal' bodies and the 'normal' spaces operate together in an interdependent relationship more like an 'ecological' system. So 'normalcy' can be seen as a critique of the ecology of organisations that make it seem as if it is normal and natural that there are some limited ways of designing buildings and institutions and some kinds of bodies that work well inside them. We need to go beyond the 'social model' of disability, a model which showed us that there are historically constructed mechanisms that exclude some kinds of people but a model which still makes a distinction between disability as socially constructed and impairment which is a real underlying problem. We go beyond that social model as a version of the individual-environment approach to a deeper critique of how we are all included in a system which relies on the distribution and gradation of abilities, as if we are things, commodities.

To go beyond that model would mean placing value on the ecological interrelationship of ourselves with nature so that the body is not cut out of the equation as something separate that could then be diagnosed as impaired or not. This therefore makes 'normalcy' an approach to disability politics that should be an ally and resource of any anti-capitalist movement or organisation that calls itself 'ecosocialist'.

As an answer to capitalism's attempt to include as many people as possible as good producers and consumers – inclusion which always still requires a measure of exclusion of those who really don't or don't want to fit in – 'normalcy' makes us ask another question, inclusion in what? For example, instead of joining the Conservative Party's hypocritical crusade against 'corruption', as if rooting out the unfortunate impediments to a competitive free market would then be truly inclusive, we should be treating what is taken to be normal in this sick destructive exploitative economic system as itself corrupt. And instead of homing in on bad behaviour in schools as the source of social problems, so-called 'classroom disruption' should be embedded in a deeper critique of the way members of the ruling class are schooled to bully those assumed to be less fit than themselves.

The term 'normalcy' also helps us question the intersection between different forms of oppression under capitalism, and of the relationship between disability and colonialism in which some parts of the world are treated as more normal than others. Here the political choice is between globalisation as a form of generous 'inclusion' into capitalist modes of production and consumption, enabling business as usual, including in a proliferation of chic niche market products, or globalisation of resistance so that another world might be built in which new consciously-elaborated ecologies interrelate with each other and in which different kinds of bodies move through different kinds of liberated space.

The choice must be posed at an international level, to include radical disability activism alongside other movements of the oppressed and, of course, and necessarily so, at a local level, at the level for example of what exclusion of children with 'special educational needs' from school tells us about the nature of schools under capitalism. Any attempt at 'radical inclusive education' must also pose this choice, between 'inclusion' in a corrupt disabling school system on the one hand and 'liberation' from ideological assumptions made about ability and disability on the other.

At stake here is what education is geared for; to the needs of a political economic system that requires each separate body to move around it and be seen as living a 'valuable' life – that road leads toward a quasi-eugenic system of exclusion of the unfit and adaptation of those who will be valuable to it – or to the needs of pupils inside the school who reflect on what their own needs are and collectively represent what is of value to them. The concept of 'normalcy' then becomes a frame for critique so that we can move from inclusion to protest, and to liberation in the field of education. It forces us to reflect on what is happening in school so that we can educate ourselves about how we need to change, change so that we can together revolutionise this world which, in different ways, disables us all.

Occupy

Occupy summed up a movement of diverse protests devoted to reclaiming and redefining spaces and symbolic forms of power. It happened everywhere, including in psychotherapy. The first national meeting in the UK of the Free Psychotherapy Network (FPN) took place in Manchester on a busy Saturday 21 May 2016, a day when many other alternative left events were also taking place. Registrations, which were free, had hit nearly two hundred the day before, and the participants packed into the main hall of Friends Meeting House to begin a task barely formulated before the meeting began but which became clearer by the end of the day, to 'occupy' psychotherapy. What it means to 'occupy' and the resonances of the term across the left and anti-capitalist movements protesting against austerity are now on the agenda. This was not the case for all the participants, but for many of them this is what was happening. How, and why?

Psychotherapy is a practice of self-exploration and, potentially, of empowerment, but under capitalism, which is the political-economic system that provoked a need for psychotherapy and fed it as a means of feeding the 'self' as a valuable commodity, psychotherapy has also turned into a tool of social control. It needs to be reclaimed by those who seek to tackle distress and want to tackle the underlying causes of distress as social causes. The project of the FPN is, very simply put, to link together practitioners of psychotherapy together to provide free or very low-cost treatment. The privatisation of distress under capitalism is matched by the imperative to make people pay for their treatment, but what is often forgotten is that the early days of psychotherapy saw many practitioners, including Sigmund Freud, founder of psychoanalysis, call for treatment to be provided free. The FPN is one way of reclaiming that history.

The day began with two powerful introductory speeches, by Paul Atkinson from London and Yasmin Dewan from Manchester, on the brutal effects of austerity on social relationships and personal experience and on the importance of enabling access to psychotherapy for all who need it. The titles of the workshops that took place in the morning and afternoon before the final plenary session were indicative of the breadth of the network, and the breadth of meanings that 'psychotherapy' has for those involved. This term 'psychotherapy' was also, in the course of the day, being reclaimed, 'occupied' to make it something more than the reduced professional label that is jealously guarded by mainstream registration bodies, bodies that also, as one psychotherapist at the meeting pointed out, do not speak out against austerity. For example, the meeting included 'psychoanalysts' of different persuasions working together, something rare to see, and 'counsellors' and 'counselling psychologists' who are often divided from each other by way of the institutional turf-wars conducted by their representative bodies. Through the day 'psychotherapy' and 'psychotherapist' were the terms used to bring participants together, to refer to themselves as a group and as a practice.

The morning workshops included one on 'service users and professionals working together', and this was an opportunity to discuss the different attempts by NHS practitioners to defend services, the strategies of 'pseudo-inclusion' by which users of services are invited on to committees in which they have no real power, and the attempts to break the binary opposition between professional and user. This last issue concerning the identity of the psychotherapist as a precious protected professional identity was something that we see combated for example in *Asylum: Magazine for Democratic Psychiatry*, and was to appear again later in the day. A workshop 'rescuing psychotherapy' focused on the question of power dynamics between therapist and the one who seeks help and who is variously referred to as a 'patient', which has medical connotations, or as a 'client' who is today under neoliberalism treated as if they are some kind of customer. A third workshop on 'mental health activist campaigning in the UK' was led by Disabled People Against Cuts (DPAC) and explored different forms of direct action against austerity and exclusion, action that has already involved members of FPN. The fourth workshop was on 'peer-led alternatives' and it was from this group in the afternoon that some radical proposals came forward about the binary opposition between healers and their clients.

Two of the afternoon workshops were led by activists from two services that already provide free therapeutic support: Trafford Rape Crisis centre, which focuses on feminist strategies for combating power and supporting women who experienced sexual violence; and by the asylum and refugee service in Manchester 'Revive', about the ways that the state repeats violence against those fleeing torture. There was a workshop on different forms of 'peer support', for those who offer psychotherapy working together, one on 'neoliberalism and psychotherapy', and one on the 'mechanics of building FPN'. The whole day was filmed by a team from the Philadelphia Association, a psychotherapy service founded in the 1960s by RD Laing.

The final workshop in the afternoon, on the 'mechanics of building FPN', sprung a surprise for the participants in the final plenary session, a surprise that has yet to be worked through. It had already become very clear during the day that alongside the psychoanalysts, psychotherapists, group analysts, counsellors and counselling psychologists were a few sympathetic psychiatrists willing to speak out against the medical model in their own profession, and, more importantly, activists of different kinds who used psychotherapy services but who were intent on making those services work for them rather than against them. Among these activists some were already themselves providing forms of 'psychotherapy', but forms not recognised by the big beasts in the registration and regulation jungle. From them came the demand that the movement include in the FPN the 'wounded healers' who draw on their own experience and offer a range of forms of support. Psychotherapy is much more than what is marketed, and then differentiated into different 'brands' which are expensive for those who want to train and get a certificate to practice. The FPN may also end up changing the way we think about what psychotherapy is. That is what happens when it is occupied, taken from those who usually define the practice and guard the boundaries around it.

This free psychotherapy network has its roots in 'Occupy' in London in 2011–2012, an occupy movement to which it now returns. Many of the key activists had been involved in the occupy events, and have since been active in the direct action protests against the government workfare schemes. Occupy was a particular strategy of resistance, a way of taking the physical spaces of power and redefining them as the space of the ninety-nine per cent instead of the one per cent with power and privilege. Some even saw Occupy as a form of psychotherapy. Occupy Wall Street in 2011 and then Occupy London protests took space, but also reclaimed the way we understand resistance. The critiques of Occupy drive home the message that we should not reduce resistance to liberal complaint or, for that matter, to psychotherapy.

The immediate link between movements inside psychotherapy and political action is what gave this May 2015 meeting in Manchester such energy. There are many other such initiatives now that the Free Psychotherapy Network connects with and overlaps with, including the 'Alliance for Counselling and Psychotherapy' which fought back attempts at state regulation, and the recently-founded 'Psychotherapy and Counselling Union'. The discussion of neoliberalism at the meeting was one way of articulating the FPN as a political project. Neoliberalism entails the stripping back of welfare provision and the demand that people pay for services, the imposition of a strong state and coercion to make people work and the incitement to individuals to take personal responsibility for social problems. As was pointed out in the course of the day, the FPN should not promise too much in terms of material provision, it still has very few members willing to give of their time, but it already functions now symbolically as a form of resistance.

This resistance is there in the three words that comprise FPN: it is 'free', for welfare and support and explicitly in support of the NHS, not part of a 'big society' which replaces state provision; it is 'psychotherapy' as a form of self-care and care for others that is explicitly against coercion and violence; and it is a 'network', bringing individual psychotherapists together and configuring their practice as a social intervention, a collective project. The link between these three terms is important; then FPN can symbolically, and materially, resist neoliberalism. In the process the FPN gave a new meaning to what psychotherapy might mean as part of social liberation. This was free psychotherapy in the sense of making it free and in the sense of making it into something freeing. FPN occupy it.

Other

This strange term 'other' speaks of who we are in relation to others, to ourselves and to the political causes we are drawn to. One of the signs that Venezuela was in crisis in 2016 was that the lights were going out. As the electricity supply failed, headlines appeared in the Western press revelling in the image of the country suffering in the blackouts. For the press outside the country, as well as for the big media companies inside it, this all, of course, has nothing to do with climate change; it has nothing to do with the scouring drought that is emptying the reservoirs and so cutting off the hydroelectricity supply, a drought that is also hitting neighbouring Colombia. And for a private press that works hand-in-glove with big business and which is pushing a neoliberal agenda for the opposition to the Maduro regime, the crisis has nothing to do with the dependence of the economy on oil, the structural dependence of the country on global capitalism, and the effect now of tumbling oil prices. These are indeed dark days for the Bolivarian revolution, and that darkness is itself linked in the press, and in the anti-capitalist left, with surreptitious imagery of what has been happening in Venezuela as something profoundly 'Other'.

The media war for and against the regime has always been, and is now increasingly so, suffused with allusions to 'Otherness', of an Other who knows what is going on behind the scenes; this could be on the side of the regime or of the opposition, each as operating on behalf of and even as instrument of the Other. This is a motif that slides quickly into conspiracy theory, and makes the political stakes of the struggle to defend or overthrow the regime particularly high, and dangerous. It is a motif that is worth spending a moment examining, for something of the Other is also present in anti-racist and feminist discourse, and there it is a useful tool for unravelling the ideological contours of colonial privilege and subaltern resistance.

In much radical cultural theory, the 'Other' has come to structure how readers of literary, film and even newspaper texts think about who they are and how they represent and relate to those from different cultures. This image of another culture as Other to the reader, a reader who is invariably positioned as exemplifying the West or as being the bearer of whiteness, is also often mapped across on to dimensions of gender and sexuality. Then, 'woman' as such comes to be figured as Other, other to the male norm presumed to be the standard by which she should be measured and to which she can never match up; and non-normative forms of sexuality are seen as Other to the presumed heterosexual cultural standard. There is always something fascinating about the Other, and it functions in critical discourse to remind us that we are beings formed out of our relationships to others, relationships that we often repeat unbeknownst to ourselves. When the link is made with psychoanalysis, the human subject itself is seen as existing in relation to an Other of language, inhabited by that 'Otherness' which operates as unconscious that subject. The imperative to detect and pin down the Other which suffuses critical discourse is sometimes suffocating and reactionary, but it also, at the same time, draws attention to something at work in and alongside revolutionary politics. There is something of the Other in the discourse about and inside Venezuela that appears in at least three ways.

First, there is the exotic representation of the site of revolutionary struggle as always somewhere else and filled with beauty and terror, the Other orientalised, very much in the way that Edward Said once described. For those who don't live there, Latin America seems to fit the bill, and Venezuela under Hugo Chávez has often functioned in this kind of way for those desperately wishing that there really could be a revolution somewhere in the world. This is the revolution as Other to the Western white subject who invests that struggle with such romantic fullness and vitality that they can never bring themselves to acknowledge that there are internal fractures, internal divisions around dimensions of class, race or sexuality inside their beloved revolution. This is the image of the Bolivarian revolution that pulls the present-day fellow-traveller into solidarity work that then covers over any faults in the Other, and so they complain bitterly about any critique of the revolution inside the solidarity movement. They complain bitterly about colonial racism when there is criticism of a regime they support, failing to see that their own silence about shortcomings of the regime they idealise is structured by a fascination with the Other that is also suspect, also at root racist. This kind of solidarity is plagued by exactly the kind of blindness that afflicted the fellow-travellers of Stalinist regimes in the 1930s, and the motif of 'Otherness' marks the intense subjective dimension of their attachment to their cause. More than that, the motif of the Other can later turn into a guilty reflexive agonising about what they have colluded with that will lead them into therapy rather than into a revolutionary reappraisal of their mistakes.

Second, as flip side, and sometimes as a reaction to this 'othering' of the revolution that can do no wrong, there is more explicitly racist demonisation of those who dare to resist their oppression and who sometimes make mistakes in the course of the struggle that are then viewed as unforgivable indications of their uncivilised stupidity and callousness. This version of the Other is to be found in the routine ideological othering of Chávez as someone who was always suspect because he was not quite white, and in the bizarre complaint that Maduro is not even Venezuelan. This form of racist othering which parallels neoconservative attempts to prove that Obama does not really have US citizenship erupts in the quite bizarre claims that Maduro is really Colombian, claims that are expressed even at the same moment that the speaker acknowledges that they are irrational. One way they deal with that contradiction is to note that it is 'other' people who believe this, and so to repeat the claim in that way, disavowing responsibility for it. This is the othering of the regime that desperately tries to overlook the fact that in the neoliberal right-wing demonstrations against Chávez and Maduro most of the demonstrators are white.

Third, while the neoliberal opposition fuelled by US American propaganda searches for the hidden dark forces responsible for Venezuela's slide into chaos, cheerleaders for Chávez, and now Maduro, often seem happy to match these supposedly deeper but quite wacky explanations for what is going on with their own. These are explanations which divide the world into a so-called anti-imperialist international alliance which includes some very dodgy characters, struggling against forces with unbelievable capacities to rig the market and even affect the weather. There is always a kernel of reality that provides the basis for the motif of the Other, and in the case of Venezuela many shortages are down to the multinational companies themselves deciding to restrict supplies. It is also present in the foreign policy of the Bolivarian regime, however, and that includes alliances with dictators ranging from Mugabe to Gaddafi to Assad, and then support for Putin's own war against Western capitalism which is simply designed to buttress the reinstatement of capitalism in Russia.

In cultural theory which draws on postcolonial, postmodern or psychoanalytic theory, there is no shortage of moralising phrases designed to recriminate against idealistic fellow-travellers of a revolution. Against those engaged in solidarity work there is the injunction to reflect on the dangers of 'orientalism', an injunction that often leads to cynical disengagement and to the idea that things are as bad abroad as they are at home, even that the main enemy is really at home, inside us. These cultural theorists besotted with the image of the Other will tell their benighted opponents that conspiracy theories simply express the false assumption that there is an 'Other of the Other'; really, a good analysis will show you, they will say, that 'the

Other does not exist' (these are two favourite slogans of followers of the French psychoanalyst Jacques Lacan). And so on. But, despite this 'othering' of politics as something strange, an othering that bedevils much academic critical theory, we can take analyses of the Other up and make it work for us. To take the Other seriously as a keyword in politics today that learns from anti-racist and feminist critique is not at all to reduce our solidarity with the attempts to build something new in Venezuela but should be to intensify it. We can engage in that solidarity work, to include solidarity with those who are also speaking out against the corruption of the Bolivarian revolution, and we can do that better if we examine the ideological assumptions that often riddle and then sabotage it.

Pabloism

Pabloism has become one name for handing over power to others to change the world rather than organising ourselves to do it. In 2015 after the general election in the UK everyone seemed to be joining something else, finding a party a bit bigger into which they could merge and lose themselves, to find some comfort there. This followed the rapid movement from one party to another before the election, and it looks like all of the left could get caught up in this game. Join the Greens, join the Labour Party to support Jeremy Corbyn as leader, what next? There is a name for this kind of thing, a keyword still popular on the more esoteric fringes of sub-Trotskyist sect political smear-mongering, and it's called 'Pabloism'. It might sound like a bad joke, but it is worth looking at what it's supposed to mean, and whether it still makes any sense now.

Michel Pablo was a leader of the Fourth International who helped steer the organisation through the difficult period after the Second World War when revolutionary Marxists were isolated and the opposition to capitalism came either from the Communist Parties (of the Third International or 'Comintern') operating under direct instruction from Stalin, or from the social democratic parties (most of which were in the Second or 'Socialist' International). A way out of this dire situation, caught between Stalinist parties dedicated to defending the bureaucracy in the Soviet Union (including defending it against revolutionary movements that were a threat to Stalin and his successors) and the reformist social democrats (who had such a very long view of the transition to socialism that they effectively lined up with the capitalist states to keep their miniscule reforms on track), would be to 'join up' with the bigger organisations.

At that time the Fourth International still operated as a democratic centralist organisation, and so the idea was that 'deep

entry' or 'entrism sui generis' into the Communist or Socialist
parties could be managed by a revolutionary leadership, and so
compromise with the anti-revolutionary leadership of those
bigger parties could be prevented. The tactic is sometimes traced
to what is called the 'French turn' which Trotsky advocated in
1934, with resonances today for left strategy in Europe.

Time and again, however, the 'Pabloites', as they came to be
known by their enemies, were faced with two problems. One was
that revolutionaries were tempted by the prospect of power in
the apparatus they had 'entered', and so 'deep' was the entry that
they often swapped their allegiances to their host party or even to
a parliament to which they had been elected. Another, deeper,
problem was that the revolutionary organisations themselves,
even still as sections of the Fourth International, sometimes
adapted their politics to the bigger parties they joined in order to
make them acceptable or understandable to the other members.

There was, then, a risk of falling into a version of the trap that
Trotsky himself had earlier noticed as 'tailism', though here it
was not merely tailing after events and fitting in with what was
already happening, working alongside forces out of our control,
but also going with the tide of new ideas on the left that were
actually usually old reformist ideas about possibilities of gradual
change or Stalinist ideas about the importance of strong charismatic leadership. Groups once allied to the Fourth International
around the world then ended up with members of parliament
who turned against their fellow revolutionaries or echoed nationalist sentiments in order to keep in with popular opinion.

The flip side of these problems was hysterical denunciation by
those following the old one true path, denunciation of anything
that looked remotely like a broad alliance with anyone beyond
the revolutionary left. This accusation was a speciality and
trademark argument made by followers of Gerry Healy, his
'Workers Revolutionary Party' and his own 'International
Committee of the Fourth International' run with a grip of steel,

fear and some violence from London. As revolutionary Marxism got weaker in relation to other anti-capitalist movements, their kind of 'exposure' of what they saw as the secretly counter-revolutionary nature of the 'Pabloite revisionists' became increasingly sectarian.

The high point (well, it was actually the worst moment) of this sectarian response was in the weirdly logical conclusion that because the Fourth International was allying with the lackeys of Stalin or of the capitalist states (by virtue of working inside the Communist or Socialist parties) it must have always already been an agent of the police apparatus of one or both of our deadly enemies; the 'Pabloites' were therefore agents of the KGB and CIA and, why not, they were complicit even in the death of Trotsky, and so they must be destroyed.

This twisted logic followed its course as the obsession with what was called 'Security and the Fourth International' led to physical attacks on 'Pabloite revisionists' because they were an obstacle to world revolution, and then attempts by Gerry Healy's true path anti-pabloites to disrupt what they called 'The platform of shame' in London in 1977. That public meeting brought together leaders of different Trotskyist traditions – Tariq Ali, Ernest Mandel, Tim Wohlforth (who is now a crime writer), Pierre Lambert (the last two labelled as 'renegades', of course, because they had dared to break from Healy), and even Michel Pablo (in a message read out to the meeting) – in a rare show of unity to object to what Healy was doing as a danger to the whole revolutionary left.

Healy's group, once one of the largest revolutionary organisations in Britain, disintegrated ten years later after revelations about sexual exploitation that the tabloid press called the 'reds in the bed' scandal, and the different fragments of Healy's own 'international' geared to destroying the Fourth International splintered further in acrimonious disputes in which the anti-pabloites ate each other while playing 'spot the police agent'. One way to annoy them and relive aspects of the worst of the past of Trotskyism is to tell someone from the Socialist Equality Party or someone selling *News Line* about the Fourth International, watch their eyes narrow and wait for the venomous accusation sputter out that you are not talking about the real one at all.

The term 'Pabloism' therefore has a weight inside the Trotskyist revolutionary left that is unfortunately defined mainly by those who don't know what it is but know they don't like it. It is a term of abuse that expands what was a tactic ('entrism') into a worldview that no one actually ever fully subscribed to. It is true that the term draws attention to a risk that goes with every attempt at creating an alliance or, still more so, joining up with a party larger than that of the organised revolutionaries. It is also a term with a history that drags the hopeless history of sectarianism on the left along with it, which is why it is either shouted in the strangled angry voice of the crackpot demanding to know why you murdered Leon Trotsky, or whispered in a sad reminder of how a party that stood against the social democrats and the Stalinists after the Second World War then degenerated. It drags the bad past and still leaves us with two problems today.

One is the suspicion it stokes about the attempt to bring together the anti-capitalist left in new forms of organisation that are no longer 'democratic centralist' and that build into their politics an appreciation of anti-colonial and anti-racist struggles as well as of feminist practice. It makes it difficult to acknowledge that the 'Fourth International' itself is no longer one unitary force, or that revolutionaries today need to work across the divisions between 'anarchist' and 'libertarian' groups to build something that is of the tradition of the 'fourth' international whilst also being of the tradition of other international struggles that it needs to absorb lessons from. Actually, many of the complaints about 'Pabloism' overlook what it often amounts to in practice. The complaints come from sectarian groupuscules that put their own organisations first; what 'Pabloism' is, for them, is the strategy of building the broadest possible alliances, including alliances alongside and even within the larger parties when those parties can be engaged in action against capitalism.

The other problem is that it names but one aspect of the life of the revolutionary Marxist Michel Pablo, a revolutionary who carried on outside the Fourth International for many years before a convergence of perspectives again before he died in Athens in 1996. This is the best 'Pabloism', of a comrade who was arrested for gun-running to support the Algerian independence struggle in 1961, a minister in the FLN government attempting to push the revolution forward, a Marxist who made at least an attempt (albeit botched) to take women's liberation seriously, and who appreciated Frantz Fanon as a comrade, who was later an activist in Chile under the Allende government before the coup in 1973. 'Pabloism' as a keyword fails to cover all of the struggles, false paths, defeats that this one individual participated in, all of which we can still learn from today.

Performativity

Performativity shifts attention from who we are to what we do. When supporters of the Spanish radical party Podemos held their 2015 national meeting in Manchester, for example, they invited a speaker from the Greek party Syriza who was clear about what we had to do, build solidarity now. It was not a question, she said, of whether Syriza would or would not win the election on one day and perhaps take power the day after, but rather that Syriza was definitely going to win and then what happened after that would depend on all of us. Enough of predictions! The question of Syriza on the edge of power entails what Judith Butler, the feminist philosopher and inspiration for queer politics, calls 'performativity'.

The performative dimension of politics is crucial to queer interventions into the construction and deconstruction of gender, that is, of the way that we become divided into the categories of 'men' and 'women' and play that division out in everyday life, and of the way we challenge and dismantle those categories. Socialist and feminist histories of the struggles of women to redefine who they are in the revolutionary process have always emphasised how women and men then necessarily radically change their relationships with each other. You cannot make a revolution when women are stuck in the home imagining all they can do is make babies, nor when men imagine that they are the only ones who will form the vanguard of the struggle out in the real world.

Butler argued that the stable gender identities much-beloved of conservative enthusiasts of the family are not as stable as they seem, that they are struggled over inside and outside the home, and that those identities of men and women are held in place not only by laws and the ideological trash peddled by the newspapers and television but also by our own 'performance' of gender. But that performance is not just like playing a part on the stage, choosing to adopt a role as the good little girl or the macho male leader. It is performative in the sense that it involves us following rules of behaviour and rules about the way we think about ourselves that are, Butler says, 'reiterating' gender, endlessly repeating it so it seems like there is no alternative way of being with each other. When a child is born, even though many infants are of indeterminate sex (and 'intersex' is the medical category used for those who just won't fit either side of the gender binary), a decision is made that 'it's a boy' or 'it's a girl', a decision that is performed by the family and then has to be performed by the boy or girl to be accorded legal and social and political rights. And that's exactly what queer politics challenges, opening up spaces for many different kinds of performance of identity, which includes those who say they are 'trans' (and reject the normative binary divide). We have to take some responsibility for this, but that is a collective activity, not one locked inside each individual agonising about how they should behave (and reduction to the level of individual identity is something that queer politics also refuses).

The performative dimension has consequences way beyond gender and sexuality, and it connects with and deepens the way revolutionary Marxists think about the relation between description and prediction in politics. This is one point where feminism can connect with Marxism. 'Performativity' is a keyword for new politics that shows us that every description and prediction is from a standpoint that is full of assumptions and values, assumptions and values about what must always stay the same and what can be changed. This 'performativity' deepens the way we think about 'performance' so that this performance is no longer just an individual choice about how we deliberately play our parts on the political stage. It also deepens the way we speak and act in such a way that 'description' and 'prediction' themselves become questionable when they smuggle in assumptions and values. Description and prediction about what is going to happen in the revolutionary process, for example, makes it seem as if there is this 'revolutionary process' going on that is separate from us, and from what we say about it, makes it seem as if our description is just some kind of neutral commentary and our prediction is just an optimistic or pessimistic guess about what is going to happen next. That fake neutral position is as much a problem in the world of politics as it is when we think we are neutrally describing someone's gender or sexuality.

The dimension of performativity draws attention to how everything we say is from a position, we are part of what we describe and that has effects, there are consequences of what we say. Here we connect with what was in the Marxist tradition called 'praxis' (which combines theory and practice in one activity). When we describe the relation between capitalist and worker as being intrinsically exploitative and dehumanising, for example, that leads us, next, to mobilise to end exploitation and assert our humanity in an understanding of what is going on that is immediately combined with changing it. This argument also opens up a range of connections with the performative dimension of sexuality, 'race' and religion, as well as attempts by the right to treat the political question as a simple question of identity.

The ideological media commentaries on what would happen if Syriza really took power had at least one thing in common; the commentators pretended that they had no stake in what they were describing and they shut out the possibility that what they were predicting had a performative dimension. At the very moment they were busy performing being experts on Greece and pretending they could guess what would happen if Syriza did this or that they also turned us into a passive audience reduced to doing little more than commenting and guessing ourselves.

Was it that we were going to simply observe these historic events, as if we are fixed in place, as if our solidarity with the

Greek people would really have no effect, as if our hope about what other people might decide to do was no more than that, a hope, a wish, consolation for our lack of power? No, our solidarity with Syriza and with all those struggling inside and alongside it for revolutionary change was as much a part of the process as was the solidarity we developed with those who were challenging the binary division into well-behaved women and men. We didn't say we hoped that things would work out well and that if, with luck, the leaders of Syriza made the right decisions we would support them. We didn't wait. We spoke and acted, performatively, asserting that this world must change, that class exploitation (and gender oppression and the manifold other kinds of misery that capitalism produces and channels to divide us from each other) must end, that with our activity we would either keep that exploitation going or we would challenge it, that with our activity we were always on the edge of power, on the edge of the possibility of radical transformation. It was not a question of if; it was a question of when. And the same applies now to solidarity with those inside Syriza resisting the betrayal by the leadership, and with those who broke from Syriza to carry on the struggle against the troika. Not only in Greece but here, everywhere, and not only in an election but in a strike, protest or solidarity event. This, and every moment, is when we as revolutionaries perform the process of transformation.

Postcolonial

Postcolonial analysis and action works in and against the legacy of imperialism. Colonialism, which was intensified by imperialism – what Lenin once called 'the highest stage of capitalism' – entailed the forcible extraction of materials and human beings and then surplus value from the supposedly as-yet 'undeveloped' world. It was a brutal process which ensured that the West actually 'underdeveloped' other countries around the world (to borrow Walter Rodney's term for what happened in Africa). Neither colonialism nor imperialism are over, but there is a new twist on the process, and a critique which tracks the way that systematic exploitation and oppression of 'the world of the third' also includes pervasive cultural imperialism as a necessary aspect of contemporary globalisation. One name for this, and it is a name that does not at all pretend that we are beyond or 'post' colonialism, is 'postcolonial'. Postcolonial critique focuses on the intimate link between coloniser and colonised, the recruitment of the colonised to the colonial project, and the material and ideological dependence of the colonial world on those it repeatedly renders as 'other' to it. It is a field of study which examines the way each economic and cultural entity is located in relation to the history of colonialism, and, as we can see in Malta, for example, it enables critical reflection and resistance to local and imperial state attempts to subjugate populations and destroy the land.

Malta is one of many emblems of postcolonialism today, expressing the contradictions of its colonial history and literally cracking apart, facing ecological catastrophe; the land disintegrates as a consequence of 'development' as those contradictions are intensified in the pursuit of profit. Malta was one of the key staging posts for Western Europe's assertion of sovereignty in the face of the Ottomans, something now celebrated for local consumption and tourist interest. Maltese as a language is written in Roman script but is very close to Arabic, with a roughly seventy per cent overlap of words, meaning that asylum seekers who make it there from north Africa can be immediately understood on the streets of the capital, Valletta. This linguistic overlap reinforces the self-representation of the islanders as being both at the centre of fortress Europe in the middle of the Mediterranean (and popular British holiday destination), and as being at the margins, south of Sicily and close to the Libyan coast. A popular discourse here, even for those who do not speak of themselves as 'postcolonial' subjects, is that the Maltese are 'hybrid', and this is also expressed in the internal resistance to the Catholic Church, internal resistance which draws on liberation theology from Latin America, the 'preferential option for the poor' underpinning solidarity and support work with migrants.

The Partit Laburista (PL) under Dom Mintoff demanded independence from Britain (which had acquired Malta in the early nineteenth century) in the 1960s, and the island became a republic in 1974, engaging in a series of nationalisations and expansion of the welfare state. These were moves supported by the Communist Party of Malta which emerged from a split from the PL in 1969 and then rarely stood against either Mintoff or his successors in elections. In fact, the PL in power has behaved like a classic rotten borough apparatus working hand-in-hand with local business interests and maintaining its grip on power through a series of personal networks and back-door deals, something that is easier to manage on an island smaller than Greater Manchester and with a population of less than half a million people. The conservative Christian democratic Nationalist Party is the opposition party, egging on the PL in its recent neoliberal turn and promising to speed up the pace of privatisation. One of the most densely-populated countries in the world, Malta has been destroying local habitats at an alarming rate, with 95% of the land now officially urbanised, and very few small pockets of green land left in the country. It is now often referred to as being a 'City State', marked in its coat of arms and now literally materially geographically a fact on the ground.

These are precisely the questions addressed by postcolonial analysis and theory, and this is precisely why postcolonialism is such a hot topic among Maltese academics and activists as they ally with the oppressed and defend their land against those forces that will otherwise end up destroying both, destroying the people and the environment already marked by the history of colonial expansion and wars of conquest.

The theoretical resources for postcolonial critique are varied. They include the attempt by the French psychoanalyst Octave Mannoni to account for both the subjection of the colonial subject to the coloniser and the master-slave dialectic of simultaneous dependence of the coloniser on those they make into their subjects. More importantly for us, it includes the critical response to Mannoni by Frantz Fanon, an anti-racist response which showed how Mannoni himself was caught in the very categories he was attempting to analyse; Fanon is one anchor point for postcolonial critique which was linked to active solidarity with the Algerian revolution and lessons beyond that. The resources also include the work of the Palestinian scholar and activist Edward Said analysing the production of the 'other' in the colonial imagination, of the process of what he called 'orientalism' which turns the colonial subjects into objects of exoticised fear; thrilling objects which are both fascinating and threatening to the coloniser. They include work by the Marxist-feminist Gayatri Chakravorty Spivak who inspired a strand of 'subaltern studies' which revolves around the position of those subject to this new phase of colonialism and asks how it is that these subjects might inhabit the forms of culture that have been imposed upon them and speak within the language of the oppressor. And, in this spirit of immanent critique which deconstructs the colonial relation and turns it around to show how fragile the position of the Western 'master' is when their slave-subjects speak back, the theoretical resources include the work of Dipesh Chakrabarty who rereads cultural texts to 'provincialise Europe', to show that Europe is not the centre of the world but is marginal to what is developing as a critique and in social movements around the world against its historical legacy. There are many others, the point being that there is no one master theorist here but, rather, a plural series of objections and rejections of what colonialism has left in its wake.

Such matters came to a head in Malta in 2015 with a desperate attempt by the government to reposition the country as part of the global knowledge economy, and to feed on the neoliberal privatisation of the university sector to attract investment. Among the government's top five development projects that threaten to turn Malta into a 'permanent building site' is the proposed so-called 'American University of Malta' (AUM) which will occupy Zonqor Point, a green site that was previously tagged for a hotel complex. This will require 'nationalisation' of 11 per cent of the land on Marsaskala and Bormla at Zonqor Point, land currently in private hands, and this will then be handed over to the private 'university'. Protesters inside and outside the existing public University of Malta, including those in the independent 'Critical Institute' registered as an NGO on the island (and which publishes the online journal *Disability and the Global South*), have been resisting these moves, mobilising over 3,000 people – refugee support, disability and environmental activists – in demonstrations against the development. The protesters pointed out that: the AUM private project rushed through by the PL is not American, it is a Jordanian enterprise run by Sadeen Education Investment Limited; it is evidently not Maltese, competing directly with the one existing university and opening up the higher education sector to private competition; and it is not even legally a university, the National Commission for Further and

Higher Education were clear on that point.

One aspect of postcolonial critique that is borne out by these recent attempts to recolonise Malta and by the resistance to that neoliberal exercise in cultural imperialism in the context of the globalised knowledge economy is that 'postcolonial subjects' are not only those who live inside the old colonies. Postcolonial studies describe, among other things, the way in which those at the margins often, in a way that is uncanny for those in the 'centre', know more about the colonisers than the colonisers themselves know. And the flip side of this is that those who refuse to be of the 'centre' and who make political alliances with 'outsiders' can all the more effectively dismantle the legacy of colonialism, anticipating the day when it really will be accurate to refer to it as something that really is 'post'.

Postmodernism

Postmodernism attempted to grapple with cultural and political changes in capitalism and with resistance. There is one thing that most Marxists seem to agree on when they are identifying their worst most dangerous ideological helpmeets of capitalism. Different competing Marxist traditions agree that 'postmodernism' is a plague which must be wiped out of the revolutionary left. But this keyword, a scare-word for many on the left, has also over the last thirty years or so actually drawn more activists into revolutionary politics than it has lured them away. It is time to reappraise the dangers postmodernism holds and look again at how it has also re-energised the new anti-capitalist movements.

Way back in the early 1990s, soon after postmodernism first appeared on the scene, socialist feminist activists wrote thoughtful and lengthy accounts of how dangerous it could be as a collection, they said, of 'theories of difference'. Postmodernism, which at this time was closely connected with 'Eurocommunist' arguments, was, critics pointed out, shifting attention from class struggle to a muddle of different competing accounts of subjectivity which effectively drew feminist activists away from a unitary socialist rebellion against capitalism into the swamp of 'post-feminism'. There was some truth in this diagnosis. In contrast, more recent harsher wilder attacks on postmodernism combine a number of different enemies to world revolution that include the German tradition of 'critical theory' and postmodernism from France, and that together function as an evil and shadowy conspiracy of what they call the 'pseudo-left'. Meanwhile, separatist radical feminists – those who believe that patriarchy can only be overthrown by gathering women together in political action away from the world of men, and well away from left organisations – have also named 'pomo' as a deadly threat. When feminists or queer theorists start playing with postmodern ideas, the argument goes, they must be disabused and their theoretical errors pointed out to them pretty sharply. Away with all your postmodern superstitions which smuggle into politics the relativistic idea that there is no progress, that all ideas are already equal could we but see it, and so that there is no revolutionary theory now that can take us forward.

But from its first glimmerings there has always been one uncomfortable aspect of postmodernism that has bothered the old left and made their complaints about it seem just a little bit, well, reactionary and even colonial. Postmodernism has been attractive precisely to those who are not at the centre, those who have had the most to lose from what postmodernist theory calls the old modern 'grand narratives' of history and scientific knowledge. It has not actually been so much that postmodernism cuts against the left and feminism, but that a new feminist anti-capitalist left at the margins, including in the old colonies, have seen in it a way of dismantling the 'truths' that hold capitalism and patriarchy in place. Capitalism pretends, and now all the more so, to be the only game in town, but postmodernism shows us that there are many more games to play against it.

India is a case in point, a place where postmodern argument has flourished. Why? On the one hand it could seem at first glance to be a playground of postmodernism, mixing together a multitude of different cultural traditions, combining political-economic forms from what orthodox Marxists would usually assume to be different 'stages of development', blurring boundaries of sex and gender and opening space to the 'hijra' as a third sex that also seems to function as a social class, and assembling religious imagery into a polytheistic carnival that subverts how the monotheistic colonial people of the book would define faith. However, looking a little closer, we can see how this regional capitalist power which is closely integrated into the global economy, and now run by a Hindu fundamentalist government, has some very clear ideas about scientific knowledge and progress that postmodernism actually helps us to unravel.

The key founding document of this theoretical tradition, *The Postmodern Condition*, was written in 1979 as a 'report on knowledge' for the Canadian government which wanted an analysis of how it could get into and better exploit the new field of information technology. One of the arguments the author, Jean-François Lyotard, made in this document was that information technology effected a revolutionary transformation in the economy and subjectivity, and this also had implications for politics which now functioned more and more as a series of 'language games'. There was therefore actually an account here of the progressive transformation of capitalism which some writers then linked with Ernest Mandel's analysis of 'late capitalism'; for literary theorist Fredric Jameson, for example, postmodernism was the 'cultural logic' of late capitalism as Mandel had described it. In this respect there is nothing necessarily 'anti-Marxist' about the analysis. It actually shows us how new forms of technological knowledge masquerading as scientific rationality operate as forms of power. Remember that India is now a centre of the tech industry and with a rapidly expanding service sector which fits the bill for Mandel's and perhaps even for Lyotard's analysis. In this use of 'postmodernism' we do not necessarily embrace it, but note the diagnosis of a new twist on ideology under capitalism.

Those who do not conform to these forms of power are then the ones accused of being irrational, and their resistance is treated as if it is a form of superstition. This is an ideological rhetorical move that Marxists have been well used to, with our dialectical-materialist analysis of capitalism mocked as unscientific superstitious nonsense, as a form of religion (which unfortunately is how it did indeed function in the service of the Stalinist bureaucracy in the Soviet Union).

In India, 'superstition' is a highly-charged term in a series of language games about faith and power that perfectly illustrates how such accusations about irrationality quickly turn around to bite those who try to use them for good progressive secularist and even, they might imagine, socialist purposes. Take the Maharashtra Superstition Removal Organisation founded in 1989, for example, which began as a grass-roots rationalist and socialist movement to oppose fundamentalist Hinduism, and which, in its early years, did get support from leftist and Dalit activists. They eventually brought an 'Anti-Superstition Bill' to the Maharashtra legislature in 2003, where it was first blocked by the Hindu right, but was eventually passed as an ordinance in 2013, four days after the assassination of Narendra Dabholkar, the founder of the Maharashtra Superstition Removal Organisation. The Bill has been taken up in other Indian States, but here's the thing; it is not being used to tackle 'superstition' at all, but rather those forms of religious practice that the state deems to be 'superstitious'. In Karnataka, the 'Prevention of Superstitious Practices Bill' is ready to go on the books (though opposed by some supporters of the Modi government who are anxious that it could cut against them). In practice, however, legal instruments like this have not been used against devotees of Hindu temples like the popular India tourist site of Balaji offering 'faith' treatments, but have, predictably, targeted those operating and visiting Muslim shrines.

The new language games opened up under late capitalism are therefore not at all free-flowing playful arenas for anyone and everyone to define reality exactly as they like, but rather deadly serious sites of combat. These are the kind of practical and ideological struggles that have always been part of Marxist politics, and that Marxists still need to be engaged in. And we have to remember also that the definition of the 'postmodern condition' that was provided by Lyotard did not actually tie it to a progressive historical narrative, as if first we had the 'modern' capitalist society and then we had the 'postmodern' one. Rather, Lyotard argued that there was a 'postmodern' moment at the beginning of every cultural transformation, and therefore that 'modernist' literature and art was, in this sense, already 'postmodern'. It is not 'post-feminism' that is postmodern, then, but feminism itself; for while 'post-feminism' pretends that the struggle against patriarchy is over, postmodern feminism treats patriarchy as a constantly mutating practice of power that needs to be combated at every level, economic, political and cultural. Postmodernism is a moment of intense reflection and opportunity. It is that aspect of it that we need to seize and define as a moment of revolutionary transformation.

What postmodernism does is to turn superstition under capitalism against itself. It unravels the truth claims of ideology, showing that much supposedly scientific knowledge that props up existing power relations, and that tells us that we cannot and should not change the world, is actually profoundly irrational. Much supposedly social 'scientific' knowledge about human beings under capitalism, knowledge about subjectivity and spirituality, is just not true, but is a collection of fictions which are enforced as if there is no alternative. When postmodernism subverts this knowledge it opens up new spaces for the oppressed to speak truth to power, and – this is what is most disturbing about it to capital, patriarchy and the old left – for the oppressed to themselves define what counts as truth grounded in their political practice so they become the subjects rather than the objects of history.

Precarity

Precarity sums up the insecurity of much employment today and the demands that we should be flexible at work, and it is both a threat and opportunity. Conditions of labour have always been precarious under capitalism. Insecurity is built into our forms of life, which are structured around the false ideological claim that each separate individual can choose to sell their time in return for a wage and that this is a contract freely entered into. The trades union movement responded to that fragmentation and insecurity with an ethos of collective bargaining, an ethos which draws on the strength of workers to act together and thereby also lays the basis for a new form of society in which the free development of each is the condition for the free development of all. What is crucial about that opening to an authentically post-capitalist world is not only that the divisions between each individual will be transcended, but that so will the opposition between the 'each' and the 'all'. But before we get there, that insecurity is being intensified, and divisions deepened, with one of the names for this insecurity now being 'precarity'.

This precarity takes different forms as a discourse describing our labour and political struggle today. Three dimensions have been noticed by anti-capitalist feminist activists: there is 'precarity' as such as the condition of life in which there is structural inequality and uncertainty; there is the 'precariousness' we experience, this ramped up as employers build threat and punishment into the labour contract; and there is the 'precarisation' of the population as insecurity and uncertainty seep into the way that people manage their own lives and even come to think about who they are as human subjects.

There is also a fourth dimension, in the claim that a 'precariat' is emerging as a new class, yet to become conscious of itself; our precarious lives are now, it is claimed, taking shape in the form of this 'precariat'. But this precarity is not the new class beloved of social democrats who think that capitalist society can be wished away, and what we need to keep focused on is part of the fabric of neoliberal capitalism. It is there in the three interlinked dimensions of precarity, precariousness and precarisation, and that's what needs to be taken seriously, including in the way it leads to new forms of struggle, including now in and with the trades union movement.

This keyword 'precarity' emerged in the autonomous Marxist and feminist struggles in Italy in the 1970s, and has been influential recently in southern Europe, particularly in Spain, where it has become intimately connected with struggles over reproductive rights; here the motif of 'precarity' has also been used explicitly by the right, and feminists have had to intervene within this discourse to combat its effects. Beyond these specific contexts, we know that 'precarity' has become one of the defining characteristics of the lives of climate refugees, raising questions for social movements in a time of the increasingly mobile global 'multitude'. And 'precarity' has become a conceptual tool to analyse, for example, the way the shift from the old apartheid regime in South Africa to the neoliberal ANC government rested on a conception of 'labour' – of control and denigration of the labour force and then of national liberation based on its dignity and unity – which systematically concealed the insecurity that linked the 'precariousness of work' with the 'precariousness of subsistence'.

Against the old profoundly ideological opposition between 'labour', as if it is the domain of men, and 'precarious' life at the margins of 'real' work, as if that was the domain of women, the feminist uptake of 'precarity' – in the Spanish activist research group 'Precarias a la Deriva', for example – has been to work with life on the margins, with the precarious, and to use that as the basis from which to do politics differently. This has also been the take on 'precarious life' from within queer theory which has always from the start been concerned with how our identities are a function of performances that are never stable and secure; Judith Butler, for example, makes this the core of her analysis of how bodies are productive and performative, inventing new forms of freedom in public assembly spaces like Tahrir Square in Egypt during the 2011 rebellion.

Queer theory notices how taken-for-granted oppositions – the gender-binary between men and women, for example – are often the real problem we need to focus on. And this is partly why queer responses to the phenomenon of 'trigger warnings' are so useful. The discourse of trigger warnings – the claim that we should prepare and protect against unexpected exposure to upsetting images or ideas that might provoke a painful personal response, even to the point of activating 'post-traumatic stress disorder' – are one expression of what precarity means today. The discourse of 'trigger warnings' on campus is, significantly, flourishing in a context of privatisation and precarity in education in which both staff and students are victimised, and so it is not surprising that a first reflex response is to try and make the campus a 'safe space'. But this reflex response rests on what queer theorist Jack, once Judith Halberstam calls a 'discourse of offense and harm' which assumes that emotional pain comes from past traumatic events that have been 'barely buried hurt', and that leads to people becoming 'hypersensitive' subjects set up for 'public performances of grief and outrage'.

What should be noticed about this discourse Halberstam describes is that the argument for trigger warnings is necessarily and symptomatically paired with a reactionary response which wants each individual subject to be strong and stand on their own two feet as separate adults; one US libertarian website which runs with the tagline 'free minds and free markets', for example, sees in trigger warnings a threat to the endeavour to train students to be 'rational members of a democratic society'. This has been music to the ears of some British libertarians who are happy to uncritically link to this website and then relate their own horror stories, to then complain that trigger warnings are 'educational suicide' or that 'Victorian-style feminists' are using them to shoot down free speech.

The problem, notice, is the opposition of terms – trigger warnings or the spectre of censorship – which plays into exactly the kind of opposition that contemporary conditions of heightened precarity prompt; either you are a tough resilient type who will ride the wave and triumph, or you are the weak vulnerable type who will time and time again fail and be reminded of your weakness as a traumatic core of what you are. And that opposition itself repeats the opposition between strong men and weak women that is the ideological stuff of patriarchal society, the ideological stuff that queer politics unravels. So, when Jack Halberstam speaks against what the discourse of trigger warnings perpetuate as a particular form of subjectivity in relation to real or imagined threat he is able to traverse the boundary and opposition between what it was to have been a weak girl and what he now performs himself to be as queer. He notices it, perhaps, as something she lived, inside the contradictions of contemporary life under capitalism that we all, to some extent, experience and which keeps most of us in our place.

Precarity as structural insecurity now affects us all, and these new conditions of work call for a collective response by revolutionaries. It is a threat, a condition for our political practice and also an opportunity. The danger is that it becomes a description that is taken up and adopted as if it were something that is for individuals separated from others to choose and embrace, and then we really do fall into a trap. The trap is of being forced to choose. To choose, on the one hand, a resilient stereotypically masculine kind of strong independent agency scornful of the harm wrought by capitalism and disparaging of those who speak about the effects of that harm. Or to choose, on the other hand, a vulnerable stereotypically feminine victim position, of the one who searches for reminders of their weakness and warnings about the things that might 'trigger' their pain. Each option in this forced-choice trap is a dead end that turns precarity into an endless neoliberal spiral dividing those who want to thrive in these new conditions from those who can barely survive them and wish they would end.

It is those conditions of precarity – not being 'precarious' as an identity or trying to make the 'precariat' into a new class – that we must together tackle and transform. That means still using the trades unions as a base for collective politics rather than seeing them simply as the old enemy and mirror image of static labour capitalism, bringing them into joint action with the new social movements and building new forms of autonomy. It will involve interventions into the trades unions to transform them so they can engage with precarious labour outside the traditional workplace – something we have already seen in some of the 'community branch' initiatives – in the very process of doing away with precarity and capitalism itself.

Prefigurative

We are prefigurative when we anticipate the world we want tomorrow in how we do our politics today. The 2015 election and rapid recuperation of Jeremy Corbyn as leader of the British Labour Party – a double-process in which victory and failure were dialectically intertwined from the start – also changes the coordinates of left politics. It represents a break from Labour's past, not only from the fairly recent neoliberal turn under Tony Blair that opened the way to the present Conservative austerity agenda, but also from the longer history of the Labour Party in power. And, crucially, it represents a connection between traditional working-class political resistance and the socialist-feminist project which was articulated in the late 1970s and early 1980s around the term 'prefigurative politics'. To be 'prefigurative' in our political work is to anticipate the authentically democratic and inclusive forms of society that we want to build as an alternative to capitalism and patriarchy (and alternative to the racist legacy of colonialism, and to the pathologising of those who are not seen as 'normal' enough to fit in as good workers).

The British Labour Party has always, even when it has come under pressure to bring about significant reforms and has in the past, particularly after the Second World War, engineered a progressive shift towards public ownership, even at those moments has prioritised top-down managerial intervention over direct democratic accountability. This is one of the lessons of the 2013 Ken Loach documentary film *The Spirit of '45* which inspired the formation of Left Unity. The film was an account of the founding of the National Health Service and nationalisation of key industries to boost economic growth, and then the attempted destruction of that spirit barely 50 years later. From the rotten Labour boroughs to the grip of the bureaucracy on the party machine to reports of document-shredding at central office to conceal the Party operation to stop Corbyn, we see not only the legacy of social-democratic politics but also a form of political organisation that holds things in place, one that has contempt for the self-organisation of the oppressed. Inside that machinery there have been honourable traditions of resistance, including of the development of mechanisms of accountability at the time of the Greater London Council (GLC) in the 1980s, for example, traditions in which there was a strong socialist-feminist current which was linked to the first appearance of the book *Beyond the Fragments* co-authored by Sheila Rowbotham, Lynne Segal and Hilary Wainwright as a book and series of meetings and interventions around the country.

But inside that machinery there were also old far-left groups like Militant that once upon a time, back in 1964, began a process of 'entrism' and got lost inside the Labour Party, unable to disentangle themselves from it until they were forced out. They started to take on the characteristics of the very Party machinery they went in to change, adapting to a little-Englander politics in line with the history of the bigger stronger social-democratic tradition, hostile to new social movements such as feminism and gay rights, and bit-by-bit turning into the kinds of apparatus that repeated power relations under capitalism rather than challenging them. We can see how important 'prefiguration' in politics is from that history of the left; from the way those groups were, as it were, prefiguration in reverse, a warning to all of us.

The point about being 'prefigurative' is that we don't wait until after the revolution to put feminism and anti-racism on the agenda, but we build those aspects of the struggle into our activity now, finding ways to work at the intersection of class, 'race' and sex (to name just three dimensions of oppression that enable and intensify the exploitation of workers under capitalism). We build, from within a disintegrating political-economic world-system, the kinds of social relations that define us as socialists, feminists and anti-racists. We develop those social relations now in our present-day forms of struggle and organisations because we have learnt that if we do not do that we will simply reproduce existing forms of power; we will just end up with a regime that is a corrupt bureaucratic mirror image of the one that we were against.

The consternation and feeding frenzy among the little left groups outside the Labour Party in the wake of Corbyn's success was a warning of what is to come, and points to a choice between different conceptions of revolutionary politics. Difference, it should be clear, should not be treated as a problem, and the choice-point between different conceptions of politics will involve sharp debates. We should bear in mind that an attention to 'intersectionality', for example, does not at all mean that differences are blurred, but precisely that we clarify and work through the oppositions between what oppresses and what empowers. An attention to the 'prefigurative' dimension of politics should include not only the new forms that we wish to build upon – democracy, recognition and solidarity – but also the way that the old forms reproduce themselves, reproduce themselves not only in the forms of their organisation but then inevitably in the content of their own political agendas.

When Militant were forced out of the Labour Party in 1997 they took on a new life as the 'Socialist Party' (SP), but it is life that simply repeats the past rather than learns from it. It repeats it in the direct-line sent from London (to the provinces and to the member organisations of its own 'international' around the world) and in meetings of the Central Committee in which members of that decision-making body are full-time paid workers dependant on the apparatus for their livelihood; it repeats it in the obedience that they demand from their members under cover of a form of 'democratic centralism' far removed from that of the Bolshevik Party before the rise of Stalin; it repeats it in the 'negotiations', stitch-ups it aims to forge between itself and other organisations; it repeats it in the front organisations like Trade Unionist and Socialist Coalition which it controls (with the Socialist Workers Party as a willing ally while it suited that group's interests), and then includes 'independents' who have no decision-making powers (which was the fate of those hitched to it in the 'Independent Socialist Network'); and it repeats it, as a horrible necessary logic of this kind of politics, in the accusations that it covers up domestic violence, protects them for the greater good of the movement against the 'diversion' from the class struggle that feminism represents to it (including, we should note, attempts to pathologise the women victims with the claim that they were 'mentally ill'). The reappearance of the signifier 'Militant' on the SP leaflets given out at the Corbyn election rallies is, on the one hand, yes, a reminder of what they call their 'proud history' of local council rebellion. And, yes, there are great militants inside the SP (as there still are in the SWP) as well as in their groups around the world, who take feminism and anti-racism seriously. But the organisation's leadership structure is also a reminder of how this tradition of politics, warped by its years inside the machine, now threatens to come back into Labour as an obstacle to the new kind of politics that Corbyn promises.

The prefigurative political struggle we face now – whether it is inside or outside the Party – is one which has to pit itself against the old apparatus of the Labour Party (that is what Corbyn himself is up against as he puts together yet another shadow cabinet which includes many career politicians who hate the idea of revolutionary change), and which has to connect Corbyn's own history with the parallel alternative history of the GLC (of which the shadow Chancellor of the Exchequer, John McDonnell, was deputy leader) and of *Beyond the Fragments*. Corbyn himself is not someone who has an explicit history of involvement with socialist-feminist politics – and some rather disgusting attempts in the liberal press have been made by his enemies to turn feminism into a tool against him – but his campaign and the trajectory of his personal struggle is compatible with, sympathetic to feminism. It is on that basis, just one out of all the many different contradictory forms of struggle that will now take place, that the call for a 'Communities for Corbyn Network' and then 'Momentum' to defend and extend his election as a real movement forward should be supported. This network could bring together Labour Party members who are with Corbyn, those activists who have joined the Party energised by what has happened, and those outside the Labour Party, including those still active in Left Unity inspired by *The Spirit of '45* and what was made possible by it. These are the grounds today for building an open inclusive prefigurative political movement that puts into practice now what it wants for another world.

Psychoanalysis

Psychoanalysis is one powerful theory and practice of the unconscious. Some revolutionaries fervently wish that there were some deep connection between Marx and Freud, and the publication of a letter from Marx to Freud could be the Rosetta Stone to decode the relationship between political economy and psychic economies, finally perhaps settling the question of the real political allegiances of psychoanalysis.

The letter exists, republished in a Mexican psychoanalytic journal in 2008, and there has been much discussion among leftist psychoanalysts in Latin America about it. There are versions in French, Italian and German, where a detailed analysis of the history of the text in archives in Amsterdam and Frankfurt weighs up what its significance might be. The letter is undated, but appears to have been sent by Marx in 1882 via Freud's then close friend and mentor Wilhelm Fliess. The letter refers to then unpublished writings on hysteria that Freud had prepared with Joseph Breuer; it tries to engage Freud in a correspondence about critical and materialist science, Marx offering to send over a copy of *Capital* for Freud to read.

Another letter from Marx to Engels has a smudged postmark which cues us into the 1882 date, and claims that Freud had sent him some papers on 'metapsychology', the surprisingly early workings on what would become psychoanalytic theory. Here Marx describes to Engels two key questions Freud is exploring: the existence of mental activities that are not conscious, which would indicate that the different social classes are not fully aware of what they make of the consequences of their actions; and the existence of a 'sexual economy' which appears as the result of investigations into the sexual lives of the bourgeoisie (which would fit neatly with their analysis of bourgeois marriage as a disguised form of prostitution, though Marx does not spell this out here).

If the dates are right then this would mean that this was old Marx, he died the following year, and was sent to a Freud in his mid-twenties, who Marx refers to in the letter twice as 'young doctor', that is well before Freud actually invented psychoanalysis. Much of the debate about the letters in the accompanying article, originally published in German in 1979, is about their journey and place in different archives, and this draws attention to a similarity between the histories of Marxism and psychoanalysis, which is that there are repeated returns to the founding texts, to interpretations and readings of those texts for clues about how things might develop. In both cases there is a contradiction between the privilege given to that writing and the practice, which in psychoanalysis would be through oral transmission of technique and in Marxism would be through class struggle.

The word 'correspondence' is a bit misleading, for there is no evidence of a reply from Freud to Marx, and the word could be a bit of a giveaway of what the later Marxist readers might be hoping for, that there is some kind of correspondence between the two theories. (The web-link to the journal *Subjetividad y Cultura* is actually 'correspondencia-marx-feud'.) Another similarity between Marxism and psychoanalysis is the degree of censorship and rewriting of history that marks each practice, and makes it more understandable that there should be such energy put into deciphering who wrote to whom.

In Marxism, of course, we know that the rise of Stalin and the bureaucracy in the Soviet Union meant that the production of the Marx-Engels complete works – the 'MEGA' – was not in safe hands. So, when David Riazanov in charge of the Moscow archives said he was doubtful about the authenticity of the letters and was purged shortly afterwards (an event Trotsky commented on in 1931), this could be taken as further evidence that there was something to hide. Trotsky was favourable to psychoanalysis, sending his own daughter Zina to an analyst in Berlin, and Stalin saw it as a decadent bourgeois fake-science opposed to dialectical materialism. In this light it makes perfect sense that a future president of the International Psychoanalytical Association, Joseph Sandler, could once have been a revolutionary Marxist and member of the Fourth International.

In psychoanalysis there is much controversy over the way its own history is written, including squabbles over occlusions and ambiguities in the first major biography of Freud by Ernest Jones, who was always anxious about links between psychoanalysis and the left, and who opted for keeping the psychoanalytic associations in Germany under the Nazis going even when they expelled the Jewish analysts. One embarrassing episode Jones glossed over in his biography was the death of Victor Tausk who committed suicide in 1919 the day after ending his analysis with Helene Deutsch following Freud's own suggestion to Deutsch that she end it. So the suggestion that the Marx-Freud letter found its way to the archives via the Tausk family could be further evidence that something was being hidden which should now be brought to light.

There is doubt that the letter is genuine – it is not – but is that really the point? Clustered around the letter are the activities of adherents of two theoretical frameworks turned into kingdoms carefully guarded by their followers as if we should know what lies at the authentic origin of each one. This 'invention of tradition' is crafted much in the same way as the invention of the tradition of separate nations is patched together, usually from external sources, and certainly well after the founding events they pretend to describe. Here we come to an odd connection between theoretical domains and nations.

We now live in a world that is divided into little fiefdoms called nation states, and so it makes all the more sense that we should think of our own individual selves as if they were sovereign territories. Freud explored the image of the self as being like a fortress which guards itself against outsiders and which makes sure to suppress any internal division that might cue the enemy into a weakness, and the 'invention of tradition' in Marxist work is designed to show how the colonial centres and their offspring are fabricated and then turn vicious if there is a questioning of how authentic they are.

What psychoanalysis and Marxism both show is that these supposedly unified and separate entities, the self and the nation, are fictional, and that often they serve to obscure conflict; the stories we tell ourselves about our origins often cause emotional pain less as our little fortress of the self is shored up against internal threat, particularly against desires of others and for others; and these stories are bound up with practices of exclusion and policing of boundaries. The fantasy of a United Kingdom or fortress Europe also, for example, then operates as more of a prison state than a paradise.

Some Marxists forget this invention of tradition when they appeal to a fictional unity of the British working class as an argument for keeping Scotland in their disunited kingdom, and they risk falling into the trap of little England mentality when they are too quick to say no to Europe. Psychoanalysis reminds us that there is no such thing as 'unity', that a wholesome harmonious society of any kind is just as much a fantasy as a wholesome harmonious self. Psychoanalysis reminds us that unconscious desire pulls in different directions, tears us apart as individuals or groups, even at the same moment that it glues us together in our collective struggle to make different forms of civilization. It reminds us of the importance of memory, both of what did and what did not actually happen in the past.

Psychoanalysis is quite Marxist, something the supposed 'correspondence' between Marx and Freud actually diverts attention from. Freud, in a 1918 speech in Budapest, called for public free provision of psychoanalysis for workers, and he actively supported the development of a welfare service and education in Budapest, Berlin and Vienna through the Sex-Pol clinics of Wilhelm Reich (who was expelled from the Stalinized Communist Third International for being a psychoanalyst and from the International Psychoanalytical Association for being a revolutionary Marxist working with, among others, activists of the Fourth International). The imposition of fixed fees and the intense bureaucratic regulation of psychoanalytic treatment were actually instituted by the Nazis when they took power in Germany and Austria, and it is that model of privatised treatment that we live with today.

The debates over the implementation of Freud's Budapest speech were international, and internationalist, calling on local state resources to be put into psychoanalytic education and treatment while dissolving national state boundaries. The rise of fascism imposed private and nationalist agendas on psychoanalytic institutions, and it broke the link between psychoanalysts, who were mainly on the left, and Marxists. The connection between psychoanalysis and Marxism will be forged again through our commitment to the disunity of each, diversity of debate and practice, and a critical perspective on the operations of the state or the orthodoxy of tradition. Contradiction is something psychoanalysts listen for in their psychotherapeutic work, and contradiction rather than unity is what enables an articulation of the unconscious life of individuals and politics today.

Psychologisation

Psychologisation turns social analysis into something only personal. The new televisual genre of 'poverty porn' not only represents what is going on in the world, but, like all pornography, it feeds into the phenomenon it describes, which today has the added ingredient of 'psychologisation'. A new BBC programme to be made by Twenty Twenty Productions called *Britain's Hardest Grafter* was scheduled in 2015 before the Conservatives were endorsed by only 24% of the electorate in the general election on a promise, pretty well matched by the other main parties, to intensify its austerity agenda. After the election, as it sank in that the Conservatives were really going to enjoy this intensification of austerity as part of a class war that they were winning, there was opposition to the BBC programme, opposition voices which pointed out that the 15,000 pound winnings would be taxed as earnings, on top of dragging the reputations of those desperate enough to compete in the programme through the dirt. Under conditions of psychologisation the assumption made by the reality television companies is that this 'dirt is good' (as the Persil soap-powder advertisement had it around the same time), it will be good for you.

The programme is in line with the austerity agenda, which is to make the poor pay for the crisis, and that will not only increase poverty but also alienation. One of the differences between classical economic liberalism of the nineteenth century, the emerging capitalism that Marx was writing about, and 'neoliberalism' today is that there is a deepening influence of psychology in all areas of our lives.

Psychology as a separate academic discipline and profession came into being as capitalism was taking root as the dominant political economic system in Europe, and it flourished as helpmeet of capitalism in the factories to observe and regulate the behaviour of workers. The early mechanistic forms of psychology were ideally suited to assembly-line production processes in which each task was broken down into separate components so that each worker's repetitive activity could be monitored. Their own knowledge of the task would also be stripped down into the barest manageable elements so that it could be relayed back to the worker in more efficient form, efficient for management and good for profit. The skill of the psychologist in noticing how people behaved and thought complemented the deskilling of the worker as they were separated from what they once knew.

Psychology separated intellectual from manual labour as it developed its own expertise in the way the mind works, and it accomplished this separation so easily precisely because it is this kind of separation that is at the heart of work under capitalism. And today there is a further separation at work, inside the intellectual labour that psychology made its own domain of study; this is a separation between cognition – rational thinking and the errors of thinking that psychologists then think they can correct – and emotion which becomes a new source of human creativity to be garnered as emotional labour. Women's work then becomes valued in the service sector as sites of labour become 'feminised', and there is a corresponding shift from the old style of psychology which was all about men (and usually only about men's work) to new forms of psychological research and expertise in which women become the ideal-typical human subject to be studied and exploited.

So now this isn't only about psychological expertise for those trained to measure other people's behaviour or to correct their faulty thinking; it is also about the way that people are required to behave and think and feel in line with popular and globalised psychological discourse. This sets them up for appropriate treatments to make them happy with their lot. That was the aim of the shameless 2006 Layard Report commissioned by the previous Labour government; Layard argued that a quick blast of cognitive-behavioural therapy would get people off incapacity benefit for six months and so save the government money. But more than that, this use of psychology as a tool frames the poor so that if they dare to resist conditions of alienation they will be pathologised, as 'mindless' or 'thoughtless' or not sufficiently 'psychologically minded', before they even get near a psychotherapy clinic. Psychologists are then impelled to go deeper than cognitions and behaviour, into the way that people feel and are made to feel about how they work and who they are.

Poverty under capitalism is intimately linked with inequality, and there have been attempts to gauge what Wilkinson and Pickett termed, in the title of their 2010 book, *The Spirit Level*. This inequality has been a source not only of attempts to update Marx's *Capital*, attempts which aim to repair capitalism instead of putting an end to it, but also to map a new spirit of capital under neoliberalism. This new spirit of capital revolves around the 'psychological' effects and even, for some enthusiasts, the idea that there are psychological causes of the economic crisis, a new spirit we should notice as increasingly widespread psychologisation. This psychologisation refers not only to a crisis of market confidence, as if market confidence were the cause of our recent woes but also to the way that victims of the crisis are expected to respond in order to count as good citizens. This sure does put a new twist on each of the aspects of alienation under capitalism described by Marx.

First, and this is the underlying premise of *Britain's Hardest Grafter*, there is alienation of each human subject from the others as people are set against each other as competitors. This first aspect of alienation is fundamental, of course, to any psychological approach that aims to discover how human beings tick by extracting them from the social relationships that made them who they are and treating each of them as enclosed self-contained 'individuals'. As always, what is 'discovered' appears as if by magic, or as if it were natural, from the conditions that are set in place by the discoverers themselves, and that's how it works in the psychologist's little laboratory experiments. Either that or by the psychologist's masters, which is how it works in industry. Nowadays, with the psychologisation of experience, the individual separated from others and competing with them for work is also told to take 'responsibility' for the conditions in which they find themselves. They will be assumed to do that when they sign their contract to take part in the television programme, for example.

Second, and the creative designers for Twenty Twenty Productions will be part of this problem, there is alienation of human creativity; what is produced is separated from the individual to be turned into a commodity. The participants in *Britain's Hardest Grafter* will be required to show how they feel about the search for work, but how they feel will be taken and represented in the narrative of the television programme so that it is no longer their own; they will have no connection with or control over what they are trying to express as they try to make sense of the spectacle that sells them as the product. The twist that psychologisation introduces into the process is that the struggle must now be seen to be an emotional struggle – personal demons, interpersonal conflicts, agony at success or failure are the stuff of reality television. The creative designers will rely on this emotional performance to make good television, and they will just as surely deskill those who provide them with raw material for lucrative entertainment.

Third, and this is where there is betrayal of our nature as human beings, there is alienation of ourselves from our bodies, from our own human nature. This always already is crucial to competition in the workplace, for each worker is at war not only against potential rivals for work but also against his or her own body as a body that might one day fail to take them to work and perform the labour necessary to get the wage. The psychologisation of everyday life hides this aspect and takes it as given that bodies will be cared for, this while the National Health Service is being torn apart and privatised. *Britain's Hardest Grafter* will only include those fit for work, not those on employment or support allowance. In this case it will be Twenty Twenty Productions that effectively function as the assessors, the media placeholders for the private companies that carry out Work Capability Assessments, filtering out those who can work so they can compete in the programme.

As ecosocialist arguments drawing on Marx have pointed out, there is also alienation of human beings from nature as such; this is why capitalism itself, not only commodity culture which sells artificial social relationships formed under the gaze of the media companies, has become, as Joel Kovel in his 2007 book of that title put it *'The Enemy of Nature'*. The question will be whether alienation will function as a warning that if we don't break from these political economic conditions, from capitalism, then we will be finished, and finish each other off in competition for diminishing resources as more of the world becomes enclosed by Capital; a Battle Royale writ large as entertainment and diversion while being an essential condition of neoliberalism.

One comedian commented after the election that the next five years after the 2015 election would be like the Hunger Games, but without the games. That's not quite right, because there are serious mind games ahead, in which the increasing psychologisation of politics will map out some of the most dangerous moves. How we respond to that psychologisation while responding politically to the distress caused by austerity will be crucial to the battles ahead.

Queer

Queer opens up gender and sexuality to challenge and change. The debate in one of the British left groups over commissioning and hosting of (what some saw as) a transphobic article and then the removal of that article by (what some saw as) an anti-feminist protest muddled together a number of quite different questions, questions that queer politics can clarify. The worst of the muddle was in the tangle of accusations about what the different actors in this drama really were, and so (it seemed) what they really must have meant. The problem is that you cannot explain away what people mean by what they are, as if, for example, because they are a woman they must say this, if they are a radical feminist they must say that, or if they are 'trans' you know what they think. Against that kind of poisonous dead-end attribution of identity (I know what you are so I know what you think), queer theory is concerned with what people actually say and do. (This was the case, for example, for revolutionary Marxists who did not ever pretend to know what Engels 'thought' as a function of his class position but instead looked at what he did in practice, those who looked to the proletariat to overthrow capitalism and in that very process abolish itself as a class.)

Queer, in the work of Judith Butler for example, shifts attention from fixed identity, especially gender identity assumed to flow directly from biological sex, to the process by which boys and girls reiterate sexed categories to be accorded the status of men or women; that is the 'performative' dimension of queer. Queer also, in the work of Judith (now Jack) Halberstam for example, disturbs stereotypically feminine motifs of 'failure' as if that signals weakness, and 'trigger warnings' that are pitched at those assumed to be emotionally fragile. The first move, by Butler, already broke from simple humanism, from the old Western Enlightenment idea that people consciously choose what they perform, and the second move, by Halberstam, took queer in a 'post-humanist' direction to connect with questions of body modification and 'trans' (those who transition from one sex to another or who live somewhere in the transition). Together, and these are only two queer theorists who have had an impact on 'third-wave' feminist politics, they have inspired and supported a new generation of LGBTQ+ activists. But queer interventions are themselves a process to be reiterated, never resting in an identity of someone who will finally declare or accept the attribution of another speaker even that they are really 'queer'.

These interventions are never-ending deconstructions of identity, continually unravelling the certainty that speakers (and their enemies) have that they are a certain kind of entity. This is precisely because identity-based 'essentialist' ideology under capitalism (you are a worker, bourgeois, man, woman, as you are, never to change who you are) is always trying to fix things in place. And this fixing in place (which also, by the way, works on the assumption of fixed identity that dialectical materialism always pitted itself against) operates not only in the field of bourgeois politics but also in the left, in feminism, in anti-racist and sexual politics. It operates, for example, when the term 'female woman' is used to block questioning of the way women are defined by way of their biology (which has historically been the way that patriarchy limited women by explaining to them what they really were and always must be), it operates when radical feminists who have an analysis of the category of women as a 'class' are accused of being 'TERFS' (Trans-Exclusionary Radical Feminists), and it even operates when queer as process slides into 'genderqueer' as a new kind of identity.

The key elements of that little outbreak of 'excitable speech' in cyberspace, which was very much in keeping with Butler's diagnosis of the performance of hate speech – an outbreak on the British group's website, internal and public email lists, online petitions and Facebook – began with the fateful decision to open

a 'debate' over trans. It then went from bad to worse: commissioning of an article on each side of the debate; publication of one
against trans (by a feminist who was not a member of the group)
before the one arguing for trans was ready; nasty personalised
comments on the site and then on Facebook (and on email lists)
pro and anti; posting of a reply for trans on the group's website
which was supposed to balance the first one against; a petition
against the group 'hosting of transphobes'; posting (following
internal leadership discussion) of an apology and trigger
warning about the article; removal by the author of the original
article in protest at this framing of her contribution; posting of a
disclaimer by the comrade who commissioned the article and
stood by it as a positive contribution and who complained of the
way the 'echo-chamber' of Facebook exaggerated opposition to
the article; removal in protest from the site of articles by other
feminist activists who claimed that the group had folded under
pressure from the trans lobby assisted by cis-men (with 'cis' in
this context bizarrely meaning that they really were men and so
intrinsically hostile to feminism).

It is easier in retrospect to plot the elements of this story as
deliberate mistakes, to turn it into a narrative of reactionaries
(whether naïve socialists trying to educate themselves, bad
radical feminists taking the opportunity to complain at
displacement of attention from the sex class system by third-
wave LGBTQ+ activists, or men who transition and then
undermine the women's movement by demanding to be included
in women-only caucuses) and progressives (well, actually the
narrative in this sorry story was mainly centred on reactionaries
and spiteful accusations levelled against each and every one).

What is for sure is that some really bad ideas about politics
were re-enacted in this process. One was setting up feminism and
trans as a debate, as if it were a binary opposition, as a dispute in
which a correct understanding would be arrived at. A first
principle of queer is that binaries like this won't do anyone any

favours, and that's why binaries are the target of political decon-struction (and, if you like, of a historical materialist analysis of how this reality has been constructed and enforced). Another bad idea was to treat the two 'sides' of the debate as distinct positions, as coherent lines that would be threaded together in one political understanding. A second principle of queer is that these different political traditions have different agendas and targets that are not ever going to be welded into one unitary whole (and the world we want to replace capitalism with is surely not going to be one governed by a single agreed idea of what is good for everyone but by diverse perspectives on life and love). Second-wave feminisms, including radical feminism, provide a critique of capitalism that we need to learn from, as do third-wave feminisms, and we will learn from them too, will take them seriously as guides to action. A third principle of queer is that identities can be a guide to action, but as what Gayatri Chakravorty Spivak, in an allied move, called 'strategic essen-tialism'; here a claim is made against oppression of an identity but not for the identity as such to fix us in place, so we are not drawn into the divide and rule practices of the dominant and colonising ideology. It is that dominant and colonising ideology that the group unwittingly reiterated, and from which it had to disentangle itself.

Realism

Realism tells us that there is no alternative and it confirms things as they are. This was the case with the stories the left told itself after the 'Brexit' referendum in 2016. One powerful fantasy on the left in Britain during the EU referendum campaign was that a vote for Brexit would enable a fundamental break with taken-for-granted coordinates of British politics. The Lexiters calling for a left 'Leave' vote surfed the wave of xenophobia stoked up by one faction of the ruling class against the other, as the battle inside the Conservative Party over who would be the next leader to replace David Cameron was played out around the fiction that one side was for and the other side was against the European Union. The truth was that neither Cameron nor Boris Johnson, former Conservative Mayor of London, ever wanted to leave the EU, and the Brexit result handed Boris a poisoned chalice as Cameron tearfully retreated. Socialists who called for a vote for 'Remain' were portrayed by the Lexiters as being the conservative realists, as those who could not bear to change the world and were content instead to support the European status quo. 'Realism' in this difference over political strategy functioned in the background as a dirty word, a keyword that would mark out those who would dare to seize what the SWP called the 'chance of a lifetime' and those who were made out to accept that there really was no alternative.

The choice over how to vote was, for some on the left, conditioned by an analysis of the balance of forces, as it was in 1975 when some of the same left forces who called for a Remain vote in this referendum judged back then that 'No' to Europe could also be a vote for a 'United Socialist Europe'. The underlying premise was that that particular 'reality' and what it was to be 'realistic' was a function of changing historical conditions. That is, after all, what dialectics is concerned with, and why it is such an important element of Marxist politics. Dialectics is about contradiction and revolution, about how the world is always changing, and that is why historical and theoretical analysis is necessary to grasp that process, history and theory that becomes the basis of a political tradition, not a grid into which the world is pressed to make it seem to be as we would like it. Reality itself is not a fixed immutable thing, and it is simply not possible to dust off the same old programme, polish off the old slogans, and expect that they will always have the same consequences. Even the terms, the keywords we use to understand reality mutate over time.

'Realism' itself is different today, has a different valence from what it had in the 1930s, say, when it could be hooked to the word 'socialist' and come to define an artistic tradition in Soviet art which pretended to portray the new post-capitalist world and, at the same time, express the capacities and hopes of the working class and its allies in the struggle to build a new state. Realism today is more tightly hooked into the word 'capitalist', and so *Capitalist Realism* (to borrow from the title of Mark Fisher's 2009 book) comes to function as a component part of a critical analysis of the way that the dynamic possibilities of capitalist society have been stalled, how its progressive potential has been exhausted, and so how 'realism' becomes a cynical affirmation of the state of things, of the world as something that simply cannot be changed. The diagnosis of 'capitalist realism' also comes to mirror what 'socialist realism' was always actually really about. The Russian revolution saw a blossoming of fantastic projects which imagined the variety of ways in which another world could be possible after capitalism, projects that broke with reality, and then 'socialist realism' was promoted by the bureaucracy with the lesson that it would only be like this, like this one world that had been instituted under Stalinism. Similarly, the ideological promise of perpetual innovation that was underpinned by 'pragmatism' in the United States during most of the twentieth century was eclipsed by the hard reality that this capitalist world is now the only game in town; capitalist realism is a name for the message that nothing can be changed, and there is nothing beyond pragmatic realpolitik.

Capitalism realism thus comes to function much as socialist realism did, closing down the idea that things could be different, and now with a twist, a trap into which those who fell in love with Lexit fell headfirst. The trap is to imagine that a dramatic break of any kind, even one following a racist campaign for leaving the EU, would really be their big chance. It was a chance, they thought, to outflank Nigel Farage's United Kingdom Independence Party from the left. The fantasy 'after Farage, our turn' was not only a fantasy that repeats the lessons of ultra-left third-period Stalinism, the disastrous parody of dialectical materialism in which Moscow dictated to the German Communist Party in the 1930s that a victory for Hitler would be just a brief prelude and signal that the time of the left was about to arrive soon after (expressed at that time in the Communist Party slogan 'After Hitler, our turn'). It was also a fantasy rooted not so much in hope as in despair. This is how 'capitalist realism' works, not simply by telling you that things cannot be changed, but also luring you into desperate attempts to kick against it, but to kick against it in such a way that you end up kicking your comrades and then kicking your own head in.

And it is more dangerous than that, for in an ironic twist of fate that fans of the dialectic who savour the sudden transformation of something into its opposite would easily recognise, things now seem even more like they were than they were before (and this is what 'accelerationism' describes). Instead of being so very different, things are actually very much the same, but worse. What was fantasised as being a 'Lexit' turns out to be cause for celebration across Europe among fascists, what was assumed to be an assertion of democracy turns out to be the very kind of individual sovereignty beloved of the new libertarian right, and what was promised to be a collective movement of autonomous and independent choice by the British working class turns out to be a delusional attempt to rip away reality and bring us face to face with dark hidden forces under the surface. It is not as if the Lexiters had not, even before the vote, already paved the way to this denouement of their stupid strategy, a strategy that was conditioned by capitalist realism and an unthinking revolt against it. And even in that revolt there were signs of compromise, of collusion, of what seemed at one moment to be of the 'Left' mutating into the agenda of the Right, of ludicrous reactionary attempts, for example, to reconfigure immigration as being about the free movement of labour as capitalist ploy, and therefore something that socialists should also be against.

While the Conservative Party panicked and backtracked, tried to find a mechanism by which it would be able to avoid the Brexit it never wanted, while it watched the markets that dictate its own politics go into freefall, while it tried to rein in the forces it unleashed and bring things back to the way they were before – to restore the 'capitalist realism' that was its guiding ideological mantra – the Lexiters were faced with a world that is precisely the opposite of what they dreamed of. After having beaten back the fascists of the British National Party and English Defence League, and after having then turned their attentions to Farage's UKIP in a bizarre attempt to impose 'no platform' on those little Englanders, they already had to appeal before the results of the vote for the Remain left not, please, to call them, the Lexiters, racist. And after the vote had been announced, they now claim to stand up to racism after having intensified it to a higher level than ever. The Lexiters themselves were not racist, it is true, but they were, during the referendum, a real pain in the arse and a liability to the anti-capitalist left. Some of the Lexit groups had already played their own little pathetic role in fuelling sexual violence in the last few years, and now they must take responsibility for a rise in racist violence. Capitalist realism has bitten them on the bum, and in their very attempts to find a short-cut out they have landed us deeper into what capitalist realism is, into the brute reality of a system that divides and rules us and persuades us that there is nothing we can do about it.

Recuperation

Recuperation neutralises and absorbs us so we become part of 'the spectacle'. Jeremy Corbyn was very clear during his campaign to be elected leader of the Labour Party in Britain; that this should not be about individual personalities, not draw us in to be mesmerised by another leader, but we should, instead, be building a movement together that would challenge the austerity agenda. It is on that basis that most supporters attended the near-on hundred large rallies around the country, and flocked into the Labour Party. In the week following his first election as leader in 2015, nearly 60,000 more people were inspired to join, and those numbers doubled and then tripled in the year after. Not to mention the little revolutionary groups who are going in to turn local constituency party meetings into mini-sect-fests. Have they all been 'recuperated', or are they just being softened up to be absorbed and neutralised in due course?

Recuperation into the political celebrity 'spectacle' of capitalist commodity culture and into the machinery of bourgeois fake-democracy could be the fate of any radical struggle. That was the danger that the Situationist International (SI) alerted activists to, and the paranoiac suspicion that what Guy Debord in 1967 called the *Society of the Spectacle* would take you in and package you up to confirm itself, even at the moment that you thought you were resisting it, was at the heart of the participation of the SI in the Paris May 1968 events. And it is still a question at the heart of revolutionary politics today as we are faced with a struggle that is ever-more mediated by forms of communication that transform the message into pulpy nonsensical bits of stuff on Facebook that we are bewitched by when we think we are simply choosing whether we 'like' it or not.

The question runs deep into the revolutionary project, separating those who have the romantic belief in something human under this alienated system that can organise itself, rise up and speak and take control (this hope appears in the May 68 slogan 'Beneath the paving stones, the beach') from those who suspect that if something becomes popular then it has already failed, even that what appears to be our salvation will turn out to be what locks us more tightly into our oppression (which appears in the Situationist response 'Beneath the beach, the paving stones', a slogan that was then spun into the reactionary sarcastic rhetoric of some of those who turned to 'postmodernism' as if that was a full-blown alternative to Marxism).

The danger signs were there early on in the first Corbyn leadership campaign in 2015, in the 2,000-strong Manchester rally, for example, where the chair (a local left-Labour newly-elected member of parliament) rather desperately introduced our hero as 'the man with the plan', a phrase she repeated at least twice before he got to the platform. The leader of Unite, the largest trades union which had nominated Corbyn, declared on the eve of the election that their candidate had actually been so successful so far in attracting new people and returnees into the Labour Party that he had already won. Or perhaps we should say, with the SI, that he had already lost, he had already got thousands of people caught up in the gears of the machine, and lost to the struggle.

One problem with rushing into the Labour Party to support Corbyn is that things are going to be very different from the heady atmosphere of the rallies. The revolutionaries are not going to be jostling alongside the reformists, debating and supporting the new shadow cabinet, keeping it on course, as if we will all be there inside some huge room with freedom to organise, be heard and make the leadership accountable. The Labour Party apparatus is a slow-burn machine, dragging through procedures and motions, testing the loyalty of its members, and slowly burning them out, until the moment when even the revolutionaries find themselves obediently sitting behind the stalls at the local constituency party jumble sale.

This is an aspect of the 'spectacle' that the SI were less attentive too, the battle of attrition through drudge-work to service the election candidates who disappear into the council or into parliament, only to appear at the next election-time to sadly tell us that things are much more difficult than they thought. This, at least, is something Corbyn himself has avoided over the years, as one of the more honourable exceptions to the rule, accountable to his local constituency Labour Party activists in Islington in north London, connected with political campaigns outside the party, holding true to extra-parliamentary activity that was always a necessary part of revolutionary struggle. And then, if the SI is right, this brave exceptional stance is all the more ripe for the recuperation – the neutralisation and absorption – of him and this movement into the spectacle.

That material reality of the organisation of space – something the new crop of enthusiastic Labour Party members will discover for themselves – was actually something that the SI did describe, in their activist exploration of the boundaries and obstacles to movement that are placed in the way of those who want to create different kinds of alliance. This activist exploration, engaging in what they called a 'dérive' through the city, a conscious drifting that usually followed the rule that we should move toward the north-west of the city they called 'psychogeography'. Psychogeographical exploration aims not merely to discover the world, but to map it in such a way as to open up new spaces for action, for movement, to anticipate, to collectively 'prefigure' we might say, a world in which there is freedom of movement, of populations, of the 'mob' seen as a creative mobile force rather than as movement pathologised by the state. The psychogeographers go to the edges, remain on the edge, remain mobile, wary of being sucked into organisations (and they are mindful, perhaps, also of the history of the SI itself in which the guiding force, Guy Debord, expelled his enemies from the organisation until he was pretty well left in a one-man band).

There are at least two lessons we need to learn about 'recuperation'. The first is that we need to build our own forces as mobile forces, able to move fast and flexibly around the edge of the main organisations. And today that means operating on the edge of the Labour Party, keeping open the escape routes for those who get disappointed and burnt-out after the first flush of Jeremy-fever dies down and the rumours begin of betrayal and failure (that after refusing to sing the National Anthem, good, Jeremy will join the Privy Council, bad; that after appointment of a cabinet that 'represents' the spread of the Party, OK, this will lead to a majority in favour of military action overseas, disastrous). The question is not whether Corbyn will be broken, but when, whether it will be by an internal Party coup or by a real threat of a military coup by those who decide he has gone too far. Jeremy Corbyn is committed to the Labour Party, he won't break from it, and so we have to be there for those who at some point will have to defend the gains that have been made by breaking themselves from this spectacle, from spectacular success flipping into spectacular disappointment.

The other lesson is that there is a paradox built into the analysis and politics of the critique of the spectacle itself. This is that pessimism and disappointment have been so hard-wired into British politics that the main response to Corbyn's success has been amazement, even among some old activists who fear that things that have transformed so rapidly might yet again turn in another more horrible direction. The possibility and suspicion of 'recuperation' – once upon a time a good analysis of the limits of revolutionary politics being absorbed and neutralised – has itself today been absorbed and neutralised into the spectacle of a disappointed cautious politics that suspects that when we find bits of the beach under the paving stones it won't be long before we crack our toes on the even deeper bedrock of hard reality, discover the impossibility of change.

Corbyn's election gave lie to the claim that the spectacle is all there is, and that our fate is to be recuperated into it. It is the rapid transformation, not only of the Labour Party but of an electorate prepared to vote for someone painted as a rabid enemy by the media, that shows us that the story that this is all going to end in tears is part of the problem. He was the opposite of recuperation for many years inside the Labour Party, and we can best continue to work against his recuperation now by mobilising for him, as far as he can go, outside as well as inside it.

Refusal

Refusal is one way of stepping outside work under capitalism to better resist it. Alongside the demand that we have the right to work, a demand which is underpinned for many of us by Marx's view of work as something intrinsically creative and humanising, there has always been a parallel demand, a little more playful perhaps, that we should also have the right to refuse to buckle under to work under capitalism. Work under capitalism, after all, is alienating, and is structured so as to distort our creativity and humanity. So it makes perfect sense to expose work discipline by insisting that we have 'the right to be lazy', a phrase used by Marx's son-in-law Paul Lafargue in a pamphlet written in prison in 1883. Lafargue was evidently not so lazy in prison, and the demand has buried in it a contradiction. Our 'laziness' or 'refusal' of work needs to be accompanied by revolutionary work to end exploitation at work, to end exploitation of all kinds. 'Refusal' thus carries with it resistance to work and the transformation of what work is.

The refusal of work is sometimes viewed with suspicion by those who are wedded to a simple trades union based notion of politics, and for autonomist Marxists this strategy of refusal also throws into question the way that the trades unions sometimes collude with capitalism and are committed to work discipline. The strategy of 'refusal' then also enables a connection between revolutionary politics inside the factory with many other kinds of resistance to exploitation outside, including with the struggles of feminists who have good reason to resist incorporation into 'work' as it is understood today. Refusal of work in this way mobilises many different kinds of struggles which can then be fed back into the realm of traditional wage labour to question the way that labour is structured, it opens a way to a different ethical sense of what it is to be a human being which rests on a multiplicity of collective struggles and a vision of what a world beyond capital accumulation might look like, one where artificial barriers between work and play are broken down, a future where we may even have better things to do than to work.

This might lead us to treat anything that turns into work or that uses the term 'work' with suspicion. This suspicion could be directed at the way sport is turned into work as part of the pernicious professionalization of collective activity which separates celebrity players from the rest who are reduced to the role of spectators. It could be directed at the way politics is configured as a kind of work today which separates the 'politicians' from those who vote them into office every few years. And it could with good reason be directed at 'sex', an activity which is already turned into a commodity under capitalism and which, as a result, turns creative and humanising activity into something competitive and alienating. And worse than that, once a feminist sensibility to power relations at the level of the personal is added to this critique, the idea that this sex should be turned into work transforms sensual contact with others into a place where women are turned into objects to be bought and sold by men. Then 'sex work' is not so much a contradiction in terms, but the expression of how deeply capitalism and patriarchy has colonised us all.

What kind of refusal of work is the refusal of sex work? These are the stakes in what have been termed 'the new prostitution wars', but the key question is what ethical position to take with the collective voices of women which does not pathologise those who engage in this practice. There is the argument that the term 'sex work' should not be used at all in these debates, that it is really 'prostitution', and should carry all of the negative connotations of that word, that it really should be pathologised. Some on the left begin with a clear account of the dimension of exploitation in prostitution, its function as big business, and its role in fuelling the trafficking of women's bodies, and that argument arrives at a call to support the 'Nordic model' for addressing this problem. The 'Nordic model' would, it is claimed, criminalise the men who purchased sex, and so close down the business altogether.

This call for criminalising prostitution also sets itself strongly against those women who speak out for the right to sell sex, with accusations that, at best, these women either suffer from some form of 'false consciousness' – they do not really know what they are saying and whose agendas they play into – or, at worst, that these are false voices, that self-organised women who work as prostitutes or 'sex workers' are puppets of the pimps; organisations like Amnesty International are on the side of the pimps, it is claimed, because that organisation argues for the decriminalisation of sex work, and are therefore agents of the most vicious form of patriarchal imperialism. This argument even spins into a complaint that 'first-world' Marxists who buy into consumerism are colluding with capitalism, and that collusion blinds them to the way that women in the developing world are being reduced to commodities; for these critics of sex work, it is women in the third world who really suffer most from prostitution.

In contrast to these claims, take the example of COSWAS, the 'Collective for Sex Workers and Supporters' in Taipei, Taiwan. This political initiative which began in 1998 campaigns against Article 80 of the Public Order Maintenance Act which was enacted, with less than 48-hours notice, to criminalise prostitution that had previously been 'licensed'. The 'licensing' itself, of course, operated under the auspices of the Taiwanese state, and divided sex workers from other women. What the COSWAS protests did through protests that included street demonstrations of sex workers was to turn moralising surveillance into an ethical question, turn individual choices into collective action, and turn pathologised behaviour and character into something that was part of the variety of ways of what it is to live a normal life. Very unusually, these public protests included trades union activists, some of whom then 'came out' as clients of the sex workers. The

People's Democratic Front, which has supported the sex workers, which includes sex workers in its ranks, has also then been able to bring together a range of different exploited and oppressed groups, including disability activists. These political mobilisations are in line with the call by the 'Global Network of Sex Projects' to decriminalise sex work, and to build a broader feminist and anti-capitalist politics from which Marxists must learn.

So, on the one side there is a 'refusal' of work that objects to 'sex work' on moral grounds, which may include the moral argument that the reduction of sex to work as such is evil; that work itself is exploitative, or that there should be a clear separation between real work and authentic loving relationships. This refusal targets individuals who are behind the scenes pulling the strings and ventriloquising the prostitutes, or it even targets the sex workers themselves as women who have made bad and reactionary moral choices. This refusal makes a clear separation between what it thinks is normal and pathological, a separation which also pathologises sex workers themselves. This would lead to a moralising, individualising and pathologising response to COSWAS that would effectively reinforce the power of the Taiwanese state, with dire consequences for sex workers and for political resistance generally.

And, on the other side there is another refusal of this work, one that takes an ethical stand which respects the different choices that women make, that points out that the 'Nordic model' fails in practice, that it actually invited more police and state discrimination against sex workers, and that maybe the 'New Zealand model' might be better. This is an ethical stand which also acknowledges that feminism is not one fixed approach, but that it operates contradictorily as a variety of feminisms, feminisms that include LGBT and Queer and more responses to sex work. Maybe this position would embrace the slogan 'Neither Norway nor New Zealand but Taiwan', Taiwan as part of anti-imperialist *Asia as Method* (the title of a 2010 book by Kuan-hsing Chen) that is also that of international struggle of the exploited, oppressed and allies. This 'method' would entail intersecting Taiwan, China, Japan and Korea in the context of colonialism and imperialism to understand how and why the 'licensing' and prohibition of sex work happened in those different contexts. This feminist refusal of exploitation looks to collective action by sex workers and their allies, and it also stands against the stigmatising of these women, working with them to find another way to eventually end the regime of work that structures all human life under capitalism today.

Spirituality

Spirituality repeats and can also transform organised religion to provide a revolutionary resource for liberation. This has certainly been the case in Mexico after the Ayotzinapa massacre in 2014. The so-called 'drug wars' in Mexico have decimated communities, closing down space for the left in the process, but have also opened up space for a resurgence of spirituality as a keyword and resource in the struggle against oppression, for solidarity, and for a better world, for liberation.

In September 2014, 43 students from the Ayotzinapa Rural Teachers' College in Iguala were 'disappeared', a disappearance that implicated not only the local drug cartels but also the regional state apparatus in Guerrero that works hand in glove with them. The timeline of this struggle – of the massacre, the 'investigations' and the protests – has revealed, even more so than the actual events, the depth of corruption and collusion of the state in the deaths. The students have, in addition, been treated by the Mexican media as being responsible, as if they themselves were asking for what happened to them for daring to study at a poor rural institution with a history of links with radical social movements. These events not only pose questions about our solidarity with the Ayotzinapa students but also of the way we embrace those who embrace religion as part of our common struggle for another world; pressing questions for revolutionary Marxists who are often atheists rightly suspicious of old feudal and quasi-fascist religion and also new-age retreats from politics.

We fight for a democratic secular world, but must be clear that 'secularism' as an obsessional hostility to religion can also be dangerous (and sometimes, in France, intensified as reaction to the *Charlie Hebdo* attacks, for example, slides into racism). The 'secularist' left that makes hostility to religion a badge of honour and sign of its loyalty to historical materialism not only often misunderstands how religion functions but also forgets the history of Marxism in times of revolutionary struggle. One glance at what are often treated by the secularists as the sacred texts of Marx where he comments that religion is 'the opium of the people' should be enough to dispel the illusion that spirituality as such is our enemy. Far from it, Marx is using the metaphor of opium precisely to draw attention to the consolation it brings to those living in alienated life conditions under capitalism. For Marx, religious suffering is both an expression of 'real suffering', as he puts it, and a 'protest' against that suffering. When he argues that religion is the 'sigh of an oppressed creature' this is because it provides something that has been crushed by capitalism, and the struggle for socialism is surely also a struggle for what is missing in this heartless and soulless world, the struggle for something precious which we name and feel in our hearts, in our souls.

The problem in many poor countries of the world that are reduced to the miserable condition of providing the raw material for the happiness of the rich is that the machinery of exploitation is intensified, intensified because it is necessary to the economic survival of communities caught up in the drug trade and, because it is illegal, subject to state repression even at the moment that the corrupt elements of the state also feed off that trade. The para-state organisations really do function as 'cartels' and we can see how the law and the state under late capitalism are not the opposite of each other, but require and use each other to survive. These are not mere assorted groups of criminals but organised systems of production that operate as caricature forms of the economic 'cartels' that govern the 'legitimate' world of commerce. Marxist critiques of the place of crime in relation to capital, as the partner in crime of big capital, anticipated, and spelled out very clearly, some of psychoanalytic arguments after the French psychoanalyst Jacques Lacan about the law being inhabited by an obscene supplement which is necessary to its function.

The messy and contradictory 'war on drugs' carried out with ruthless inefficiency by the Mexican state is actually a war against its own people, and the drug cartels are as much used by the state as part of the apparatus of oppression as they are treated by the state as rival power-bases. The current crisis in Mexico then expresses the underlying contradictions of capital accumulation, but refracted through the dependence of Mexico on the world economy, including the dependence of the rich on the kind of herbal or chemical solace that they can buy to relieve their suffering, this in place of a political critique that would turn that suffering into protest. As the other side of the coin, the poor communities that suffer the depredations of the corrupt forces of 'law and order' often turn to the drug cartels to dispense justice. They turn to the drug cartels not only as a form of protection, even of protection against the forces of the state, but for alternative forms of religious expression of their suffering (and their protest against it). That is why so many of the cartels are held together by quasi-religious systems, of the worship of Santa Muerte (Saint Death), for example.

Then, against the background of accusations that the left has failed to respond to this situation – a failure that is, in part, a consequence of the repression meted out by the state and by the drug cartels – religious activists have stepped into the struggle. Many of the key figures in the protests against the disappearance of the Ayotzinapa 43 are radical priests, and so the events have seen a revival of the fortunes of 'liberation theology' in this part of the Americas. Liberation theology was a crucial resource for many radicals in Brazil, and in the Spanish-speaking countries in other parts of Latin America from the 1960s, putting into practice what was termed a 'preferential option for the poor'. The election of Pope Francis as a character more sympathetic to this theological tradition has also given inspiration to a new generation of radicals. The problem is not so much in Mexico that religion is the opium of the people but that opium is the opium, and religious suffering as protest then has to be forged in the struggle against the drug cartels and the state. Some communities, such as the one in Cherán in Morelia, have been taking forward that double struggle as an example to the left.

This is also an opportunity to reconnect radical political struggle with revolutionary Marxist history that has long been concerned with bringing about a world in which 'historical materialism', far from being the quasi-religious belief system it became in the Soviet Union under Stalinism, will one day become outdated and unnecessary, bringing about a world in which there will be possibilities for new forms of spiritual development and enlightenment. The Bolsheviks, before Stalin seized power and betrayed the revolution, were not, for example, always defined as 'atheists', did not make atheism a condition of membership of the party. In fact, many members of the Bolshevik Party at the time of the revolution were religious believers, including about fifteen per cent followers of Islam (and up to seventy per cent in some regions). Revolutionary Marxism was not seen as the opposite of religion, but as a condition for the free enjoyment of religious rights, and it was only after the rise of the Stalinist bureaucracy suspicious of organisations outside its control that there was a crackdown on religion, including on Islam and Christianity, a crackdown running alongside a corresponding resurgence of anti-Semitism. Radical resources operate in every religion, Islam, Christianity, Judaism, and more, and even, we might dare to say, in the kind of atheism that is open to collective dimensions of human experience beyond the confined prison of the self that neoliberal individualism locks us into.

The current revival of religious discourse should not therefore be seen as a threat, but as a resource, and it is in this context that we can appreciate why activists turning to 'ecosocialism' might then follow through their journey and arrive, in the case of the

Jewish anti-Zionist activist Joel Kovel (for example), at Episcopalian Christianity. The journey clearly does not necessarily lead away from revolutionary struggle, but can deepen it, can deepen it even where there are some dramatic conversions from one 'religion' to another, conversions that enable the spiritual suffering to turn into protest.

Stalinism

Stalinism was the bureaucratic degeneration and reverse of Marxist politics. The August 2015 'Liberation Day Tour' by the Slovenian band Laibach in Pyongyang, the first public performances in the capital of North Korea by a 'Western' rock band, poses a question about the nature of Stalinism today, how it functions as an institutional iron cage for the subjects of Supreme Leader Kim Jong-un and how it perpetuates itself as a cultural form. The keyword 'Stalinism' is not only an accurate characterisation of the bureaucratically degenerated regime in the Soviet Union up until the fall of the Wall in 1989, and for a series of other dictatorships that drag the name of communism through the mud. The term Stalinism, as a consequence of the crimes of the bureaucracy, is also the name for a set of practices on the left that presage the intensification of oppression instead of the liberation of humanity; it is an authoritarian perversion of our revolutionary struggle for a better world.

The Democratic People's Republic of Korea (DPRK) choice of Laibach is surely evidence of systematic misrecognition, misunderstanding, not only of what Laibach are but also of how the regime itself figures as something which is the absolute reverse of anything 'democratic'. Laibach rubbed the faces of the DPRK leadership in their hypocritical betrayal of socialism precisely by revealing the truth of the authoritarian cultural imagery and institutional practice that sustains the apparatus. This was a bitterly joyful repetition of how Laibach 'over-identified' with the post-Tito regime in Yugoslavia, specifically in Slovenia, as part of the process of resistance that unrolled with the appearance of the punk movement there in the 1980s.

Laibach was born under Stalinism as an internal critique of it, confronting a regime that claimed adherence to Marxism, and showing how false that claim was. Marxism aims for the expansion of democracy, up against the limits of capitalist exploitation and then through a necessary break from those limits in proletarian revolution. This promise is betrayed by Stalinism; democratic centralism inside the workers' movement is replaced by centralisation of decision-making and prohibition of opposition. Marxism is concerned with change, deep change in which understanding the world necessarily entails changing it. This commitment to dialectical movement rather than to discrete fixed essences is buried as the Stalinist bureaucracy crystallises. Social relations become fixed in place, often with an appeal to identity categories such as 'the proletariat' and, of course, its leadership. For Marxists, the self-determination of associated producers reworks notions of autonomy so that human rights become defined in relation to freedom understood relationally. Stalinism, in contrast, turns political struggle into a tool of the pragmatic needs of the bureaucracy (Moscow under Stalin himself, Beijing under Mao as a replication – at moments less so and at moments more so – of Stalinism, and so on through the smaller client states of the Soviet Union and China).

Marxism is a self-consciously internationalist movement which pits itself against the imperialist and global ambitions of capital to segregate the workforce. Against this, Stalinism revived nationalism through the motif of 'socialism in one country' and by way of appeal to national sentiment in each country where a variety of home-grown bureaucracy ruled. Marxism restores not only meaning to creative labour but also provides a meaning to the development of capitalism, and then to the forms by which it may be transcended. Stalinism responds with simple appeals to authority and the closing of debates around the interpretation of history in line with one correct account. This totalisation also serves, of course, to ratify the power of the bureaucracy as the interpretative tool through which historical determination can be judged and measured. The historical narrative Marxism provides is one that learns from the past so as not to repeat it and provides a means by which past struggles against exploitation find redemption. Marxist history is therefore also historical intervention in which combined and uneven development is characterised by unexpected connections and leaps which bring history alive again in the revolutionary process. This conception of history is betrayed by Stalinism which must rewrite the past in order to favour the standpoint of the leadership. This fixity of sequence replicates the fixed position of the bureaucracy, and it serves to justify alliances with the so-called 'progressive bourgeoisie' of capitalist economies friendly to that leadership. It serves to fix the narrative into sequences of stages of development so that they culminate in present-day arrangements.

Marxism enables and requires collective resistance to capitalism, and resistance to the strategies of divide and rule by which opposition to capitalism is rendered into individual, ethnic or nationalist complaint. Stalinism turns this resistance into obedience to a command-structure, a form of authority in which various forms of populism and state-sponsored re-articulation of power relations are seen as the most effective means of change. Marxism values collectivity, collective activity as the basis for participation which is not reduced to simple equality or equivalence of each individual's voice but of subjects constituted in such a way, in relation to one another, as to be able to understand and change the world, through its own praxis. The bureaucracy replaces this with a cult of the personality in which great leadership individualises resistance and subordinates it to party and state discipline. Marxism is an open self-transformative process of inquiry and change. The reflexivity necessary to Marxist analysis as a form of intervention is evident in its progressive recursive engagement with other social forces such as feminism and, more recently, ecological movements. Stalinism, in contrast, operates on the assumption that some version of science will save the day, in its most grotesque forms as an identitarian so-called 'proletarian science'. For full-blown Stalinists who turn Marxism into ideology, their pretend 'scientific' dialectical materialism is the path to accumulating unquestioned truth about society and nature. Under Stalinism in the Soviet Union, for example, the 'family' was reinstituted as emblem of the nation. Today this ideological perversion of Marxism reappears in claims, even among some parts of the left, in a form of Stalinist sexual politics, that there is an unchanging biological truth about the nature of what real 'men' and real 'women' are.

Marxism is a theoretical and practical articulation of the working class as it grasps the nature of alienation under capitalism and constructs its own zones of freedom. It aims to overcome alienated conditions of production through a revolutionary process in which there are qualitatively greater degrees of free association, in which the free association of each is dependent on the free association of all. Stalinism only offers the barest comfort in the humiliating deference to elders and betters. Then, on top of all this, the Stalinists resort to lies and slander to label those who resist its version of 'Marxism' as being agents of capital, 'Trotskyites' or even 'fascists'.

When we call someone a 'Stalinist', it is sometimes to draw a direct connection between their politics and the bureaucratic apparatus that benefits from it (and which sometimes determines that politics). That apparatus was once in power in many countries of the world – the so-called 'socialist' countries which stifled dissent – and so operated as a state apparatus (as it still does in North Korea today). And often, in a more offhand and imprecise way, we say someone is acting like a Stalinist or is using Stalinist tactics when they tell lies to smear their enemies. No left tradition is immune from bureaucratic degeneration, even Trotskyism, and there are sectarian fragments of this movement that has used lies and violence. That kind of bureaucratic machination usually does go hand-in-hand with centralisation, instrumental use of people for short-term political goals, occasional petty appeals to nationalism, appeals to authority, appeals to fixed essences and identities rather than attention to processes of change, and claims to one truth about those essences and identities that the leaders define in their own interests.

Laibach's apparent 'fascism' was always actually its uncanny reverse, a device to reveal how close Stalinism always was to what it triumphantly proclaimed itself to be liberating the world from, how close Stalinism came to turning the promise of socialism into something barbaric. Laibach fascinated the regime in Slovenia even at the very moment that the band was suppressed and accused of representing Western decadence. And the same happened in the DPRK; while Laibach mixed North Korean folk tunes with melodies from the 1965 kitsch anti-fascist film *The Sound of Music*, the narcissistic fascination of the regime with the group that appears to be a mirror image of itself also enabled the staging of critique, the closest to public critique that Stalinism in the DPRK had permitted so far. The regime was playing with fire, and this could even, just as when Laibach played with the Yugoslav regime, be part of its undoing.

Standpoint

Standpoint sees the world against power rather than with it. Every revolutionary movement against capitalism has at some point come up against psychiatry, either in the attempts by the forces of law and order to rule out revolutionary change as unreasonable protest to be explained away as pathological, or in the use of medical authority to lock away activists mad enough at exploitation and injustice to take steps to end it. Then it becomes clear that psychiatry views the world from the standpoint of those with power and that we need to build on the standpoint of the oppressed to see how that power works, how it works at the level of political institutions and inside our own sense of ourselves as alienated and powerless.

Psychiatry has always had at its disposal the authority of medicine, which functions not only as a discourse in which people are told that they are 'mentally ill' or that their distress in conditions of alienation and crisis is a kind of 'disease'. The titles of the two Bibles of Western medical psychiatry – the *International Classification of Diseases* (overseen by the World Health Organization) and the *Diagnostic and Statistical Manual of Mental Disorders* (produced by the American Psychiatric Association) speak volumes about what assumptions psychiatrists make about their approach to our unhappiness at the conditions we live in, and what they will say about us when we protest against those conditions.

The discourse is actually itself very important, as we can see from two examples where assumptions from medical psychiatry seep into popular culture. The first is in media images of the death in 2015 of the former leader of the Liberal Democrats, Charles Kennedy, from a major haemorrhage linked to alcoholism or, as a statement from the family put it, from his 'battle with alcoholism'. This might be better than the insinuation in the reactionary *Daily Mail* newspaper that he was hounded to death by the Scottish Nationalists, but this alcoholism is then linked in the media to addiction and then to addiction as a form of illness. There were reflections in the press on the way that Kennedy's problem was trivialised and made fun of, and that is something that also increases the distress that those labelled with a 'mental disorder' suffer; but then it was out of the frying pan of popular prejudices about madness into the fire of medical psychiatry when there was an insistence that alcoholism, like all addictions, is a 'mental illness'.

There are deadly consequences of this line that mental distress is a matter to be dealt with by medical psychiatry, which is that the logical next step is to offer medical treatment, and then to enforce that treatment if those who are so labelled refuse to take it because they are assumed not to be able to reason well enough about what is good for them. The second example makes this explicit, and concerns media discussion of the death of the US mathematician John Nash, someone well known as the main character in the 2001 film *A Beautiful Mind*. In that film Nash, played by Russell Crowe, is shown saying in 1994 at the time of his Nobel-prize nomination that he put his recovery down to improved medication. But this was a downright lie, as Nash himself made clear, for he stopped taking his medicine nearly twenty-five years earlier. The National Alliance on Mental Illness duly praised the film for pushing drug treatment for schizo-phrenia, and it turns out that there was pressure on the screen-writer to doctor what they knew to be the truth in order to fit with the medical psychiatric standpoint.

Psychiatry has the edge on psychologists (who are not medically trained, even if they now have rights to prescribe medication in many countries) or psychoanalysts (who clung to medical authority for many years but now function as a 'talking cure' sideshow to those with the power to diagnose an ever-increasing number of disorders). What psychiatry has, and this is

what makes it big business to be avidly courted by the pharma-
ceutical companies, is the power to label, prescribe and incar-
cerate people who are sick of their lives under capitalism, patriarchy and racism, but who are then told, and their families told,
that they are simply 'sick' in the head.

This is why the so-called 'anti-psychiatrists' connected quickly
with the left and feminism and anti-racist movements, and
sought to understand not only how this political-economic
system drives so many of us mad, but also how capitalism, which
pretends to be an organised rational system, is actually deeply
irrational. That irrationality is oftentimes invisible to those who
benefit from it, which is something that standpoint feminists
noticed and made the basis of their approach to knowledge and
power. These activists turn around the simple assumption made
by those who misread Marx and who treat people who don't
agree with their analysis of capitalism as suffering from so-called
'false consciousness' (a phrase Marx never actually himself used).
Against that simplistic view of the working class and the
oppressed as being dupes of ideology, the standpoint feminist
argument is that those intoxicated by power are the ones who are
unable to see how the world is; the powerful see it only from their
own limited perspective, a perspective which justifies their
privilege. Instead it is the standpoint of those who are on the
sharp end of power who can really see how it works.

This standpoint argument has always been the basis of revolutionary politics which builds on the awareness that the exploited
and oppressed can build from their own collective resistance
'class consciousness' of their position, collective resistance which
is also an anticipation of a better world beyond capitalism. It was
also the basis of the 'consciousness-raising' workshops in the
Women's Liberation Movement from times of second-wave
feminism that worked with what women already knew of their
conditions of life ruled by men so they could themselves work
out how to better understand patriarchy by changing it,

overthrowing it.

Critical analysis of psychiatry's claim to be scientific illustrates very well the main arguments of standpoint feminism; that supposedly 'objective' investigations are underpinned by research questions that are in line with stereotypically masculine attempts to 'predict and control' behaviour, which itself is a profoundly 'subjective' and partial approach to understanding human beings. In place of the pretend-objective 'God's eye' view of ourselves that Donna Haraway explores in books like her 1989 *Primate Visions*, which is about the 'experimental' and 'observational' torture of animals, we need a 'science from below' which shows how knowledge is put together. Then standpoint feminism connects directly with a historical materialist analysis.

Radical feminist anti-psychiatry activist Bonnie Burstow in her 2015 book *Psychiatry and the Business of Madness*, for example, shows how this standpoint argument can become the motor of an activist exploration of the way that psychiatry works as part of what she calls 'institutional ethnography'. This approach works with those who have been made to live inside the institutions that psychiatry rules, whether those are institutions as mental hospitals or institutions that implant themselves in communities, and it works with people to map the territory of those institutions, to work out what their internal shapes are. This leads to a question for those who want to change the world, about what we should do with mental hospitals and whether, at a time of deep cuts in state welfare services, we should defend them and imagine that it would be possible to reconfigure them as places of asylum.

Some psychiatrists are able to make use of the asylum as a base for political work, as Frantz Fanon showed during the struggle for Algerian independence at Blida-Joinville. But the place of the asylum as prison-house or refuge is contested by critical psychiatrists, as it is by psychiatric system survivors. In France, for example, the asylum was a place of safety for anti-fascist fighters during the Second World War, while in Italy the asylums were used by the fascists to imprison their enemies. That difference between French and Italian responses to psychiatry has led to a debate among activists, and to the particular shape of the 'Democratic Psychiatry' movement which developed in Trieste and which still today inspires *Asylum: The Magazine for Democratic Psychiatry*.

The Trieste movement emphasised the way that the institution of psychiatry did not only operate in the mental hospital, but also that the political struggle to do away with asylums required a deeper process of 'deinstitutionalisation'. The many voices of 'anti-psychiatry' and 'democratic psychiatry' build on the different standpoints of those who have been subjected to the mental health system, not all of whom draw feminist or Marxist conclusions from their own analysis. But the practice of 'deinstitutionalisation' in Trieste and in the Asylum movements works with the logic of 'institutional ethnography' that radical feminist research has made possible, and shows that the standpoint of those who are diagnosed, medicated and incarcerated must be part of the broader struggle for liberation from the rule of capital.

Structurelessness

Structurelessness is the diagnosis of power that returns when it is simply wished away. The first meeting in Manchester of 'Momentum' – the group set up after the election of Jeremy Corbyn as leader of the Labour Party in 2015 – looked like it may be the last. Fortunately it was not, but there were bad signs that recuperation of Jeremy was being sped along by institutionalisation. Many there meant well, but activists who have lived in the Labour Party a long time as well as the hopeful newcomers were caught in a contradiction, between structure and an attempt to avoid it. A young career-track politician from London called 'Sam' quickly told the meeting what they already knew – that Momentum was set up to organise in the Labour Party in support of the new Jeremy Corbyn leadership – and then the splits started to open up. Each division revolved around the very questions of democracy and 'new politics' that Corbyn's election promised. And each bitter attack was made in the name of a new 'openness' in the Labour Party that recalled the old debates prompted by anarchist feminist activists nearly half a century ago over the nature of 'structure' and what Jo Freeman in a classic little 1970 pamphlet called *The Tyranny of Structurelessness*.

At a time when the women's movement was experimenting with consciousness-raising groups and an attempt to do away with structure altogether, 'structurelessness' became the implicit progressive alternative that promised to do away with all forms of organisation, bureaucratic organisation that kept people out of leadership positions and even any form of organisation that would hinder, they thought, full participation. Freeman named this implicit ostensibly super-democratic alternative, named it in order to lay bare what the problems were. She pointed out that whenever left and feminist organisations claimed to offer a free and open space for people to talk, they invariably concealed a hidden structure. This hidden structure returned often unbidden, even despite the best intentions of those involved, to silently shut up and drive out those who did not conform to it. This was the 'tyranny' of pretend structurelessness that functioned as the weird mirror image of the structure of obviously authoritarian 'democratic centralist' far-left groups, including anarchist groups that railed against democratic centralism in theory while enforcing it in their own practice.

Then, as now, it was usually women who were excluded from political discussion and political leadership as a result of the tyranny of structurelessness, and as feminist theory and practice has developed to take into account Black feminism and LGBTQ+ politics, it has been clearer that this tyranny benefits not only men but every dominant group. The result is that each and every power relation that the left and feminist activists have aimed to overturn has actually been reproduced in their own organisations. What is important to note now is that this reproduction of power works in two ways. It works in the way noticed by Jo Freeman: that the pretence that there is free and open debate, and the illusion that there are no 'structures' if we just all wish to make it so, actually enables dominant power structures to click into action again. It also operates through bureaucratic obsessional following of rules which privilege those who have already prepared their scripts in advance and intervene as a block inside other organisations they plan to capture and bend to their own agenda. Both these aspects of power, of structure and structurelessness, work in tandem today, and we can see this double-operation at work inside the Labour Party.

An apocryphal story circulated in the north of Britain about a young woman comrade who joined a Left Unity branch to find that many of the activists were there to promote their own little organisation. Escape from this wretched situation opened up with the election of Jeremy Corbyn, so she gave up on Left Unity and joined her local branch of the Labour Party to find that same little organisation spouting the same line, they had now moved in from Left Unity to the Labour Party with a new front organisation. There were those who ridiculed 'safe spaces' in Left Unity, and put their ridicule into practice in almost every meeting, ensuring that only those with very thick skins – or those with bodyguards around them who were from their own organisation – returned after being subjected to what these very structured sectarians like to call the 'cut and thrust of political argument'. These people can be friendly enough chatting before and after the meeting, but behave very differently when following orders from the leading group inside their own organisation when they think they should be implementing a 'line'.

It is true that the 'safe space' policy that was much-discussed in Left Unity – not least because of the antics of the organised groups intent on taking over local branches or simply raiding them for new recruits – risked turning clear decision-making structures into moralising procedures. Left Unity itself accumulated a series of local, regional and national 'committees' and an extensive range of 'policies'. For some wishing to do away with structure altogether, that has made it seem at times to be more like the Labour Party that it was attempting to supplant than a genuinely new movement that did politics differently. It was, nevertheless, a brave attempt to break with the past, one that should still be supported, and Left Unity is still one of the places from which to support Corbyn.

The 'safe spaces' became a fetish for the sectarians who know very well how to mobilise to get their own motions voted through one of the layers of the organisation and how to get their members on the committees. They know it so very well not because they are individually clever but because they are obedient to their own organisation and to the leadership organisation inside their organisation. That will be the 'central committee' or the 'national committee' that passes down the line agreed at the last congress, they will say, and which tells them how to push the line through. This strategy can work very well for these groups inside local party branches of larger more open parties like Left Unity, and it is worse when there are no clear and open rules governing the meeting. In those conditions the little left groups who are not at all ashamed of structure, contemptuous even of what they see as the 'touchy-feeliness' of new politics, are able to drive away those who want a more intuitive engagement with the issues or those who are not confident in arguing a 'position', perhaps because they are actually thinking it through while discussing it with others. The reason these groups hated the 'safe spaces' policy was not because it hindered open debate but precisely because it facilitated it. The ground-rules set a structure which the sectarian groups saw as an obstacle to their free-market survival-of-the-fittest form of politics which they wanted to play out in a field that was, if they were lucky, apparently 'structureless'. Against this structurelessness there is, it is true, always the danger of what one response to Freeman's article called 'the tyranny of tyranny'.

There will undoubtedly be attempts to purge these small organised groups – organisations inside the organisation – from the Labour Party and we need to keep open the space for the issues to be debated. One problem is that it seems that some little groups that have embedded themselves in Labour Party branches are now just as keen to exclude the newcomers as the big old apparatus. Towards the end of the Momentum meeting there were demands for an open democratic structure. If you want to be on the committee, the meeting was told, you can talk to 'Sam', and the chair of the meeting accidentally referred to the group as 'Monument'. There had been an open discussion, 'structureless' it seemed, in which the hidden structure of traditional Labour Party politics was in command, exactly as Freeman many years ago could have predicted. Lack of structure is the feeding ground for undemocratic and exclusionary politics, and Momentum might yet ensure that little if nothing of the Corbyn revolution is taken forward. For those who have jumped into the Labour Party and are hoping that Momentum will be a vehicle to support Corbyn, good luck, but also, at the same time, keep your links with those outside who are trying to find new ways of working that take that dialectic between structure and structurelessness seriously so that it may, in practice, be transcended.

Subjectivity

Subjectivity provides a different way of describing personal experience as part of social structure and takes us beyond the division between the strong individual and followers. Can Jeremy Corbyn do no wrong? Well-known newspaper friend of the working class and the struggle for progressive leadership of the Labour Party (not) the *Daily Telegraph* recently reported that Jeremy Corbyn is, perhaps, more evil than his enemies suspected. Corbyn does not even give his cat a name, calling it simply 'The Cat'. The newspaper said that Corbyn greets his cat with 'Buenos Dias, El Gato', a respectful designation that honours the nature of the animal but, of course, robs it of any particular personhood. What could be worse than that? But perhaps this story is more telling than it seems, cuing us into an aspect of politics that Corbyn has assiduously avoided cultivating – the cult of personality – and drawing attention instead to the role of 'subjectivity' in revolutionary collective activity.

This question of subjectivity breaks completely from the assumptions about politics that underpin the training of reporters in the bourgeois press. When the BBC, for example, is asked to tackle the question of 'bias', its reporters, who have always operated on the basis that their task is to present a 'balance' of opinion from different leading politicians, appear mystified by the idea that their own political positions might have any influence on the choices they make and the way they home in on personal rivalries to try and make things accessible to their readers or viewers. If we play their game of the reduction to personalities (in line with some form of strategic essentialism) for just a moment, the nauseating BBC journalist Nick Robinson is a case in point. But the problem is not so much that Robinson is chums with traditional party leaders, and was President of the Oxford University Conservative Association; rather, the main problem is that his presentation of political issues, and this is the model of presentation that is followed by other junior reporters at the BBC, always frames the report about what this or that leader is 'thinking', 'feeling' or 'intending' to convey to their audience. His individual style exemplifies the problem, and it reinforces the idea that political leadership should be about individual personality characteristics.

This reduction to 'personality' and then the production of personality cults in media reportage, celebrity politics which obscures the key issues and excludes ordinary people from politics altogether, is in line with dominant ideological preoccupations under capitalism; individual strivers who make the country wealthy versus individual failures who hold us back. But at the very same moment as this reduction to the individual is intensified under neoliberalism, new forms of political resistance have emerged that use quite different ways of speaking about what the 'personality' is. The question of subjectivity also breaks from assumptions about the importance of 'personality' in the old left, assumptions that have often unfortunately carried on down from the personality cult around Stalin to the antics of the little would-be Lenins in the myriad of revolutionary groupuscules that function more often than not as obstacles to revolutionary change.

With the reformulation of individual personality characteristics as being aspects of 'subjectivity', we are able to pick up some of the older Marxist debates about the 'role of the individual in history'. This was once a question which revolved around the dialectical interaction between what a political activist brought to a social movement and what historical forces were thinkable, historical forces that are often nowadays spoken of in terms of what Foucault and some feminists call the 'conditions of possibility' for certain forms of knowledge. The 'tradition of all dead generations weighs like a nightmare on the brains of the living', as Marx once had it, and this includes the very idea that social change should be brought about by leaders strong enough to wake the masses up.

An opening to the problems that the old way of posing the question led to was posed by Georg Lukács after the 1956 Twentieth Congress of the Communist Party of the Soviet Union where the new leadership attempted to present a balance sheet of the dangers of the 'cult of personality' after Stalin's death. Lukács quite rightly pointed to the problem as being not only that of the 'personality' but also that of the 'organisation'. It was, after all, the party apparatus that had produced the cult of personality, and this apparatus operated like a 'pyramid' in which many 'little Stalins' who were treated like objects by the leadership in the top layers became the 'creators and guardians' of the cult of personality around Stalin himself.

Instead, and building on this internal critique of the Marxist tradition, and extending reflexive developments of a more open Leninist theory of organisation, the question of subjectivity in politics is central to new forms of organisation and transformations of consciousness. In this way subjectivity as a keyword for a different kind of politics connects more easily with notions like 'intersectionality' than do more fixed and commonsensical terms like the 'self'. In line with this conception of subjectivity let's acknowledge the variety of ways it is described rather than pinning it on to one particular bright theorist.

It appears in the development of psychoanalysis as an account of the self that questions the reduction of explanation to the conscious manipulative 'ego' as centre of reason and action; psychoanalysis rests on a conception of the human subject as divided; divided between consciousness and the unconscious, and divided at the level of the unconscious, an unconscious which links each individual to others in contradictory lines of identification and hostility. You are not exactly who you think you are, and this opens the way to an emphasis on what is actually said, said to and with others, rather than looking to the miniscule master in the head who is able to decide what things really mean.

It appears in the development of systems of ethics concerned not so much with what an individual self-conscious subject intends – a 'prediction and control' model of politics which values political leaders who operate like masters of themselves and then of others – but with Alain Badiou's description of 'fidelity to an event', to events which we together build the conditions of possibility for. The key question is then what responsibility we have for what we have created, even if we were not individually there, as part of our tradition of struggle – of the Russian Revolution in 1917, for example – and the way we draw out the lessons of that. Here 'subject' itself may be thought of as individual or collective, or somewhere between the two, not confined to the individual body.

And it appears in the more recent descriptions of action which also break from psychoanalysis, and which provide some of the grounding concepts for autonomist Marxism in which the 'collective subject' is conceived of as constituted through a multiplicity of 'lines of fracture' which operate in and against, subversive of and disruptive of disciplinary power (this way of looking at things comes after the work of Gilles Deleuze and of Hardt and Negri). The 'multitude' is, in this sense, the creation of a new form of subjectivity in which we might participate as individuals, but it is something distorted, sabotaged, if we try to make that multitude conform to a disciplinary theoretical grid or to one individual will.

The orchestrated complaints about Jeremy Corbyn from the moment he was first elected – a drip, drip of interviews with career politicians bitter that they had never made it to the top of the pyramid rolled out on television and in the newspapers at the rate of several a week – was that he would not be a strong enough leader to win the election in the next general election. Such a 'leader' should, they assume, be able to avoid negative attention from the media, an aspiration that is pie in the sky if you pose any kind of challenge to commercial television and the big business press industry. But Corbyn and many of his supporters inside and outside the Labour Party have always made it clear that the election inside the Labour Party should not, to start with, be about finding a strong figure that would provide top-down leadership. Rather, it should be about using the election campaign to build a different kind of politics in which ordinary members of the Labour Party and trades union activists and those in different social movements can be brought into activity on their own account, speaking for themselves, creating the structures in which they would be heard and making the new 'leadership' democratically accountable.

Jeremy is not a charismatic powerful leader that the old form of politics loves and is able to contain and control, not a 'personality' with the strength to show us the way and tell us what the limits are to what is possible. In some ways yes, but, more importantly, no, he configures himself and his team and his wider group of supporters, and then the radical movement around him in a different way, beyond petty individual characteristics and entailing a broader sense of subjectivity altogether.

Trans

Trans both reproduces and transgresses gender and other binaries. The keyword 'trans' is radical and controversial; it provides a point of common struggle for new revolutionary movements, and it operates as a point of division between the 'old' new left that has solidified in various political currents over the past fifty years and the new social movements, movements for whom LGBT and a progressive elaboration of new unstable identities marked in that letter series with different initials – to add Q for Queer, for example – also reflect back and unsettle what the old new left was beginning to take for granted. To take something for granted as an orthodoxy is not exactly 'bureaucratic' in itself, but it does begin to sediment one fixed dogma about who can be treated as good 'allies' of revolutionary socialists, dogma which the new LGBTQ+ movements have progressively cracked open. They replace bureaucratic assumptions about what counts with properly political interventions in capitalism, and in the left itself. In the process, 'trans' shows us something about the nature of bureaucracy and politics as such.

Trans as a movement has radically evolved from denoting 'transsexual', a medical category concerned only with transition from one kind of body to another, to signifying 'transgender' as an overall umbrella term to cover a range of different ways of connecting gender and sexual identities to the body and disconnecting them from it. It problematises forms of gender segregation we can too-easily take for granted. It is now a crucial component of revolutionary struggle around the world, taking slightly different forms in different places, for four reasons.

First, it puts on the progressive political agenda a basic democratic right of an oppressed group to be able to live and speak about their experience without fear of violence, even death. Often the danger they face is linked to precarity and sex-work.

Many in the trans community simply want to live safely, and they have no interest in sexual politics as such, still less in revolutionary politics (as is the case for many members of oppressed groups). As we well know, that violence can be extreme, and the political dimension of our response to that violence needs to include not only defence of trans people from threat but also the ideological battle against attempts to minimise the threat. Second, trans activists who are politically mobilised to defend their rights and to explicitly connect their own personal political struggle with their LGB and other comrades are making a demand on the basis of their identity. This is a claim for a right to be included which opens up democratic space to difference, to more difference. And, at the same time as they make that identity claim, they destabilise it, they mark and question the very notion of identity in radical politics.

There are two further reasons why trans is important to us; these are not, unfortunately, positive reasons to do with the progressive dynamic of trans, but rather in the response we must give to the reception given to trans among some of our comrades and on the right. The third and fourth reasons, then, are conditioned by the backlash, and the urgent need to defend the rights of trans people and to work with trans activists. This reaction comes in at least two forms that are linked by way of the motif of bureaucracy as an insidious alternative to authentic political struggle.

The reaction, this is the third reason why we must take trans seriously in our politics, is more often obviously bureaucratic, for it follows in the wake of the Stalinist suppression of difference for the glory of a supposedly 'united' movement against capitalism. That Stalinist reaction, which once upon a time included the suppression of homosexuality and the accusation levelled against lesbian and gay activists that they were some kind of unconscious police agents serving decadent Western culture against the straight left. This accusation itself, of course, served the interests of the gerontocracy in the Soviet Union, the real hardened old 'left'. Here it is easier to see how a bureaucratic mindset which is dead-set against the proliferation of movements that would disperse and invent identities in struggle, and see that diversity of resistance as a source of strength rather than weakness, actually reflected and reinforced a particular kind of social apparatus. Bureaucracy in the Soviet Union, and in other pretend-socialist states, as well as in the Communist Parties that served it around the world, was a way of approaching protest that clamped down on anything that might disturb the interests of the apparatus as an actually-existing material structure of social relations.

However, alongside this reaction to trans, which is easily understandable given what we know about Stalinism, there is another equally reactionary and in some ways more disappointing and pernicious reaction that comes from some of those who we would, in other times and still in other progressive campaigns, see as our comrades. We include here some of those who identify themselves as 'feminist' but who have a fixed idea of what 'feminism' is as a political perspective operating in one singular biologically-based pure form that is suspicious of the wider domain of third- and fourth-wave 'feminisms' which are deliberately plural in their self-designation and in their practice. This is the kind of feminist reaction that is sometimes too-quickly smeared in the term 'TERFs' (Trans-Exclusionary Radical Feminists), a term we briefly cite here because it is used by some trans activists against those who treat them as enemies rather than as allies. This kind of reaction runs alongside the attempts to roll back the gains of the LGBT movements by even suggesting that the 'T' be dropped (and the Q simply forgotten).

The fourth reason our politics is also trans politics comes from the challenge posed by the pervasive recuperation of alternative social movements by capitalism, a recuperation that fuels, with good reason, the suspicion of a good few trans-hostile feminists.

This recuperation (and those second-wave socialist feminists and radical feminists who are suspicious of what trans means are right to be critical of what is happening) includes the turning of gender and sexuality into a commodity. And it includes the incorporation of this niche identity into corporate bureaucratic alternatives to politics, with the recruitment of Caitlyn Jenner to centrefold propaganda and the Republican Party in the United States as a case in point.

The critiques of trans have to be taken on board, have to be included in the way we work with trans and with trans activists as our comrades. These critiques, well-noted by socialist and radical feminists, include: the enforced segregation of the sexes and reinforcement of that binary as part of the 'transition' process in which those who move across the binary play out their new identity in even more caricatured gender-stereotyped ways; the enforcement of forms of gender identity into which people are locked as they attempt to claim and defend them against attack; the agenda of the private medical companies pushing sex-reassignment surgery which reduces transgender to 'trans-sexual'; and the sexualisation of children encouraged by the medical companies and linked propaganda apparatuses that seek to reduce the age at which transition might be 'chosen', usually really chosen by the targeted parents.

But, the reality of trans is actually that the segregation and enforcement of chosen gender identities based on an idea of what a real biological sex might be is only one aspect of what trans experience and activism includes; as the trans and queer use of the term 'cis' indicates, much of the trans movement is not concerned with moving from one side of the gender binary to the other at all. Rather, there is a fluidity of gender and sexual identity which is the nightmare of any bureaucratic attempt to categorise and define what they really are as boy or girl. The ethos and practice of the trans movement operates as a critique of hierarchy, against a hierarchical and bureaucratic image of social organisation as something vertical, top-down power. Against this it encourages a transversal and more horizontal network of networks, a model form of the kind of revolutionary organisation that historicises gender, operates as a critique of culture, and anticipates the kind of society we aim to replace capitalism with. Trans, for all of the disputes it has unleashed inside feminism (and inside the socialist movement), is a hinge-point between those of us who still think we are straight, on the one hand, and contemporary revolutionary 'feminisms' on the other. We have something to offer trans as a movement that has always opposed bureaucracy and we have something to learn from it as an already anti-bureaucratic politics.

Transition

Transition today enables a connection and reframing of the distinction between reform and revolution. It is a commonplace assumption, an ideological assumption, that slow reforms are the way to go if you want a stable sustainable lifestyle, and that revolutionaries aim at a permanent revolution that entails perpetual turmoil. This opposition between reform and revolution conveniently overlooks the fact that the Russian Revolution in 1917 was actually quite peaceful; more people were killed in the Eisenstein reconstruction on film ten years later than were actually killed during the storming of the Winter Palace. The revolution certainly involved dramatic transformations, but the real turmoil came later, after the allied intervention by the combined armies of the capitalist world intent on provoking civil war that, they hoped, would overthrow the democratically elected Bolshevik regime, a regime based in the Soviets rather than in the corrupt bankrupt parliament devoted to war, the First World War. It also overlooks the fact that contemporary shock capitalism itself as a feature of its normal everyday functioning precisely relies on continual and increasingly violent slumps and booms in the economy that disrupt the social fabric and which repeatedly kick-start capital accumulation; that's what wars and imperialist interventions are usually about today. Revolutionary politics has always been about 'transition', a term that poses new questions to revolutionaries who call themselves ecosocialists today.

An attempt to bridge reform and revolution, and to rethink what each is about, as well as the relationship between the two, is at the heart of the 'transition town' movement, a movement rooted in ecological politics. It looks at first glance a bit tame, 'reformist' we might say, but it actually keys into and forces us to expand on what we meant by 'transition' in the old 'Transitional

Programme' drawn up by Trotsky in 1938 which attempted to revive revolutionary internationalist politics in the Fourth International. The transition network was built from local initiatives to grow alternative systems of sustainable food production and changes in consumption that would be ecologically responsible. It then expanded from a first base in Totnes in the south of England around the world, always first based in communities and only then making links between them. The food production initiatives include 'permaculture' – a form of production that is based on the recycling of material in distinct closed ecosystems – and so it immediately connects with the attempts to defend 'food security' that have also been at the heart of new revolutionary movements across the world.

The ethos of the transition movement is thus grounded in a profound change in the way that the material world is organised, with small-scale agricultural initiatives designed to replace big-business industrial-scale farming, as well as what some adherents would see as a quasi-spiritual transformation of values. This is something that revolutionaries today should recognise as being consistent with a socialist feminist 'prefigurative' politics that aims for a process of change that anticipates in its very form the kind of world we want to build as an alternative to capitalism. The demand for a change in lifestyle now thus operates as part of a 'transition' which reworks the counterculture movement and turns it from being an idealist hope for a better life into authentic practical initiatives which lay the basis for what a socialist society might be like.

Does this mean that the transition town activists are not really 'revolutionary' because they pretend that their revolution is happening now, and because they don't formalise what they are doing as being a small-scale series of incremental changes as part of a programme which has in its sights the evils of capitalism and its necessary destruction? No. The transition towns are also increasingly energised by environmental degradation and by the threat posed by climate change. Unlike some of the hopeless attempts by 'scientific socialists' to put the clock back and pretend that the destruction of nature by capitalism has either not happened or that it could easily be put right once world revolution has been brought about by the vanguard party, the transition town ecosocialists are trying to find ways to reconfigure what human life on the planet will have to look like as a result of the momentous geographical changes that have already taken place in our 'Anthropocene' era, an era that is thought by geologists to have commenced in 1950. In other words, they focus on the here and now, and they have an eye to the broader geopolitical historical context in which they bring about change.

A moment's reflection on the way that the 'transitional programme' has actually functioned for many of the revolutionaries who might be quick to scorn the hippie ethos of the transition town reformists would remind us that the right programme on its own has not been so successful quite yet. The transitional programme should function as a 'method', that is, it should enable us to key into the actually-existing hopes of the exploited and oppressed and build into our political engagement with different social movements a series of realistic demands that bring people up to the bars of the cage; not so they learn what is impossible, disheartened, but precisely so they demand the impossible of capitalism, a life free of want and violence, a life that they have already started to build for themselves and that they will all the more energetically defend against the attempts by the capitalist state to beat them back. In practice, the transitional programme itself too-often functions as, at best, idealist wish-fulfilment – the 'demands' for a sliding scale of wages and so on are polished off and wheeled out as if they will have a magical result – and, at worst, as manipulative unrealistic demands that we pose simply because we know that they cannot be met. We are gradually starting to learn that 'ecosocialism' does not simply mean patching in some new 'transitional demands', but it changes the way we conceive of the revolutionary process and the end point we aim for.

What is striking about the 'transition towns' is that they are actually rebuilding, within the wreckage of austerity capitalism, networks of support and, crucially, physically sustainable structures of production and distribution that operate very much like the broader conception of 'soviets' in the revolutionary Marxist tradition. We have always known that there will be a period of 'dual power' in which the old capitalist economy coexists with and competes with and tries to suppress the new socialist forms of life that could and should replace it. Transition towns in their own careful thoughtful way function as forms of dual power, early forms but forms that materially sustain the kind of alternative economy we want to build after the overthrow of capitalism. And transition towns are on the agenda now as a response to the attempt by the capitalist state to impose austerity, strip back the welfare state and make local communities pay.

In Manchester, for example, the so-called 'Northern Powerhouse' will see a transfer of powers to administer the cities but with a dramatic reduction in resources, and with the emphasis placed on big business as driver of the process. The scam that is called 'Devo Manc' promises to deliver reforms that will shift the balance of power from London to the regions and to the cities networked together across the north of England. It has been enthusiastically embraced by the Labour council in Manchester on the pretence that local people will have more say over the control of resources, but it will actually be predicated on massive investment and tighter integration into the needs of the world capitalist economy, with the airport as the key hub and Chinese capital as the controlling influence. These are 'reforms' that will be profoundly disruptive, a local version of shock capitalism that will destroy key elements of the local infrastructure and result in greater poverty for the mass of the population; this is a recipe for Manchester to become the centre of what critics of the government scheme see as the 'new northern poorhouse'.

Against these violent reforms, perpetual disorganisation and mass misery, the subjection of people to forces beyond their control, the seemingly slow and modest initiatives of 'transition city Manchester' are actually more humane and more revolutionary. They enact their own version of 'transition' that is one way of implementing a materially-effective 'transitional programme'. It is not the transitional programme exactly, but revolutionary ecosocialists should be learning from what is happening on the ground and linking it with similar movements around the world that have also already transformed Marxist politics, linking with it to help it become even more 'resilient', 'sustainable' and also, at some point, self-consciously and actively anti-capitalist.

Wages

Wages draw attention to new forms of slavery under capitalism and to demands that unravel it. There must have been many listeners of the British Radio 4 soap opera *The Archers* who laughed out loud when Rob Titchener, the father of Helen's new child born of his rape of her in 2015, decided that he should call his new son 'Gideon'. 'That's lovely,' purred his mother Ursula, happy that he should name it after his grandfather. But there are many who weren't fooled, and knew something of the subtext. Rob succeeded in destroying Helen's friendship with gay Ian, the chef at Grey Gables hotel and country restaurant in Ambridge, the fictional village in 'Borsetshire' where the soap is set. Rob is a reactionary who not only abuses his women and dislikes gays, he loves fox-hunting, and planned to send Helen's other son Henry to public school. And so, the name 'Gideon' confirms him as a rotter; why else would he want to name his son after the then British Chancellor of the Exchequer, multi-millionaire George Osborne who is lined up to be Baronet Gideon Oliver Osborne, as Labour MP Dennis Skinner never ceases to remind us whenever he refers to this aristocratic thug as 'Gideon', one who now functions as one more mirror for evil Rob. The subtext surely is that Rob is a Tory. Rob might, listeners hope, be done for the new offence of 'coercive control', but his insidious suffocating behaviour raises a question as to what might have saved Helen from all this; would she have been safe if she had retained her independence by being given a wage for all the domestic and emotional labour she has been carrying out as Rob's slave? The notion that 'wages' might be the key to the liberation of women, even that payment of some kind might be empowering for all, has been gathering steam recently. But will this keyword 'wages' really unlock us from wage-slavery and its associated forms of power?

The call for 'wages' has been on the agenda for some feminists for many years, the most well-known advocates being activists with Wages for Housework, a movement launched by Selma James in Padua in 1972, and the argument has taken on new life through a series of interventions by the Italian feminist Silvia Federici who then turned around the demand to argue that it might also function as a more radical critique of women's labour that one might call 'Wages Against Housework'. Federici's 2004 book *Caliban and the Witch* showed how violence against women and suppression of spirituality was bound up with the brutal development and enforcement of capitalist social relations in Europe. The point, Federici argued, is that the whole of society is becoming turned into a capitalist factory machine in which domestic labour and the oppression of women has become a crucial component globally. The idea that 'wages' might be demanded for labour that is currently unpaid, labour that is absolutely necessary for the reproduction of labour power in the home, has been taken in a number of directions. It bears fruit outside socialist-feminism in the call for a Universal Basic Income which the Green Party UK has signed up to, and also, in more discretionary welfare mode, underpins the UK Government's Personal Independence Payment for long-term ill health or disability which has now replaced the Disability Allowance. This should make us pause and think about whether this is all as progressive as it seems.

It is not so much that the call for 'wages' is itself problematic, but what happens when it is concretised and turned into social policy and a government programme for getting people to stand on their own two feet and to take responsibility for their lives as individuals isolated from each other. This, after all, was exactly Helen Archer's problem when she became wrapped up by boa constrictor Rob, isolation. The Personal Independence Payments, to work back from the worst of the concrete 'wages' programmes, is attractive to some people with disabilities or mental health problems precisely because it does give them some control over their own lives. In that sense, the idea is a clever one, for it does what it says on the tin. But that lure of 'control' comes with some long-term material and ideological costs. The material costs are clear, as those in the 'Disability Visibility Project' have long argued, with the assessment for Personal Independence Payments passed from one private company to another working under the imperative to reduce costs to the government. The bottom line is to make the poor and the disabled, and anyone who will not subject themselves to conditions of wage-slavery, pay for austerity. And the material cost agenda is intensified by the ideological argument that once these people have been given the money they should stop bothering the state and stop complaining. This is payment to shut up and give up your claim for welfare, for support, or for a world which does not 'disable' people who cannot work.

This logic tracks up to some of the more popular versions of a 'wages' for all argument on the left in proposals for 'Universal Basic Income', and was topic of intense debate in the radical left-of-labour political party Left Unity. The proposal that the party adopt this demand as part of its economic strategy fell, precisely because it would entail a shift of emphasis from welfare provision for all to the provision of payment in return for being thrown at the mercy of the marketplace. Left Unity, which was founded to defend the National Health Service, was particularly sensitive to the implications of this call for a basic wage for all, and was right to reject the proposal. After all, if everyone has been paid enough to make their own choices about housing and health, why not then allow them to pay for whatever health provision they like – the way is open to a marketplace of health. Left Unity would have been left without any coherent argument against the privatisation of the health sector. Wages for all in practice here boils down to the privatising of services as much as it boils down to the privatisation of personal choice.

And so, paying Helen Archer a wage would not have enabled her to assert her economic rights. Once she had been paid off she would have been at the mercy of her new husband. We should notice, furthermore, that in this particular case, as listeners of *The Archers* will be well aware, Rob had actually left his own job and was the one who was dependent on the new shop at Bridge Farm, and so on the Archer family, that is Pat, Tony and their daughter Helen. If economic control was all there was to 'coercive control' then Rob would have been dealt with long ago. The thing is that it is not.

The point about coercive control, and this is the point to the narrative of Rob's increasing control over Helen's life, is that this is power which has some relation to economic wage-slavery, but it actually operates according to the logic of a master-slave dialectic in which the slave desperately wants recognition from the master. As a materially and symbolically structured power relation, there is enforcement of that desperate condition. That master-slave dialectic is spun in one direction under capitalism in which the worker must sell their labour-power in order to live. That's where the punishment of the poor in the government's austerity agenda kicks in. And it is spun in another direction under patriarchy which today accompanies and intensifies abuse under capitalism in the UK. Which brings us back to Wages for Housework, and demands that seem at the one moment explicitly economic – they really are arguing for a 'wage' to be provided to all women who labour – but at the very same moment the slogan functions as a symbolic demand. Treating it in this way helps us address power without reducing the demand to an economi-sation of every aspect of our lives, an economisation that, when it comes down to it, we should oppose. That symbolic demand mobilises women as workers to struggle alongside all those who work and those who cannot. Even if the extrapolation from Marxist analyses of wage-labour to labour in the home is true, and even if it is not, what that symbolic demand for wages expresses is a demand that patriarchal power be taken as seriously on the left as the power of capital.

The Archers, which began broadcasting in 1950, has the largest audience of a radio soap opera in the world, 4.77 million. The average age of its listeners is 56 (younger than the membership of some Trotskyist groups). The audience has been appalled and enraged by Rob's treatment of Helen, and impelled to action, sometimes charity action. Helen's trial in 2016, after she stabbed Rob after he goaded her that she would only be free after she took her own life, has been covered in many newspapers. The actor who plays Rob has described how he researched the role, and the scriptwriters have been working with domestic abuse charities to get the narrative right. Rob's abuse has put domestic violence on the political agenda for a small but not insignificant part of the electorate. The storyline has been so successful that there were security concerns at the annual fete in the real Suffolk village of Monks Eleigh when it was announced that the actor would be a guest there. Some people evidently confuse the symbolic aspect of this abuse and control with the real world, but even in their confusion they are speaking out for the right reasons.

The notion of 'wages' can operate as an analytic tool for a socialist-feminist politics to address the oppression of women, but that does not mean that it is a solution to problems of power, just as Marxist analyses of 'wage-slavery' do not exhaust our analyses or our action against different forms of oppression. And Marxists do not at all want a world where everyone gets wages, our vision of life under capitalism and patriarchy is more radical than that. A wage would not save Helen, but the demand for a wage connects with the political questions that are opened up by her plight and for an audience that wants her plight to end. Against the Tories in Ambridge, and for a socialist-feminist revolution across Borsetshire!

Whiteness

Whiteness makes power relations visible by colouring them in. Racism is bad and ugly. This is what everyone on the left knows well. But when we only name the problem in that way, it is easy to slide into a liberal discourse in which we all agree that we are against bad and ugly things. Attempts to expand descriptions of the problem to include 'institutional racism' went some way to addressing the sense that some white liberals had that they were being personally attacked, poor them, that their very experience of the world was being undermined. However, this reassuring shift from persons to institutions then led many leaders of institutions ranging from schools to police forces to cheerfully announce that they were tackling this institutional racism. Then there was a bizarre slide back into the personal realm again as everything and everyone learned to confess that they were institutionally racist. Another way of tackling this problem is to shift focus to 'whiteness', to notice that white is not the absence of colour, but a particular kind of taken-for-granted fleshy tone that counts some people in and some people out. Colouring in whiteness is a strategy that can complement anti-racist politics, but it is also a strategy with a double-edge. We need to cut through this in a quite different way, perhaps, facing what is real about it and developing a strategy that is more 'surreal'. To do that we might learn something by connecting with Claude Cahun, who was 'white' and 'non-white' and fought at the boundaries between the two.

One of the problems with 'whiteness' is that it is all but invisible to those who inhabit it, those who enjoy their comfort with being white with such ease that they do not even notice that they are white. Then the problem becomes named as being 'black', with the focus on forms of disadvantage and exclusion suffered by black people, encouragement to them to overcome the obstacles they face instead of examining exactly what those obstacles are. One way of turning things around is to name what the activist and scholar Sara Ahmed, author of the 2010 classic *The Promise of Happiness*, calls the 'walls of whiteness'. The 'walls of whiteness' appear as the 'shiny surfaces' that public relations departments polish up to reassure the public that they really are inclusive. These shiny surfaces may include friendly images of black people on advertising for courses or services, and in this way the walls of whiteness which actually keep black people out are, paradoxically, peopled with images of those they exclude. This shiny surface demands that those who people it, whether black or white, are 'happy', and so happiness itself becomes part of the architecture of whiteness, and is then an architecture that terms like 'racism' spoil; those who notice and name racism are the bad ugly spoilsports who are stopping people from being happy.

Ahmed's work draws on the black lesbian feminist Audre Lorde, among others, and develops a detailed analysis of the forms of language and experience that this whiteness involves, and so her reading is a version of standpoint, phenomenology or the investigation of direct experience that is then accused by those who do not want to be disturbed and named as benefitting from racism as being 'too subjective'. Speaking about 'whiteness' as part of the apparatus of contemporary racism does mean drawing on experiences of exclusion, turning that experience into a resource, 'speaking truth to power' as Audre Lorde had it in her 1977 interventions about silence and action. But, as Ahmed and a new generation of black feminists have asked, do these 'declarations of whiteness' really do what they say they do; that is, are they 'performative' in the way we would expect radical political analysis to be, changing the world at the very moment of interpreting it; or are they 'non-performative', leaving the world of whiteness in place?

Claude Cahun's declaration of whiteness was performative,

for it was a declaration and deconstruction of whiteness at a time and place that framed her as a Jew. It was a frame she broke using surrealism. The surrealist movement in the first half of the twentieth century had its origins in 'Dada', a subversive playful artistic intervention into bourgeois culture in central Europe that celebrated its centenary in 2016. The main figures in Dada and surrealism that are remembered and commemorated are usually men, but many women were involved, and they made of it an activist critique of capitalism that was also often a critique of patriarchy. Dada, and the Cabaret Voltaire in Zurich which became one of its centres of operation, is part of our heritage of democratic and socialist politics.

Surrealism into which Dada mutated is also part of the specific heritage of Trotskyism. Some surrealist artists like Salvador Dalí became part of late twentieth-century commodity art culture, and it was a journey for Dalí that began with him selling out to fascism in Spain, for which he became known by the anagram 'Avida Dollars'. And some aspects of the surrealist reach into the unconscious using psychoanalysis have tended to simply reproduce sexist imagery instead of challenging it, a tendency that has made surrealism itself a poisoned chalice for some revolutionaries in the British section of the Fourth International in the 1970s when tempted to recycle some of the old well-worn motifs in the movement as a so-called 'surrealist challenge' to the left. But many surrealists in the 1930s were on the left, and many were sympathisers of, or then even members of the Fourth International. André Breton co-wrote with Trotsky a 'Manifesto for an Independent Revolutionary Art' in 1938, for example, which drew on surrealist arguments, and also connected with the non-psychoanalytic magical realist tradition in Mexico; the manifesto was signed by Breton and Diego Rivera who had provided refuge to Trotsky in Coyoacan, and ended with the slogan 'The revolution – for the complete liberation of art!'.

Claude Cahun's surrealist subversion of bourgeois culture around axes of gender and race led to her direct involvement in the surrealist movement and in the Fourth International. She was born Lucy Schwob in Nantes in 1892 the granddaughter of a rabbi from Frankfurt, but eventually settled on the sexually ambiguous name 'Claude Cahun' after some time experimenting in different kinds of relationship and with different forms of identity. Her partner was Suzanne Malberbe who became known as 'Marcel Moore', and they worked together on art projects and politically. She was, Michel Löwy points out in his 2010 essay on Cahun's Marxism in the book *Morning Star*, one of the only revolutionary women photographers in the surrealist movement, active in the Association des Ecrivains et Artistes Révolutionnaires in the early 1930s and one of the leaders of the left opposition inside that organisation, involved in protests against fascism through the 1930s. She moved to Jersey in the Channel Islands in 1937, but remained politically active, joining the International Federation for an Independent Revolutionary Art in 1938.

Claude Cahun's subversion of whiteness and of generalised racism took at least two forms. First, many of her self-images play on the ambiguity of masculine-feminine – her man's dress, shaved head and monocle apparently disturbed even the surrealists like Breton – and on what she was as a Jew, as something presumed to be white, but not quite. Some of the images push the whiteness itself to an extreme point of identification with stereotypes of the vampire-like uncanny Jew that at one moment is portrayed in anti-Semitic Western culture as being outside the pale of white civilisation and at the next as being dangerous precisely because the Jew hides, passes for white. Cahun's surrealist subversion of anti-Semitism embraces what is bad and ugly and shows us how it works. Cahun's second act of subversion took place in Jersey where, under Nazi occupation from 1940, she engaged with her partner Marcel in guerrilla-artistic attacks on the German soldiers. Claude and Marcel were known to their neighbours as the 'two sisters', and passed for many years under the occupation as harmless eccentrics until they were eventually arrested. The German occupation forces became convinced that there was a large-scale resistance movement on the island after being unable to track down bizarre messages to the soldiers that urged them to turn their guns on their officers, messages left in coat pockets, thrown through open car windows, or placed inside packets of cigarettes. Here there were surrealist elements of the messages, but the political strategy of appealing directly in propaganda to the soldiers was a Trotskyist one that had been enacted in Belgium, France and Germany. When arrested, Claude and Marcel were sentenced to death, and the German detention report notes that their house was full of 'ugly cubist' paintings and 'pornographic materials'. This was 1944, and they were eventually released with the end of the occupation and died some years later, Claude in 1954, Marcel in 1972, much of their artwork having been destroyed by their captors.

A deeper interpretation of 'whiteness' that does colour it in, acknowledge it and disturb the boundaries between what is white and non-white is also necessarily an anti-racist political struggle. Black feminist activists today know that from working through their own experience of living as bodies of colour, and their own experience of being told that they are the bodies of colour because they are not white. That is a 'phenomenological' political-theoretical resistance, reaching into experience and turning it into a resource. And, but, there was once and could be again another political-theoretical strategy of resistance that goes beneath what is given to us in this world as 'real', and that disrupts it. Surrealism once did that. That is why surrealism was once of such importance to the Fourth International. And that is why we should remember and honour the work of our Jewish lesbian-feminist anti-fascist surrealist comrade Claude Cahun.

Young-Girl

Young-Girl is a sexualised ideological motif and tool of consumerism. Her body takes the form of a commodity, a thing to be bought and sold, and she is invited, incited to be a beguiling youthful object targeted by the media and then marketed as a representation of all that is desirable, marketed to everybody else. This is 'Young-Girl' who enjoys shopping, indeed her life is organised by consumer culture, and for whom nothing is serious. She trivialises politics, and instead treats everything as 'cool'. This 'Young-Girl', according to the collective Tikkun, is the quintessence of the subject-object of contemporary capitalism, for while she is passed around the advertising media networks as a thing, she inhabits the body that is sold to her and in that way becomes a certain kind of subject, the perfect subject who knows her place; she is what Tikkun calls 'the anthropomorphosis of Capital'.

Tikkun identified the figure of 'Young-Girl' and then described and sarcastically mocked this figure at great length in their *Preliminary Materials For a Theory of the Young-Girl* first published in French in 1999. The collective no longer exists; they produced a few manifestos at the end of the 1990s and then dissolved in 2001. Fragments of the collective then reappeared in the Claire Fontaine art collective and in the 'Invisible Committee' which published the 2009 manifesto *The Coming Insurrection*. This later manifesto called, among other things, for the blocking of high-speed rail links, part of a strategy through which those who wanted to oppose Capital should 'jam everything'. The French state reacted in 2008 when they raided a house in Tarnac village and accused the ringleader of planning to destroy railway property and of directing a terrorist group.

Tikkun's influence lingers on in their name for the current crystallisation of the feminisation of capitalism, the way that women become sucked into the circuits of production and consumption and, at the very moment that they are cynically used to 'connect' with customers and give some erotic allure to products on the marketplace, told that this is the way they can be free. Tikkun picked up and recycled motifs from the Situationists' concern with recuperation, with the way that resistance has been turned into 'the society of the spectacle'. The spectacle, that which Tikkun renamed the regime of the 'semiocratic authorities' – those who are masters of 'semiotics', the science of signs in society – now directs its attention on a particular kind of subject, Young-Girl. The spectacle draws that subject in as the kind of being that will be 'happy' under consumer capitalism and will be more than willing to enact what the group called the 'imperialism of the trivial'.

A surprising aspect of this description and critique of Young-Girl is that Tikkun insist that she-it is not gendered, that this Young-Girl is also to be found in the pages of glossy men's magazines and in the aspirations of slick high-power professionals. They too, those who care for their muscles just as young girls are expected to want for silicone implants, are manifestations and living desiring embodiments of Young-Girl. There have been doubts as to whether this is all really so progressive. A translator of *Preliminary Materials* claimed, for example, that the original French text made her feel sick, that the text, from first exposing the way that Young-Girl was used by capitalism, then slid into a voyeuristic and sexist contempt for young girls themselves. The descriptions of the lurid way that the fantasy of Young-Girl had become a staple of consumerism were themselves turning into part of the problem Tikkun described. Feminist responses included pointing out that Young-Girl both 'parodied and mirrored misogyny'. Was there any space left for young girls themselves to be resistant self-conscious agents – in the figure of Riot Grrrl for example – or would this itself always become part of the spectacle, be turned into just another easily-marketable aspect of 'girl power'.

Which brings us to FEMEN, a movement that champions freedom of expression of young women, all women it would say, and does that by exposing and celebrating bodies which are then rubbed into the face of power, through spectacular insurrections against patriarchal institutions. FEMEN was founded in 2008 in Ukraine, initially to protest against sexual exploitation, particularly prostitution of young women who left the country to work abroad. The protests quickly involved topless young girls intervening in demonstrations or exposing themselves at public events with slogans written across their bodies. Russian imperial power in Ukraine was one high-profile target, including during a topless ambush of Putin who was being accompanied by Angela Merkel at a trade fair in Hanover, where protesters with 'Fuck the dictator' daubed across their torsos jumped over the security fence. Inna Shevchenko, one of the protesters at that event, part of a small group that had moved from Kiev to Berlin, claimed FEMEN were the 'shock troops of feminism'. In 2013 most of the leadership fled Kiev altogether following attacks by the authorities there and particularly, FEMEN claim, by the Russian security services. France then became the largest centre for FEMEN, staging protests in 2015, for example, against Marine Le Pen. The group had gained a lot of publicity in 2013 after a Tunisian supporter, Amina Sboui, was arrested in Tunis after a topless protest under the slogan 'Fuck your morals'. The 'Amina the FEMEN' case was supported by other socialist and feminist organisations in Tunisia, but with some reservations about the group's tactics, and Amina left FEMEN shortly afterwards, accusing it of Islamophobia.

The Amina case raised questions not only about FEMEN's tactics in what they referred to as their 'topless Jihad' but also about their broader political strategy and forms of organisation. There were plenty of protests against the Russian Orthodox Church in the early days of the movement when it was still mainly located in Ukraine, for example, but not so many against home-grown religious institutions, and when they turned their attention to Tunisia it seemed that some religions were worse than others. This has prompted suspicion that FEMEN's protests about the prostitution of Ukrainian young women trafficked abroad – protests that appear to include attacks on sex-workers themselves – were more than tinged with nationalism. There are even claims that FEMEN's involvement with the 2013 Maidan protests in Kiev and other cities – a contradictory movement that saw internal conflicts between the revolutionary left and neo-Nazi groups and also politically divided feminist intervention – was problematic, even that they were involved in the Odessa massacre a year later. This would be after they decamped to France leaving behind, they themselves say, barely forty activist members in Ukraine. The movement's supporters are clearly politically disparate, but there are powerful reminders here that women can be mobilised for fascism and defence of the nation state, as they can be against it.

Likewise, there are contradictory accounts of the founding of FEMEN, some reports tracing it to a woman Anna Hutsol, and others indicating that the leadership in the early days, at least, was directed by a man, Victor Svyatski. A 2013 documentary *Ukraine Is Not a Brothel* included interviews with FEMEN activists that showed them being politically-directed and instructed in how to protest, when and where. The claims about Svyatski's leadership have since led to some acknowledgement of his role and defensive accusations by Inna Shevchenko that this story is part of an attempt to undermine FEMEN.

What is irrefutable, evident in every protest, every publicity shoot that they themselves organise, and every marketing image for products on the FEMENshop official store, is that only stereo-typically feminine young white able-bodied women are the object-subjects of their form of 'feminism'. And in a world that valorises the young female body and demands that she display it, these young girls do exactly what they are told, and they speak back with their demands for 'freedom' written on their bodies.

FEMEN takes the motif of Young-Girl to its logical conclusion, but with a twist which is entirely compatible with a neoliberal emphasis on individual agency, and even with the promotion of forms of rebellion that play the rules of the game and re-energise the market. This is serious, marking a shift from a trivialisation of politics to making it one of the sites of action. This incitement of agency operates on the terrain of gender, religion and nation, enabling the destruction and reorganisation of capital accumulation under conditions of 'disaster capitalism'; Naomi Klein writ small, here written on the body.

While Tikkun saw Young-Girl as an idealised form of being who, for contemporary consumer society to function, needed to be cherished and protected – mobilised, for example, to warrant heightened security over her physical and moral health and something which leads to an increase in what the collective saw as the power of 'Police' alongside 'Publicity' – this new Young-Girl seems to speak for herself. These objects whose bodies are unwrapped and sold as commodities under capitalism are no longer compliant and trivial. But they still take up the position that has been given to them, and they speak from within it, a defiant force that confirms the very forms of patriarchal power it claims to disrupt.

Zionism

Zionism is racist expansionism as a false response to anti-Semitism. And anti-Semitism is always present around it. The day before Rania Masri spoke in Manchester in March 2015 about Boycott, Divestment and Sanctions (BDS) against Israel, jazz saxophonist Gilad Atzmon announced that the plugs had been pulled on his concert at the Royal Northern College of Music the same week. Atzmon blamed the 'Zionist lobby', George Galloway tweeted that the cancellation was 'a book burning', and an audience member in Masri's talk raised the issue, suggesting that this was a case of censorship against anti-Zionists. 'Zionism' means different things depending on the political position of those using it as a term of abuse or identity, and confusion about what it means has some deadly consequences.

Masri had made as the core of her talk an analysis of the intimate connection between the brutal treatment of Palestinians by the Israeli state, the racist murders of Black people in the United States and increasing sexual violence. She argued that colonial domination always entails violence against women, and she cited the Black lesbian feminist Audre Lorde to call for an ethics of connection between the oppressed. Zionism, she said, was 'ethnocratic' domination, a form of apartheid in which one group of those defining themselves as Jews has claimed the land of Israel as their own, as theirs by right, and is intent on reducing the Palestinians to nothing. She described the way Israeli racism is expressed in sexual abuse of Palestinian women and against children. For her it was clear, Zionism is racism.

There is a tragedy at the heart of Zionism as a political project, a tragedy that has then expanded incrementally as it has been implemented and defended. It is a term that has a history whose meaning has changed in the last century. Zionism was actually, in the early years of the twentieth century, a response to racism, an attempt to define an identity and a safe place for Jews subject to anti-Semitic pogroms in Eastern Europe. It was not a religious response but a secular one running parallel with and at times in debate with revolutionary socialist politics. While Marxism offered a politics which explicitly opposed anti-Semitism in the name of internationalism, an approach which most often dissolves identity, Zionism was one of a number of nationalist responses to oppression that made identity into its centrepiece, an identity that turned from being a progressive force into a reactionary one when it was implanted in Israel.

Zionism was a response to anti-Semitism, and still is. Anti-Semitism, as revolutionary Marxists ranging from Abram Leon (in his 1950 posthumously published book *The Jewish Question* after his murder by the Nazis) to Ernest Mandel and many others besides argued, is the legacy of pre-capitalist forms of political-economic organisation and, with the rise of fascism, an aspect of capitalism itself which reveals its nature as something barbaric. The logic of capitalism under threat was to mobilise murderous hatred against the Jews, against those who were assigned a specific economic function as capitalism developed, who were locked into the role of money-lender. The enemy of capitalism was then personified by the Nazis in the figure of the 'Bolshevik Jew'. With the founding of the State of Israel, and today as it occupies more and more Palestinian land as a settler-colonial state, Zionism as a mistaken response to anti-Semitism becomes deadly to anti-Zionist Jews inside Israel who oppose the occupation and support calls for BDS, and those activists are then accused by the Zionists as being 'self-hating', with escalating calls for the murder of 'Palestinians and Leftists'.

Zionism is a nationalist and expansionist ideology that feeds on anti-Semitism, drawing on it, tolerating it when necessary to legitimise its own racist laws which exclude the Palestinians from their own land. It is in this particular sense that it is correct to say that Zionists make use of the Holocaust; many Zionists continuously evoke the Holocaust to evoke fear among Jews that the same will happen again, that they must leave Europe to be safe in Israel (which is a really bizarre and irrational argument), and to silence, through accusations of racism and by evoking guilt among non-Jews, those who dare to speak out against what Israel is doing to the Palestinians today.

And Zionism also reinforces anti-Semitism, sometimes deliberately and instrumentally (as in its collusion with attacks on Jews in Arab countries to persuade them that they should come to Israel), and sometimes as the mirror image of what it denounces (in its own attacks on leftists and liberals who object to the excesses of the occupation). Here the worst of the inevitable intersection between racist violence and other forms of violence, including sexual violence, are once again evident. Just as Jews were both demonised and feminised, treated as subhuman in histories of Christian anti-Semitism in Europe and rendered into passive victims in the ideological justifications for the Holocaust (a toxic irrational mixture of them as manipulative and pathetic), so the assertion of the macho Zionists in Israel entails the demonisation and feminisation of Palestinian 'terrorists' and those who support them (again, of the enemy as devious and so all the more dangerous).

Then there are forms of 'anti-Zionism' which fit the bill of Zionists who are quick to accuse anyone who supports the Palestinians of being anti-Semitic. It should be no surprise that there would be, as with every most ridiculous aspect of left politics in times characterised by our weakness and so also then by our stupid sectarianism, those who will step in to back up what Israel accuses its enemies of. Atzmon is a case in point, and his championing of 'anti-Zionism' should be seen for what it is, the kind of argument that is uncannily close to what it pretends to expose. With respect to sexual violence, for example, the reaction by Atzmon to the protests inside the Socialist Workers Party following rape accusations against Martin Smith as a 'Jazz lover' was to claim that Smith was the real 'rape victim' being brought down because he didn't obey 'his tribal masters' or the 'Jewish demand' to ban Atzmon. Galloway was also on form with his own defence of Atzmon, a comment which followed the list he gave at a speech of those who, he said, were victims of the Paris attacks on *Charlie Hebdo* and the Jewish supermarket as 'shoppers, workers, workers in a shop, police officers, Muslims, Christians, atheists, journalists'. There is no mention of the Jewish victims.

With false friends like these, it is all the more important to insist that the struggle against Zionism is also necessarily a struggle against anti-Semitism, which is why Palestinian activists have denounced Atzmon, and why we should not put our energies into supporting him. The anti-Semitic attacks on Jews by so-called 'Islamofascists' not only play into Islamophobic racism, not only turn anti-Zionist political struggle into a religious war, but also directly reinforce Israel, forging a close identification between Jews and Zionism. That close identification between Jews and Zionism is crucial to Israel's attempt to present opposition to it as anti-Semitic, and that identification is broken every time Jews speak out for and with Palestinians. A Marxist and intersectional analysis of Zionism, very much of the kind that Masri offered in her talk, is crucial to enable us to avoid a twin evil. We stand against anti-Semitism which is poisonous to the BDS movement, and we stand against the Israeli state which, among its other crimes, endangers Jews everywhere, something which only solidarity with the Palestinians can address. This solidarity must be solidarity with all the oppressed that enlarges and so also strengthens the struggle against exploitation internationally and in each separate national context. This is the kind of solidarity that a reworking of 'Zionism' as an old keyword enables us to build as a new revolutionary keyword today.

Revolutionary Keywords for a New Left

The keywords in this book speak of new ways forward that have emerged through anti-capitalist struggle and a number of different crises. These are crises that we should see as opportunities rather than only as problems. The question is how to reconfigure them so that they speak for us rather than against us, how they might enable us to rebuild resistance to a contemporary capitalist order based on systemic and systematic exploitation and oppression. These crises are opportunities precisely because they intersect with each other, and to grasp how they intersect is a key task. These crises do cause problems for some of the underlying assumptions some on the left have got used to making about politics, underlying assumptions about the nature of revolutionary change. The effect of these crises may then be disturbing and demoralising, and it is tempting to respond by trying to go back to opposition to capitalism as usual. But at the same time, these crises open up new ways of relating radical theory to practice, of linking theoretical reflection to the world, to changing it.

These current crises entail some significant ruptures between dominant frameworks and institutions on the one hand, and some new alliances among the anti-capitalist opposition on the other. We can set these four levels of crisis against the background of a political-economic order, capitalism, in which crisis as such is endemic; it is an order that provokes and feeds off disorder. Capitalism needs shock after shock, disruption and misery to break people and make them ready to accept each new transformation of the system to yield more profit. This political-economic domain sets the conditions for the intersecting crises we are concerned with here, though they do not directly reflect those conditions. That is one reason we need theory. We need to be able to step back and analyse what is happening, and when we

251

face new unexpected transformations of capitalism as it re-energises itself at the cost of our health and our lives we use theory condensed in new analytical concepts to do that.

This book is about what we can do with those intersecting crises, and about the new vocabularies that have been emerging to articulate political practice with theory. These new vocabularies of resistance have been grounded first in political practice, and then they have been elaborated theoretically. Some of these new keywords that have appeared in the last fifty years draw on academic debate; they draw on concepts formed in activist spaces in and between the academic disciplines, for example. They speak of political practice and they also speak of crises in the social and human sciences. There are, of course, attempts by some academics to appropriate these arguments and turn them into something that those inside the universities will recognise as valid 'social science'. And there are corresponding attempts by some political activists outside the universities to resist these new vocabularies by complaining that they are merely academic. One danger is that in doing that, old activists find an excuse for not taking them seriously, for avoiding new theory, for not thinking.

Changing contexts

There are four aspects of the changing contexts for resisting capitalism that have to be articulated, that need to be grasped as they intersect with each other. The time frame I will use to sketch these is the century of revolutions that begins in 1917 with the October revolution in Russia, and I divide this century into a first fifty years that ends in 1967 and fifty years which brings us up to the present day. 1917 is a year which opens up some new ways of working through where we have got to and where to go next. It is the next fifty years, from 1967 to the 2017 anniversary of the October revolution that lays the basis for questioning, extending and re-elaborating Marxist analysis alongside other forms of theory.

The first aspect of context is the consolidation and disintegration of the Soviet Union. 1917 provides an anchor point for it marks a significant moment in history. It is so important to us that '1917' also operates as one password in left political debate. The first fifty years after 1917 saw the consolidation first of the revolutionary regime in Russia and then of the bureaucracy, first the Bolshevik seizure of power and the flourishing of debate under Lenin, and then the closing down of internal party democracy as the police apparatus crystallised around Stalin. We see a consequent shift of emphasis in the phrase 'democratic centralism' from an emphasis on democracy to an emphasis instead on centralisation. This is a process of consolidation of the Soviet Union as a false alternative to capitalism which demanded obedience on the part of those who were members of the Communist Parties organised in the Third International (the 'Communist International' or 'Comintern'). It is a process that provoked debate among those who broke from Stalinism and who suspected that this 'alternative' was itself, at best, a bureaucratically degenerate workers state or, at worst, a form of state capitalism. We should acknowledge here that both Lenin and Trotsky played an ambiguous role in the consolidation of the bureaucracy during the time of military mobilisation to defend the revolution, under 'war communism'. This ambiguous role had profound consequences after 1967 both for Trotskyists and for those on the libertarian left who wanted a deeper historical analysis of what 'Marxism' itself meant after, for example, the tragic events of Kronstadt (the rebellion by sailors in the fortress near Petrograd who had first supported the revolution and then been incited by the counter-revolutionary forces to turn against the Bolsheviks).

You can see here already that it is impossible to review this history without using a series of passwords for participating in left debate, passwords like '1917', 'Bolshevik' and 'Kronstadt' that enable us to discuss and dispute with each other. These passwords are charged with effect for those who hear and use them. These are terms that still today either evoke romantic nostalgic images of the good old revolutionary times, as if a return to 1917 would solve all our problems, or which spark suspicion and doubt about organised political opposition to capitalism, suspicion of any parties that might make the mistakes the Bolsheviks made.

The fracturing of the Stalinist fake alternative to the rule of capital began way before 1967, of course. Stalinism was not a monolith, and there was vicious disagreement about how to maintain the power of the bureaucratic layer that formed in the early 1920s. Other local bureaucratic rival power blocs appeared in Eastern Europe – Yugoslav self-styled 'self-management socialism' became one important resource for how to think critically in and against Stalinism – and in China. Something important then happened in China in 1966 and for the next few years, events during the so-called 'Cultural Revolution'. The Stalinist bureaucracy there both revealed itself to be a harsh caricature of the Soviet model it defied and, with Mao taking the lead in the events to mobilise support for his own position in the Communist Party, some leaders also cynically incited new revolutionary student movements to the left of the bureaucracy. The Cuban revolution in 1959 had already provided another pole of attraction within and against Stalinism, and that had forced some realignment by the Soviet bureaucracy to maintain control over Communist Parties directed from Moscow through the 'Cominform' as successor to the Comintern from 1947. One question the Cultural Revolution posed in China, and then in similar movements inspired by it that mimicked the activities of the Red Guards, was the relationship between knowledge and power. This relationship between knowledge and power is something that recurs again and again as new revolutionary keywords have developed to make sense of the past and open new paths to the future.

The second aspect of context concerns what counted as culture on the left, or what came to function as left culture. The 'Cultural Revolution' marked a shift in the axes of left critique, with 'culture' itself now operating as a battleground. But even before that break, with 1967 as a turning point when the student revolt in China began to galvanise other movements around the world, the first fifty years of revolution after 1917 saw mobilisation and then demoralisation in the field of culture on the left. This mobilisation and demoralisation was crucial to the success and failure of revolutionary movements inside Russia and worldwide.

Inside Russia, and across the domain of the Soviet republics from 1917, there was experimentation with new social forms, experimentation which included socialisation of childcare and the reconfiguring of the family, and new forms of culture including architecture, music and art. Crucial to sustaining and spreading the revolution, for example, was 'Agitprop', but the revolution in art also included many figures who were not actually Bolsheviks. The work of Kazimir Malevich, founder of Suprematism, is just one case of an art movement which became part of the revolutionary new wave. This impact of the revolution in art continued and proliferated through the 1920s and 1930s, eventually including the surrealist movement. That was an art movement which rebelled against Stalinism and even briefly, under the leadership of André Breton, connected with Trotsky who appears to have actually written most of André Breton and Diego Rivera's 'Manifesto for an Independent Revolutionary Art' while he was in exile shortly before his death in Mexico.

Outside Russia, and apart from surrealism, which was viewed with suspicion by those who were members or fellow travellers of the local Communist Parties loyal to the Soviet Union, culture was absolutely vital to maintaining left movements. Reading groups operated alongside cycling and walking clubs, and there were many different special interest groups that drew in artists and writers and which provided a context for circulation of avant-garde Soviet film and literature. These were forums for cultural production and consumption that made the claim that Russia was the centre of a new post-capitalist world more credible. It is important to remember that Marxism was not conceived in these years as merely a critique of political economy or as a theory of the party as a 'Leninist' organisation. Marxism encompassed a range of diverse cultural practices. What it meant to speak of 'ideology' thus went far beyond a simple critique of 'false consciousness', as if individuals who had different ideas about society were simply mistaken. The focus on ideological production as part of the so-called 'superstructure' of society was not at all seen as secondary to the transformation of the real economic base. In fact, there were repeated reminders that the field of 'spiritual production', as Marx himself named it, had a reciprocal effect on the field of economics. We can see this even in Stalin's argument that language was not simply part of the super-structure and in Trotsky's many interventions in popular culture, art and literature.

The third aspect of context concerns transformations that were taking place in capitalism itself. These were transformations that sharpened the sense of those working in the field of Marxist theory that the traditional categories of analysis had to be reshaped. There was, first, the argument that Marxism as such was a theory and practice of class struggle that was particularly relevant to capitalism, as a theory that was formed under capitalism in order to comprehend and overthrow it.

The consequences of this argument included accepting that other forms of oppression – those concerning gender, for example – may need other specific forms of theoretical analysis and political organisation. There was recognition that Marx had not completed his analysis of capitalism when he died, and there was plenty of work to be done to address questions of consumption alongside production, to take just one instance. The consequences of this argument included the thought that what counts as a

'Marxist' critique may in fact er'
analysis beyond classical po?
the critique. That is where some
tions have been so valuable. An¢
critique was the acknowledgement t.
oping system of production, one which ¸
it spread around the world, and was ada
impact of different technological developmeı.

and transfo
called 'e
includes
'feminiı
organiı
critiø
coı
mı
aø

One important consequence of this ackno¸
capitalism was continually transforming itself waṣ
that a 'third industrial revolution' had changed tı.
manual and intellectual labour operated in the pı
process. The first industrial revolution rested on steam
and laid the material basis for early capitalist production.
second industrial revolution enabled the spread of capitaliṣ
through the development of the railroad and telegraph system.
This second industrial revolution also provided the impetus for
and much Agitprop imagery for the Russian Revolution,
including Lenin's claim that Soviet power plus electrification
would together effectively amount to communism. The third
industrial revolution based on automation of the production
process saw the rise of the service sector, a vast array of new institutions relying on 'people skills' in shops, call centres and leisure
industries. This had profound consequences for the way that
Marxism intersected with resistance to other forms of oppression.

The rise of the service sector saw the re-entry of women into
the workforce – they had always been there as the core of the
workforce at the beginning of capitalism – but now they were
there not merely as manual or clerical workers, not just participating in the old traditional male workforce. This new workforce
in the service sector is valued for particular abilities, capacities
for the care of others which are crucial to the building of affective
links between commercial enterprises and their customers. The
increasing emphasis on intellectual labour becomes augmented

ormed in the service sector by a focus on what has been
motional labour'. In this way late capitalism also
and exploits women as women, but this so-called
sation' of production in the service sector and in other
sations is very different from feminist critique, feminist
ue which then necessarily becomes a crucial component or
plement of Marxist analysis. In fact, the suspicion among
ny feminists on the left has long been that this feminisation
tually re-energises capitalism and buttresses patriarchy.

The fourth aspect of changing context which intersects with
these first three – the consolidation and disintegration of the
Soviet Union, the development of forms of left culture, and the
internal transformation of capitalist production with the rise of
the service sector – is the transformation of the left opposition to
capitalism itself. The re-emergence of internal critique with the
left opposition to the Soviet invasion of Hungary in 1956 led to
calls for and then interventions in what then became known as
the 'new left'. Left non-Stalinist or anti-Stalinist intellectual
forums (in which we can include the reorganisation of *New Left
Review* in 1962 and the foundation of the *Socialist Register* in 1964)
did not immediately include feminist critique alongside Marxist
arguments. But by the late 1960s, the emergence of an
autonomous women's liberation movement was forcing feminism
on to the agenda, including inside the left. 1967 is often marked
in the history of the women's liberation movement as the year in
which first important meetings took place in the United States,
and from 1967 these kinds of meetings took place around the
world.

The so-called 'new left' drew together a range of different
resources to comprehend how Marxism in practice in the Soviet
Union had turned into an ideology of the state apparatus. It also
looked to innovative theoretical frameworks to build resistance
to capitalism. These analyses and practices entailed quite
different theoretical reference points, often way beyond or even

antagonistic to Marxism as such. In many Marxist groups there have been consequent attempts to take on board feminist arguments and radical debates over sexuality, culture, racism and, more latterly, ecology. Each internal transformation of what counts as 'revolutionary' has changed the language of Marxism, the keywords it uses to define itself. This has connected revolutionary Marxists with movements that describe exploitation and oppression in quite distinctive ways, leading often to incomprehension about what is happening, and sometimes genuine puzzlement and constructive debate.

The Place of Theory

Before our 'revolutionary century', that is, before 1917, a good deal of radical knowledge production, of theory that connected directly with the process of not only interpreting but also of changing the world, occurred outside academic institutions. Gentlemen scholars and scientists were usually men, usually men of independent means. When they were not rich, they either needed wealthy patrons to support their work or they drew on the resources of local clubs and societies. Marx's dependence on Engels sending banknotes through the post from Manchester to London was just one case toward the end of the nineteenth century of radical work being funded by well-wishers and by those in solidarity with the need to develop independent forms of organisation.

The October revolution not only divided Marxist revolutionary knowledge production from forms of academic work outside Russia that pretended to be more 'neutral' and properly scientific, a split that seemed to separate proletarian from bourgeois institutions. More importantly, it intensified the separation in both domains, that is, inside and outside the Soviet Union, between the academic apparatus and revolutionary 'praxis', between academic description and theory directly interwoven with the activity of changing the world it interpreted. The rise of the Stalinist bureaucracy and the caricature of scientific research to be found in the wacky 'proletarian science' of Lysenko's genetics, for example, had the effect not only of determining what would count as knowledge inside the Soviet Union. It also deepened the ideological separation outside the Soviet Union between so-called 'traditional intellectuals' (who were supposed to be disinterested in the subjects of their research, and so better adapted to producing objective knowledge which took the existing world for granted as something that could not or should not be changed), and 'organic intellectuals' who were obviously and more immediately responding to the needs of the class they were part of. This is a distinction that was important to the work of the Italian Marxist Antonio Gramsci. Traditional intellectuals are content to describe the world without taking a stand, and so they effectively give legitimacy to the way things are. Revolutionaries are organic intellectuals who develop theory in alliance with the exploited and oppressed to end capitalism itself.

Early attempts to directly link revolutionary theory and practice inside the Soviet Union, to develop an institute of 'red professors' after the revolution, were eventually suppressed. After a series of purges of Trotskyists in the 1920s and 1930s this particular institute which initially functioned under the auspices of Agitprop was finally abolished in 1938 and its functions absorbed within the central committee of the Communist Party. That institute was initially seen as one base, an alternative to the universities, from which to build a cadre of progressive academics. In the fifty years after 1917, however, the university became one of the most important sites for knowledge production, and so the separation of the academic apparatus from revolutionary praxis was accompanied by an enclosure of knowledge by the university. It became a university system that inside the Soviet Union had to show loyalty to whatever was in fashion in social science, and outside the Soviet Union had to adopt the posture of the traditional intellectuals. Radical academics in Western European universities had a little more leeway for critique, but the so-called 'visible college' of radical social scientists in the 1930s often defined and constrained them within an understanding of 'socialism' linked closely to the Soviet Union that turned them into scientific fellow-travellers of their local Communist Party.

The separation between Eastern and Western blocs functioned to enforce the separation between the academic apparatus and revolutionary praxis. This was something that was often invisible to those within the network of the so-called visible college until critics of Stalinism fleeing Eastern Europe made it more visible when they tried and failed get an academic post; the fate of Isaac Deutscher, revolutionary three-volume biographer of Trotsky who failed to get an academic position when he fled to Britain, is a case in point. But this separation also enforced other forms of separation and enclosure which defined how academics understood what 'science' and 'social science' were. In the Soviet Union the 'science' in question was assumed to be resolved by dialectical materialism of some kind, and outside it in the bourgeois universities it often took the form of 'positivism', sometimes pragmatism or empiricism. Under the banner of 'order and progress', positivism is an approach to scientific knowledge that endorses the idea that social science simply accumulates knowledge about the world. It is an ideal approach to scientific work for traditional intellectuals. That slogan 'order and progress' that expresses so well the spirit of positivism even served as a slogan that became important to nation-building. In Brazil, for example, Auguste Comte's slogan is still inscribed on the flag. In the United States, pragmatism, a 'can do' approach to knowledge that is simply concerned with what works, operated in line with an optimistic frontier spirit that valued any knowledge that delivered the goods. And in Britain, so-called 'English empiricism' (which was actually one of the fruits of the

Scottish Enlightenment) valued only what can actually be observed, and once again knowledge then served to ratify what we already know to be the case, scorning activity that would take us to a world beyond the one that already exists.

What these forms of academic knowledge have in common is an assumed separation between scientific Enlightenment as the province of the West and the so-called 'uncivilised' world. Then there is a harnessing of knowledge to the colonial project so that Marxism also comes to operate as part of the academic apparatus. This assumption about history and geography is played out in the broad sweep of historical development propagated in Stalinist 'stage theory', a distortion of Marxism in which first there is slavery, then capitalism and only then socialism. This sequence underpinned a theory which not only ratified the Soviet Union as leading edge of civilised 'development' but also became a useful tool of Soviet diplomatic manoeuvres in relation to different regimes. The local Communist Parties were instructed to support this or that supposedly 'progressive' bourgeois force against reactionary elements and put off the struggle against capitalism as such until later on, effectively blocking such struggle. This distortion of Marxism continues today with the added tragic spectacle of former admirers of the Soviet Union under Stalin justifying the twists and turns of capitalist Russia's foreign policy under Putin. The colonial project of the academic apparatus is then also played out in both Western and Soviet forms of anthropology and education with attempts to 'understand' in order to better manage backward cultures rendered as 'other' to the West.

There is a further separation that should be noted, and it takes us from the world of the gentlemen scientists before 1917 to a conception of science linked to the stereotypically masculine endeavour to predict and control phenomena. Part of the struggle to democratise the university system after 1967 then necessarily also became a feminist struggle to assert the value of women's subjugated knowledge and to link this struggle with the anti-colonial project. Critical reflection on the role of the university as an academic apparatus entailed expanding the domain of the exploited and oppressed to include their 'allies', allies that turned the 'red bases' inside the universities during the student protests of the 1960s into bases for many different kinds of revolutionary movement.

The student protests in the universities and the colleges revealed, among other things, the gap between radical theory inside the academic institutions and 'praxis', theory linked directly with practice which would impact upon the real world outside. This was something that was already apparent to those who were excluded from the universities or who refused enclosure by them, but became more obvious in the response of some radical professors who wrote about Marxism to the protests. The very task of connecting academic knowledge with activity spoke of the separation between theory and practice that had been operating in German 'Critical Theory', for example. The complaint against so-called 'structuralist' theory in France, that it replaced change with an abstracted philosophy of order, drew attention to the same problem. The attempt to develop forms of 'autonomist' Marxism in Italy grappled with exactly that issue. In Britain, the field of intellectual work was so impoverished, left in the hands of the conservative 'traditional intellectuals', that one of the projects of the academic left was to import continental European Marxist theory as an urgent task (and that's what *New Left Review* was up to for some time).

What these developments point to is the importance of a vocabulary for the left, a shared language that enables us to carry out analyses of capitalism that entail change, analyses that define our political tasks. Now we will turn to the way the very map of 'keywords' for radical politics has changed. The changes, the transformations in definition and the tasks that are then mapped out for us, are as important as the continuity in struggle. The continuity in struggle is still crucially important, of course, and we should learn the lessons of history in order that we do not simply repeat it. We must learn the lessons of history, but those lessons lie as much in the competing systems of revolutionary theory inside and alongside Marxism as in the events they describe. That revolutionary theory is articulated in language, and how we describe the world has consequences for how we think we can change it. We have access to the events themselves through the forms of language used by radicals to make sense of the world, and the changes in left language have subtly altered how we conceptualise political-economic structures and the historical process. We can begin to map how the language of the left, and not only the 'social-scientific' academic left, has changed by examining the clusters of 'keywords' that define progressive discourse. It is exactly in that way that we will come closest to an understanding of the world that really enables us to change it.

Keywords before 1917

We can begin by briefly mapping keywords of progressive culture prior to our revolutionary century, prior to 1917. One way of doing this is to take up fifty of the terms defined by the 'cultural Marxist' Raymond Williams in his book *Keywords: A Vocabulary of Culture and Society* in 1976. His book, a rather academic reflection on progressive culture, traced the historical origins and changes of terms like 'capitalism' and 'equality' over the course of several centuries. He showed not only how the meanings of the terms have changed but also how they began to interlink to provide the basis of a socialist culture. 1976 was a convenient point in time for Williams to be able to reflect on and describe for us how this vocabulary had taken on a certain kind of shape before 1967. The book began as an appendix cut, before publication, from his earlier 1958 book *Culture and Society*. The historical scope of the project is much grander than that, and this is why it is also useful to cue us into terms that come to be embedded in culture before 1917. Williams is useful here precisely because he embeds his analysis in broader social and political transformations of culture as capitalism is gathering strength and becoming the dominant system in Europe and then globally.

I will take fifty keywords defined by Williams from about a hundred that comprise his book, and I select these because they most directly concern the intersection of social scientific and socialist politics. I leave aside, for example, other terms he explores like 'behaviour', 'dramatic', 'empirical', 'literature' and 'sensibility'. These are all terms with a history, and it's worth bearing in mind that they each then carry with them particular culturally-specific assumptions about the nature of the world and about historical change itself. The term 'sociology' appears in the book, and is relevant to our discussions of the place of social science, but it actually tends to obstruct rather than take forward the project of the left, as can be seen in the fate of some left groups who are led by sociologists. Sociology as a way of describing the world which is embedded in the universities actually operates much of the time as an alternative or rival to that project of the left. This is an issue that we need to reflect upon, and is part of the problem of academicisation, the turning of our practical knowledge into academic description.

Two aspects of Williams' keywords are important here. The first aspect is what they each are as such, and through them you can get a sense of what begins to become important in a culture in which socialist politics figures as a theory and practice. But the second aspect, which is even more important, is how they cluster together to define the terrain on which we argue and act. You might object to the inclusion of some of these terms and other terms may occur to you that you think should be included. Then you might also object to the map I give of them. But here goes, and here, in *Figure 1: Keywords before 1917*, it is only a first sketch which clusters together keywords into ten groups of five.

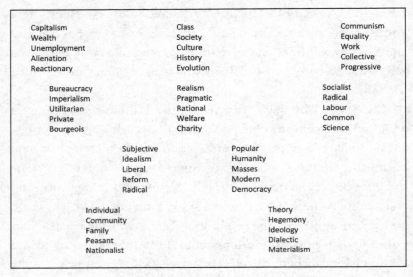

Capitalism	Class	Communism
Wealth	Society	Equality
Unemployment	Culture	Work
Alienation	History	Collective
Reactionary	Evolution	Progressive
Bureaucracy	Realism	Socialist
Imperialism	Pragmatic	Radical
Utilitarian	Rational	Labour
Private	Welfare	Common
Bourgeois	Charity	Science

	Subjective	Popular
	Idealism	Humanity
	Liberal	Masses
	Reform	Modern
	Radical	Democracy

Individual	Theory
Community	Hegemony
Family	Ideology
Peasant	Dialectic
Nationalist	Materialism

Figure 1: Keywords before 1917

A first cluster defines phenomena, beginning with 'capitalism', that come to operate as negative terms. They each mark out characteristics of the world that are problematic. As socialist politics takes shape in the nineteenth century a range of other keywords become connected with capitalism, of which we can mention 'wealth' and 'unemployment' – two terms that are not necessarily bad things for the classical political economists Marx was arguing with – and 'alienation' (our separation from our own creative activity) along with what it is to be 'reactionary'. These are terms that begin to anchor progressive politics. On the other side there are keywords that cluster together an image of what is positive, what we would aim for; this is named as 'communism' and is pitted against terms from classical political economy like 'equality' and 'work', and it offers the hope of 'collective' activity which is named as 'progressive'. These are terms that still today provide the grounds for much left political debate, terms we need to use to be able to maintain and develop a left culture. These are passwords that someone coming into revolutionary politics in a campaign or as a member of a group uses in a way that makes the same kind of sense to their friends, their comrades in struggle. It is enough that they make the same kind of sense, even if there are disputes over exactly how you define them. Those disputes are the life-blood of the left when they are carried out in comradely and respectful ways.

Then there is a cluster of terms that operate alongside the bad things, helping to fill out an analysis of what exactly is wrong about them, terms like 'bureaucracy', 'imperialism' and 'utilitarian' (concerned only with what is most efficient to keep production and society running smoothly), as well as what it is to keep property as 'private' and the naming of what is 'bourgeois' in society and culture that is dedicated to justifying capitalism (and to name the bourgeoisie as the ruling class under capitalism that displaces the old aristocratic masters under feudalism). This cluster is mirrored by terms which define what is progressive, which include 'socialist', a 'radical' tradition which takes 'labour' as a reference point, that which is devoted to what is kept in 'common' and which can be described using 'science'. The mirroring does not operate on a one-to-one basis in which what is bad can be directly pitted against what is good, or what might replace it. This isn't how the map is being patched together. What is interesting about the other clusters of terms is that some of them define the terrain on which the political battle takes place – terms like 'class', 'society', 'culture', 'history' and 'evolution' – while others are more obviously unavoidable terms over which there is a battle of ideas, for meaning, which will define how they will come to operate in progressive or reactionary discourse; these words would include terms like 'realism', 'pragmatic' and 'rational' and phenomena like 'welfare' and 'charity'.

In some cases the terms are recognised to be problematic, and the battle to reject them as they are commonly understood becomes an urgent task, as is the case with 'subjective', 'idealism', 'liberal', 'reform', or 'radical'. (What is 'subjective' as concerning what someone perceives or feels about the world is linked with 'idealism', an approach which treats ideas about the world as being more important than the world itself.) In other cases there is an assumed positive value to the terms which need to be reasserted, as with 'popular', 'humanity', 'masses', 'modern' and 'democracy'. Some terms Williams defines become part of the apparatus of progressive analysis, and take on a positive meaning within left discourse, and here we find terms like 'theory', 'hegemony' (the domination of certain assumptions about the nature of society), 'ideology', 'dialectic' and 'materialism'. Other terms draw attention to phenomena that are rather suspect and that need to be grasped precisely in order to locate and analyse them; here we find terms like 'individual' and 'community' as well as 'family', 'peasant' and 'nationalist'.

In many cases, and this is one of the surprises in Williams' book as well as one of the points of the cultural analysis he provides, the terms have a much longer history than we might suspect, and so they carry with them a value or meaning that then affects how we understand, use and debate, how we work with them or against them. This also, at the same time, makes it difficult sometimes to recognise that these are quite particular terms that define how we understand ourselves as wanting to stand against power. One of the points to notice about these clusters of terms is that there are still some important battles taking place as to what each of the keywords means. Very few of them are unequivocally good or bad when they are used before 1917, and what we now recognise as the socialist tradition in politics has to bit-by-bit fill them with progressive content. Then we can better understand the things they are referring to so we know better how to agree or disagree with the judgement that is being made about them.

An important part of the struggle for us on the left over these keywords still concerns how we fill them with capitalist or communist sense. That is, many of these keywords, even though they are fifty that I have selected as relevant to left discourse, still also operate within the more general field of liberal bourgeois politics. That is a kind of politics that accepts the existence of capitalism within the terms the bourgeoisie would prefer, and chatters about the terms, as in the mainstream newspaper columns. These keywords mean something also to us on the left, but we have to insist on their particular meanings for us as we articulate them together in socialist, feminist and anti-racist politics. The key task today is to examine and work through revolutionary keywords from fifty years of struggle after 1967, and so to engage with the innovative forms of knowledge that developed in the new social movements. But before we turn to the constellations of keywords that are now redefining left discourse we need to show what this new vocabulary of the left was building on and transforming after 1917.

Keywords of the first fifty years after 1917

The legacy of the first fifty years after 1917 lives on in the language and practice of left movements and organisations, and so in the way we relate theory to practice. This is, in part, precisely because October 1917 operates as a key reference point in our left discourse which anchors our analyses and then from which unfolds our understanding of what capitalism is. These fifty keywords I draw from my own reading and history in left politics since the 1970s, and so they are even more schematic and partial than the list I gleaned from Raymond Williams. And these keywords, of course, are refracted through the way politics has developed since 1967, that is in the last fifty years of political struggle. Where we are now cannot but filter the way we under-stand the past; that is also why history itself is a battleground of the left. Summaries and prospects for revolutionary struggle have been shaped by these terms, but we must ask two questions about these clusters of keywords. The first is whether they are sufficient, and then the second which naturally flows from that first question is what new keywords we need to use now to map again what capitalism is and how effective opposition to it should be defined. These keywords operate as windows on the world, they enable us to see the nature of capitalist society and other forms of oppression, and they operate as a frame, they restrict what we have been able to describe and how we can intervene.

As we cluster these keywords emerging after 1917 together – in *Figure 2: Keywords after 1917* – we notice three other aspects about their interrelated meanings. The first is that the clusters are more easily organised in a grid, they both fall more neatly into a spectrum. They seem to define more directly what we are against and what we aim for in left struggle. The second aspect is that these clusters are more closely tied to the particular struggle against capitalism as such, they either come to define it as the main enemy or they function as adjuncts to the struggle against capital. Instead of simply defining what it is to be 'progressive', they begin to spell out what it is to be anti-capitalist. The third aspect is that they either explicitly or implicitly become more closely tied to academic definition, and here we see the conse-

Capitalism →	Bourgeoisie →	Democracy →	Proletariat	→	Collectivism
Imperialism	Reification	Reform	Class		Planning
Exploitation	Utopianism	Science	Industrialisation		Soviet
Commodity	Fabianism	Entrism	Leninism		Marxism
Individualism	Stalinism	Feminism	Trotskyism		Bolshevik
Colonialism →	Nationalism →	Maoism →	Internationalism	→	Liberation
Reaction	Populism	Castroism	Dialectic		Communism
Fascism	Pragmatism	Humanism	Theory		Materialism
Oppression	Anarchism	Syndicalism	Revolution		Progress
Feudalism	Ideology	Socialism	Party		Practice

Figure 2: Keywords after 1917

quences of the institutional and semiotic capture of left debate by the universities. In some cases it is even possible to trace a direct line through the series of five terms which mark what is bad and what is good.

I will give two examples of series that run from one end of the spectrum to the other through the different clusters I describe. For example, we can start with 'capitalism' as part of a cluster of five interrelated keywords that define our enemy and that includes 'imperialism', 'exploitation', 'commodity' and 'individualism'. Alongside these quite specific markers of malevolent characteristics of capitalism we have other terms that define how we understand 'feudalism', 'reaction', 'fascism', 'oppression' and 'colonialism'. In left discourse this second cluster of five keywords comes to be understood as a set of equivalent terms expressing dangers inherent in capitalism.

From 'capitalism' we can trace a fairly direct line from that negative end of the spectrum to the 'bourgeoisie' as the capitalist class, as a reactionary force which facilitates, in some way or another, the continuation of capitalism. The bourgeoisie is one of a cluster of keywords that define such reactionary forces, and so alongside bourgeoisie we can include 'reification', 'utopianism', 'Fabianism' (a theoretical frame used by social democrats to justify why we shouldn't move things along too fast) and 'Stalinism'. Again, their meaning is closely bound up with capitalism as such, and then alongside them are terms that also indicate reactionary forces like 'nationalism', 'populism', 'pragmatism', 'anarchism' and 'ideology'. Just as we can trace a direct line from 'capitalism' to the 'bourgeoisie' as structural enemy and force that expresses and benefits from capitalism, so we can trace a fairly direct line in some other keywords among the clusters of associated terms, from 'colonialism' to 'nationalism', for example. This is the second of the two kinds of spectrum that organises the keywords into something which is much more like a grid than the clusters in Williams' list that organise political-cultural debate in the previous fifty years.

We then notice two clusters of more ambiguous keywords, those which are less immediately progressive or reactionary, those that mobilise political battles to define them as part of the enemy or as what we must include in socialist struggle. A first cluster of ambiguous terms here may include 'democracy'; the struggle to define and redefine it is quite directly linked to its place in relation to 'capitalism' and the 'bourgeoisie', it slots neatly into a series with those two terms. That is, it slots into the spectrum I began to map out. But alongside 'democracy' we find 'reform', 'science', 'entrism' and 'feminism' which cannot each be easily mapped across either to what we want to avoid or what we want to aim for. Similarly, in the second cluster of five terms 'Maoism' can be linked in a series with 'colonialism' and 'nationalism', but the other four keywords that cluster with it – 'socialism', 'humanism', 'syndicalism' (a reliance on trades union organisation alone for social change) and 'Castroism' – do not each directly flow in a series from other specific negative terms.

Progressive terms that are directly related to the nature of capitalism and that mark out forces that will enable us to overthrow it include this cluster of five terms: 'proletariat', 'class', 'industrialisation', 'Leninism' and 'Trotskyism'. 'Proletariat' here stands most directly in a sequence leading from 'capitalism' to 'bourgeoisie' to 'democracy', and functions as agent of change which will then facilitate 'collectivism' as part of a cluster of terms that define where we are heading. That next cluster will include 'planning', 'soviet', 'Marxism' and 'Bolshevik'. Alongside the cluster of terms concerned with agency we also find 'party', 'revolution', 'theory', 'dialectic' and 'internationalism', the last one of which, 'internationalism', continues the series that runs on a spectrum from 'colonialism' to 'nationalism' to 'Maoism', and then, beyond 'internationalism', and following that logic toward something even more progressive, we arrive at 'liberation'. This 'liberation' clusters with substantive end points we aim for that include 'communism', 'materialism', 'progress' and 'practice'.

This clustering of terms, the categorising of them as directly associated with critique and overthrow of capitalism or as running alongside that immediate aim, and the linking across the clusters of some other keywords that seem to run in a sequence draws attention to the language we still use today on the left. There have been long-running disputes over where some of these terms stand, whether 'feminism' is reactionary or progressive, for example, but the clusters of terms together set a frame in which those who enter left politics know roughly what is being referred to when they hear their own comrades or members of rival organisations use them.

This clustering, categorising and linking does, admittedly, look like an academic exercise, and that is itself part of the point of this argument as well. On the one hand, yes, it repeats and exaggerates a process by which left debate has become linked to academic forms of argument, but when you look at this grid you can actually see a little more clearly how the terrain of debate is already organised in academic terms. This is part of the problem, one of the elements of the crisis of the left we need to take seriously. Our language of struggle has been tied to academic discourse. This is one of the legacies of the map of keywords we inherited from the fifty years of struggle against capitalism after 1917. Even for those who have never been part of university institutions, the networks of terms they have learnt to use as they navigate internal discussion bulletins of organisations they belong to, or position papers and motions that emanate from one of these organisations, function as systems of academic as well as activist keywords. They together define the culture of the left, in the meanings they carry and in the network of relationships that lock them together.

That culture of the left through these last fifty years of our revolutionary century is changing rapidly, and new keywords have forced themselves into the awareness of the left. These new keywords redefine the world, reflecting changes that have taken place in the world itself. The left organisations still debating and intervening within the clusters of keywords they have inherited from the first fifty years of world revolution with 1917 as their anchor point have, to varying degrees, resisted some of the new keywords, sometimes violently so. But these new revolutionary keywords to which I now turn are crucial to defining how we understand power and knowledge today, and how we act in and against it.

Revolutionary keywords now

The last fifty years have seen repeated reference to 'crises' in the field of the social sciences. For those of us who are Marxists this should not be a surprise. These 'crises' in the academic realm may be viewed as mere political reflections at the level of super-structure of enduring economic crises which are endemic to capitalism. But there is an even deeper connection between these political crises and economic crises. That is, the left itself has been undergoing crisis after crisis at the level of organisation. These crises were anticipated in the first revolts against the Soviet regime after 1917, revolts in which anarchism and the 'left opposition' led by those who came to define themselves as 'Trotskyists' played a major role. And, after the Stalinist repression and show trials in the 1930s we saw these crises of left organisation – a crisis of the bureaucracy itself – repeated, for example, in the uprisings of the East German workers in 1953, in Hungary in 1956 and then in the Prague Spring which actually began in 1967 before coming to fruition before it was crushed a year later. Revolts inside and against the Soviet bureaucracy also gave a particular character to the anti-colonial and anti-capitalist movements in Eastern Europe, in China and in Cuba.

Those crises of organisation were then also repeated inside each of the parties that defined themselves against Stalinism, inside the Trotskyist organisations, for example, that claimed but failed for many years to disentangle 'democracy' from 'centralism'. These organisations often remained trapped in what they saw as a 'democratic centralist' vision of the 'Leninist' party which enabled the leadership to hold on to power. But then, very soon after 1967, the crises deepened, and it is here that we see a challenge to the dominance of a particular way of defining what revolution itself is. Sometimes this challenge included attempts to redefine Marxism as something that had from 1917 tended to treat it as something distinctively European, a real problem for us internationalists, and sometimes the challenge demanded attempts to redefine the revolutionary tradition as having to include feminism alongside Marxism.

The lesbian, gay and then bisexual and transgender movements, and, later, the emergence of ecological politics on the left also impacted on the revolutionary parties. As with Black and feminist politics, these new movements spoke of struggles that had first been developing outside Marxism but they then progressively redefined how we interpreted and sought to change the world. Some left groups have responded to those challenges, and some networks by virtue of their transnational character have enabled a transfer of ideas from one local context to another, speeding up the process by which revolutionary politics may be re-energised by, rather than simply stubbornly resisting, these new movements.

These were also crises of political perspectives that were disrupting the grid of socialist and 'social scientific' under-standing. Many of the new revolutionary keywords that have appeared since 1967 have, on the one hand, been possible because there have been radical sites for theoretical work inside the academy, and, on the other hand, they have had an impact on the left because some of the academics that have been working with the new concepts have also insisted on linking them with practice. The boundaries between the inside and outside of the university have, at some moments and for some kinds of politics, solidified. That solidification has, it is true, had the effect of privileging academic modes of argument over immediate political strategy. Theory, which was always crucial for those of us wanting to understand the workings of power, did undoubtedly become part of the problem when this theory became abstracted and reified, became a tool for mystification and exclusion rather than a weapon in the hands of the exploited and oppressed. But, at the same time, new generations of left and feminist and anti-racist activists have also used the university as a resource and dissolved some of the boundaries between the inside and the outside of the classroom. It is that dissolving of the boundaries that has also helped to disturb the grid of keywords that developed in the fifty years after 1917. These new revolutionary keywords disturb the academic grid that held the vocabulary of socialist politics in place after 1917 and then well beyond 1967.

These new clusters of keywords are beginning to create a new vocabulary for the left, but they also have the effect of shifting focus so that 'crisis' is no longer seen as something external to us, happening only in the domain of the economic, and no longer concerning only the political 'crisis of revolutionary leadership' (which is often a magical formula for Trotskyist groups). The very notion of leadership and of traditional organisational forms of left politics is also thrown into question. These keywords operate alongside but then transform our understanding of the keywords we inherit from our traditions of struggle from before and relayed through the often-repeated 'lessons' of 1917. They were gathered during a continuing project which notices words being used, and we test out how they work in practice, usually in domains of political analysis that are connected but slightly to the edge of the main topic. That is, the research question in this process of accumulating the keywords in this book was whether they were able to draw attention to something different that the old socialist vocabulary does not address. Many of these keywords come from the intersection of Black and feminist activism, or from other political struggles that had already been impacted by those forms of theoretical practice. I will group the fifty new revolutionary keywords into ten clusters. This is a first sketch of the list, in *Figure 3: Keywords after 1967*. This is, of course, work in progress.

```
Discourse
Agency                Realism
Subjectivity          Precarity
Identity              Recuperation                              Performativity
Multitude             Feminisation                             Standpoint
                      Ecosocialism                             Refusal
                                       Antagonism              Occupy
                                       Event                   Postmodernism
                                       Identification
                                       Queer
                      Islamophobia     Cis
                      Homonationalism
Globalisation         Young-Girl
Spirituality          Wages                                    Pabloism
Fascism               Psychologisation                         Campism
Stalinism                                                      Prefigurative
Zionism                                Transition             Structurelessness
                                       Appropriation          Intersectionality
                      Normalcy         Otherness
                      Trans            Psychoanalysis
Neoliberalism         Whiteness        Eurocommunism
Empire                Justice
Postcolonial          Animals
Accelerationism
Academicisation
```

Figure 3: Keywords after 1967

First there are general questions about the nature of emancipation that force a questioning and updating of traditional Marxist politics. These questions are marked by keywords that will be familiar from traditional left discourse, but are themselves being redefined; they include 'discourse', a term I have been using through this essay, 'agency', 'subjectivity', 'identity' and, more obviously a newcomer, 'multitude'. These keywords prompt a rethinking of an enduring historical process that we on the left have to address, and they also have an impact on the way more long-standing keywords from the 1917 to 1967 period of revolutionary politics are understood; those would be a second cluster of keywords like 'globalisation' and 'spirituality' as well as terms like 'fascism', 'Stalinism' and 'Zionism'.

Then there are keywords that are designed to grasp either the intensification of power under capitalism or, perhaps, deeper changes in the nature of capitalism itself. In the third cluster that deals with intensifications of power, that in some cases involve qualitative changes in the way that power operates, we find terms like 'neoliberalism', 'empire' and 'postcolonial' as well as 'accelerationism', and 'academicisation' as that which reflects on the place of these new terms in university and independent left discourse. In the fourth cluster are those which name some deeper issues such as 'realism', 'precarity' and 'recuperation' as well as 'feminisation' and 'ecosocialism'. It would be possible to place many of these terms on a dimension ranging from those that define problems and those that point to solutions, and so would help us feel at home in the old grid. However, many of them are conceptual markers of debates across the range, and they disturb rather than confirm traditional politics we have inherited from before 1967. They point to something entirely new, both in the shape of concepts and also in the language we use to try and link them together.

The next two clusters concern new phenomena, by which I mean either emerging ideological motifs that we need to take seriously or new dimensions of oppression that have been revealed to us. The distinctions between these two aspects, between ideological processes and underlying oppression, are not always clear cut. So, on the one hand we are faced with what we have learnt to name as 'Islamophobia', 'homonationalism' and the phenomenon of the 'young-girl', and there are the questions concerning 'wages' and 'psychologisation'. On the other hand we now notice better through new revolutionary keywords oppression around dimensions of 'normalcy', 'trans', 'whiteness', 'justice' and even the status of 'animals'.

Some of the new revolutionary keywords give us useful tools for analysis, and it is still an open question as to how they impact on Marxist politics. In some cases they can be drawn into that politics, and in other cases they cause problems for it; terms here in a seventh cluster include the notions of 'antagonism' and 'event', and those concerning 'identification', 'queer' and 'cis'. Then there are those terms that are tools for analysis that are also keywords in other movements inside and outside the academic world that we need at different points to connect with; those would include, in cluster eight, 'transition', 'appropriation' and 'otherness' as well as things that have still not been well handled yet by the left such as 'psychoanalysis' and 'Eurocommunism'.

The last two clusters, nine and ten, are practices that we need to learn from. Some are new practices and approaches to resistance, such as 'performativity', 'standpoint', 'refusal', 'occupy' and, an old favourite the left has already learned to love to hate, 'postmodernism'. Some concern issues that directly affect how we practice our organisational politics, and they would include familiar terms from the past of our tradition that have a new relevance today, such as 'Pabloism' and 'campism', and those from other traditions that will change the way we work, such as 'prefigurative', 'structurelessness' and 'intersectionality'. This 'intersectionality' is one term that, for sure, divides the old left from the new revolutionary left.

Paths and tasks

Most of these new revolutionary keywords that have emerged in the last fifty years of socialist politics are more fluid than the ones that were held together in the old fifty-year social-scientific grid that took shape after 1917. And, as well as being less substantial in themselves, as clusters they tend to desubstantialise our politics as such; that is, they trace questions of process rather than fixed substances, and they together shift attention from the nature of capitalism as a thing that can be easily defined into a set of relations. The politics they demand is also, as a consequence, concerned more with relations and relationships, something that has often tended to unnerve traditional left organisations.

I hope you will disagree with the terms I have chosen and marked as 'keywords' and with the way I have mapped them. I have not been able to argue in detail for each of them here or to show why they can be linked together in the clusters I have described. It would have been even more tedious to do that than it has been here. I suspect that in some cases you can guess why I have selected and grouped them as I have, and they express political choices that are bound up with the way I have sketched out the four aspects of crises. When you object, it may then be through wilful puzzlement which refuses to see history as I do, or perhaps it really does not make sense to you. I have not been as clear as I wished, but in some cases the issue of clarity is precisely part of the problem I am addressing here. Our different theoretical traditions of explanation and, more importantly, our different conceptions of socialist politics cut up the world in different ways. We cut it up in language and we use keywords in distinctive ways in order to do that.

These terms speak of a 'crisis' but they also perform it. They enact a crisis inside the left as it struggles to grasp what they point to and they work through what it means for the old categories of analysis and action. The task, however, is to work with these new revolutionary keywords not as abstract academic terms that can be defined and puzzled over one at a time. Rather, it is to notice how they are being put to work in political struggle, and to assess what effects they have. A trap which is set by the old grid of socialist and social-scientific politics is that we take for granted the relationship between the academic and the real world. Then we end up treating social-scientific description as the kind of alienated nonsense we would expect to be produced by academics separated from real political struggle. And then the risk is that we idealise what we think of as 'real' struggle as if it appears to us exactly as it is, and all the more so if we abandon theoretical frameworks that we imagine to be contaminating our understanding of that reality. The other side of the trap is that we feel so comfortable with the theory that we have taken on wholesale from academic description and use this second-hand knowledge to keep framing and reframing all the new terms that come our way. This is also what happens when left groups that imagine they have escaped academic discourse actually end up repeating it. Then their socialism is 'social-scientific'.

Instead, these new revolutionary keywords provoke a crisis of academic representation which also pits that academic discourse against itself, to turn it into theory useful for our practice. Now we need to learn how to use these keywords in order to under-stand how the world has changed and how we can work inside that process as an opportunity to change it for the better, and, at the same time challenge the power relations that hold its peculiar forms of exploitation and oppression in place. There are conse-quences of each of these keywords that are already being worked through in practice, that much is clear from the way they have been deployed in this book, but as they are linked together something even more radical happens that has consequences for each left organisation. The way the battles will be fought out in each group will vary; some groups more resistant or welcome to the challenges posed than others.

We have seen some groups and social movements on the left opening themselves to these ideas, but they need some encour-agement. They still need to be challenged to work these ideas into their own politics, and transform some of their own political assumptions and organisational practices in the process. It includes treating these new keywords as revolutionary resources rather than as obstacles to social change, opening their publica-tions to these ideas and linking to analyses that question the old ways of doing things. It includes, as practical steps, shifting from centralised decision-making to horizontal networks, respecting the autonomous organisation of the oppressed, and putting resources into enabling the youth in the organisation to effectively operate as the leadership, leadership of a different kind as well as different composition to the parent organisation.

Those internal battles will, as they have already begun to be, be intimately connected with a re-energising of the whole of the left as inclusive anti-racist, feminist and ecological, and as embracing a host of other contradictory struggles against exploitation and oppression. The tradition, the memory, the organisation of the left is necessary to this process, but it has to learn what it takes today to be really revolutionary, to take on board these revolutionary keywords to build a new left.

Further Reading

These further readings, with web-link suggestions to complement them, do not map one-to-one on to the keywords in this book. And some of these readings illustrate some problems with these debates rather than neat ways to resolve them. What is most important now in these texts is to explore further how the different ideas link with each other, and so many of these references span the different debates around each of the keywords. This reading list with the web-links is also available at: http://tinyurl.com/he8jwna

Achcar, G. (2006) *The Clash of Barbarisms: The Making of the New World Disorder*. Boulder: Paradigm Publishers; London: Saqi. [This detailed analysis of the so-called 'war on terror' shows how Western intervention constituted the Islamic fundamentalist organisations as both enemy and partner of imperialism to destroy the left. An interview with Gilbert Achcar about the themes in the book after the Paris massacre is here: http://www.democracynow.org/2015/1/9/gilbert_achcar_on_t he_clash_of]

Ahmed, S. (2010) *The Promise of Happiness*. Durham, NC: Duke University Press. [This book includes the classic essay 'Feminist Killjoys' by Sara Ahmed, a motif taken up by many other feminists as a critique of all the various forms of enjoyment that buttress power and violence against women. See also Ahmed's essay 'Walls of Whiteness' here: https://mediadiversified.org/2014/04/22/walls-of-whiteness/]

Anievas, A. and Nisancioglu, K. (2015) *How the West Came to Rule: The Geopolitical Origins of Capitalism*. London: Pluto Press. [This study shows how capitalism is grounded in territorial control which intimately links the fate of the 'West' with, in Walter Rodney's term, the 'underdevelopment' of the rest of the world. An interview with the authors about Eurocentrism is here: https://viewpointmag.com/2015/12/01/towards-a-radical-critique-of-eurocentrism-an-interview-with-alex ander-anievas-and-kerem-nisancioglu/]

Arruzza, C. (2013) *Dangerous Liaisons: The Marriages and Divorces of Marxism and Feminism*. London: Resistance Books. [This book provides a detailed overview of the range of different debates at the intersection of Marxism and feminism, including the impact of Black feminism and queer theory. The ideas in the book are explored further by Cinzia Arruzza here: http://www.internationalviewpoint.org/spip.php?article3718]

Bourne, J. (1987) 'Homelands of the mind: Jewish feminism and identity politics', *Race and Class* 29 (1): 1–24. [Jenny Bourne's article was a controversial intervention into identity politics that got a bad reception from some anti-Zionist Jewish feminists in the UK. The questions of identity and the way it is addressed as something 'intersectional' is explored in a different context in Sharon Smith's 2013 'Black feminism and intersectionality' here: http://isreview.org/issue/91/black-feminism-and-intersectionality]

Burstow, B. (2015) *Psychiatry and the Business of Madness: An Ethical and Epistemological Accounting*. London: Palgrave Macmillan. [This book is produced from years of radical feminist political activity in and alongside the psychiatry and disability movements, drawing on the voices of the oppressed to explore how the psychiatric apparatus appears from the standpoint of those subject to it. The arguments are linked with contemporary political struggle in *Asylum: The Magazine for Democratic Psychiatry* which can be accessed here: http://www.asylumonline.net/]

Butler, J. (1990) *Gender Trouble: Feminism and the Subversion of Identity*. London and New York: Routledge. [This is one of the classic grounding texts for what became known as 'queer theory' and, more importantly, of 'queer politics' in 'third-wave' feminism that was expressed in HIV/AIDS activist movements like ACT UP. The argument in the book is explored further here in relation to Islam and secularism in a 2009 text *Is Critique Secular?* by Talal Asad, Wendy Brown, Judith Butler and Saba Mahmood: http://escholarship.org/uc/item/84q9c6ft]

Chen, K. (2010) *Asia as Method: Toward Deimperialization*. Durham, NC: Duke University Press. [This book provides a 'standpoint' argument of a quite different type, grounding the political resistance to imperialism in Asia on the terrain of intersecting histories of China, Japan, Korea and Taiwan. The global context is also addressed in relation to Western feminism and imperialism here: https://www.opendemocracy.net/deepa-kumar/imperialist-feminism-and-liberalism]

Combahee River Collective (1977) 'History is a Weapon'. [This document was written as one of the founding texts of Black feminism, making a strong standpoint argument for autonomous collective organisation. The text is available here: http://historyisaweapon.com/defcon1/combrivercoll.html]

Davis, A. (1981) *Women, Race and Class*. London: Women's Press. [Angela Davis, once a member of the Communist Party of the United States of America, and campaigner against the 'Prison-Industrial Complex', works at the intersection of different forms of exploitation and oppression in this book; Chapter 13 of her book, on 'Women, Race and Class: The Approaching Obsolescence of Housework: A Working-Class Perspective', is available here: http://www.marxists.org/subject/women/auth ors/davis-angela/housework.htm]

Debord, G. (1967) *Society of the Spectacle*. Detroit: Black and Red. [Guy Debord, the leader and master of the 'Situationists', provides a polemical analysis drawing on Hegel and Marx of the way that radical action is 'recuperated'. There is an illus-trated guide of his argument here: http://hyperallergic.com /313435/an-illustrated-guide-to-guy-debords-the-society-of-the-spectacle/]

Ebert, T. (2009) *The Task of Cultural Critique*. Champaign, IL: University of Illinois Press. [Teresa Ebert takes on a number of different cultural theorists, including Slavoj Žižek, from a feminist and Marxist standpoint; her 1995 essay '(Untimely) Critiques for a Red Feminism' is available here: https://www.marxists.org/reference/subject/philosophy/works/us/ebert.htm]

Fanon, F. (1967) *The Wretched of the Earth*. Harmondsworth: Penguin. [Fanon's book, which was published in France with an incendiary introduction by Jean-Paul Sartre and promptly banned, is a classic of anti-colonial and postcolonial writing. It is work that needs to be taken forward with feminist critique, with one attempt here: http://postcolonialist.com/culture/reading-mis-reading-frantz-fanon/]

Federici, S. (2004) *Caliban and the Witch: Women, the Body and Primitive Accumulation*. New York: Autonomedia. [Silvia Federici writes in the Italian autonomist tradition that takes that Marxist politics in a more explicitly feminist direction than, for example, Antonio Negri. There is an interview with her here: http://endofcapitalism.com/2013/05/29/a-feminist-critique-of-marx-by-silvia-federici/]

Firestone, S. (2015) *The Dialectic of Sex: The Case for Feminist Revolution*. London: Verso. [Shulamith Firestone was one of the inspirations for a 'radical feminist' strand of 'second-wave' feminism; the first chapter of her book 'The Dialectic of Sex', which was originally published in 1970, is available here: http://www.marxists.org/subject/women/authors/firestone-shulamith/dialectic-sex.htm]

Fisher, M. (2009) *Capitalist Realism: Is there no alternative?* London: Zero Books. [Mark Fisher's book addresses the way that neo-liberal capitalism today presents itself as normal and natural; it is an analysis that can be situated in relation to 'new materialist' feminist theory articulated by Karen Barad which precisely aims to show how what is normal and natural is constituted as such; she outlines this argument here: http://quod.lib.umich.edu/o/ohp/11515701.0001.001/1:4.3/—new-materialism-interviews-cartographies?rgn=div2; view=fulltext]

Foucault, M. (1981) *The History of Sexuality, Vol. 1: An Introduction.* Harmondsworth: Pelican. [First published in 1976, Michel Foucault's *History of Sexuality* was intended to be the first volume of a six-volume study that could eventually, perhaps, have addressed feminism. There have been claims that Foucault himself named neoliberalism and then became rather fond of it, a claim rehearsed here: https://www.jacob inmag.com/2014/12/foucault-interview/]

Fraser, N. (2013) *Fortunes of Feminism: From State-Managed Capitalism to Neoliberal Crisis.* London: Verso. [Nancy Fraser is quite clear that she is still a feminist, despite the attempts to misrepresent her as arguing that feminism as such has failed because it has been recuperated under neoliberalism, and she makes her feminist commitment clear in her 2014 article 'How feminism became capitalism's handmaiden – and how to reclaim it' available here: http://www.theguardian.com/comm entisfree/2013/oct/14/feminism-capitalist-handmaiden-neoliberal]

Freeman, J. (1970) *The Tyranny of Structurelessness*, http://www.bopsecrets.org/CF/structurelessness.htm. [Jo Freeman specifically addressed contexts in which some 'consciousness-raising' groups claimed to have dispensed with power, and her arguments are complemented and critiqued in Cathy Levine's response 'The tyranny of tyranny' which is available here: http://libcom.org/library/tyranny-of-tyranny-cathy-levine]

Greenstein, A. (2015) *Inclusive Radical Pedagogy: An Interdisciplinary Approach to Education, Disability and Liberation.* Abingdon/New York: Routledge. [Anat Greenstein links the development of critique and practice around what is called in the United States 'normalcy' with questions of education and liberation; further attempts to link disability activism with feminism have been made here: http://disabilityintersect ions.com/2014/03/why-feminist-disability-studies/]

Guerin, D. (1973) *Fascism and Big Business*. New York: Monad Press. [Daniel Guerin's analysis of the rise of fascism, first published in 1939, focuses on the way that, despite the claims to be anti-corporate, fascism arises as a strategy of last resort for the bourgeoisie to destroy capitalism; an extract from Guerin's book is available here: https://www.marxists.org/hist ory/etol/writers/guerin/1938/10/fascism.htm]

Haraway, DJ (1989) *Primate Visions: Gender, Race, and Nature in the World of Modern Science*. London and New York: Routledge. [This important book by Donna Haraway locates feminism clearly in relation to the exploitation of animals and the destruction of nature; Haraway's 'cyborg manifesto', which takes the analysis in the direction of the relationship between women and technology, is available here: https://www.stump-tuous.com/comps/cyborg.html]

Hardt, M. and Negri, A. (2000) *Empire*. Cambridge, MA: Harvard University Press. [Michael Hardt and Antonio Negri, a key figure in the Italian autonomist tradition, provide an analysis of capitalism as intrinsically global, and the book, which was followed by *Multitude* in 2004 and *Commonwealth* in 2009, became important in the 'Occupy' movement. As well as taking distance from Marxist analyses of imperialism, it also had little to say about feminism, which is reasserted here in the argument for Wages for Housework by Selma James: http://www.globalwomenstrike.net/content/selma-james-and-wages-housework-campaign]

Henley, N. (1979) *Body Politics: Power, Sex, and Nonverbal Communication*. Englewood Cliffs, NJ: Prentice-Hall. [Nancy Henley shows how women are expected to take up less space than men, both in big public spaces and in more intimate settings, and to have a different relation to time; it is an analysis that provides some context for the changes in production analysed in Alex Williams and Nick Srnicek's 2013 '#Accelerate manifesto', available here: http://criticallegal-thinking.com/2013/05/14/accelerate-manifesto-for-an-acceler-ationist-politics/]

Hochschild, AR (1983) *The Managed Heart: Commercialisation of Human Feeling*. Berkeley, CA: University of California Press. [The US American feminist sociologist Arlie Hochschild shows how women's stereotypical capacities for 'care' become instrumentalised under capitalism with the rise of 'feminisation' of industry in the service sector, which is something Silvia Federici addresses in her 2010 article 'Wages Against Housework' available here: https://caringlabor.wordpress.com/2010/09/15/silvia-federici-wages-against-housework/]

Kelly, J. (1992) 'Postmodernism and Feminism', *International Marxist Review*, 14, pp. 39–55. [Jane Kelly's feminist critique of postmodernism homes in on the 'theories of difference' that run through a range of different 'postmodernist' approaches to language; the article, which was written before many feminists reworked these theories for themselves, is available here: http://www.internationalviewpoint.org/spip.php?article2737]

Klein, N. (2008) *The Shock Doctrine: The Rise of Disaster Capitalism*. Harmondsworth: Penguin. [Naomi Klein has combined scholarly analysis with socialist, feminist and environmental activism in a number of books, including in this one on the way that capitalism requires the systematic destruction of human resources in order to rebuild itself and stimulate profit; raw materials for the book are available here: http://www.naomiklein.org/shock-doctrine]

Knight, C. (2016) *Decoding Chomsky: Science and Revolutionary Politics*. New Haven, CT: Yale University Press. [Chris Knight shows how the deep split between Chomsky's academic work on linguistics and his political commitment actually has dire consequences for both aspects; an earlier journal article version of the argument in Knight's book is available here: http://www.chrisknight.co.uk/decoding-chomsky/]

Kollontai, A. (1977) *Selected Writings of Alexandra Kollontai*. New York: Norton. [Alexandra Kollontai, one of the most radical of the 'first-wave' feminists, was one of the Bolshevik leaders who put energy into the abolition of the family and the recon-figuration of personal relationships in the Soviet Union; an essay reclaiming Kollontai for contemporary Marxist feminism by Teresa Ebert is available here: https://www.solidarity-us.org/node/1724]

Kovel, J. (2007) *The Enemy of Nature: The End of Capitalism or the End of the World? (2nd Revised edn)*. London: Zed Books. [Joel Kovel's argument for 'ecosocialism' is grounded in a detailed description of the way that capitalism in a variety of different contexts must devote itself to the destruction of nature; the question which is touched on in the book, and which needs more work, is how ecosocialism connects with ecofeminism, a question addressed here: http://www.internationalview-point.org/spip.php?article2407]

Laclau, E. and Mouffe, C. (1985) *Hegemony and Socialist Strategy: Towards a Radical Democratic Politics*. London: Verso. [Ernesto Laclau and Chantal Mouffe were, with Stuart Hall in Britain, driving forces in theory of what was known at the time as 'Eurocommunism', and they both now provide resources for new social movements like Podemos. They link ideas from linguistics and Lacan's psychoanalysis with the work of the Italian Marxist Antonio Gramsci, whose prison writings are available here: https://www.marxists.org/archive/gramsci/prison_notebooks/]

Leon A. (1950) *The Jewish Question: A Marxist Interpretation*. New York: Pathfinder Press. [Abram Leon was a Trotskyist murdered by the Nazis, and his book was published posthumously on the prompting of the Belgian economist and secretary of the Fourth International Ernest Mandel; one of Mandel's own texts on 'the Jewish question' is available here: https://www.marxists.org/archive/mandel/1946/07/jews.htm]

Lorde, A. (1984) *Sister Outsider: Essays and Speeches*. Berkeley, CA: Crossing Press. [This book by US American Black socialist lesbian feminist Audre Lorde includes the 1977 essay 'The Transformation of Silence into Language and Action' which is also available online here: https://shrinkingphallus.word press.com/the-transformation-of-silence-into-language-and-action-by-audre-lorde/]

Löwy, M. (2010) *Morning Star: Surrealism, Marxism, Anarchism, Situationism, Utopia*. Dallas, TX: University of Texas. [Michel Löwy's book provides a passionate description and defence of the variety of different challenges to orthodox Marxism from within the surrealist movement. It takes forward the arguments made by Trotsky in a document signed by André Breton and Diego Rivera in their 1938 'Manifesto for an Independent Revolutionary Art' which is here: https:// www.marxists.org/subject/art/lit_crit/works/rivera/manifesto. htm]

Millett, K. (1977) *Sexual Politics*. London: Virago. [Kate Millet was one of the key figures in 'second-wave' feminism, arguing in this book for a radical feminist critique of dominant cultural resources which buttress patriarchy, which she defines as the domination of women by men and of younger men by older men; the second chapter of Millett's book is available here: https://www.marxists.org/subject/women/authors/millett-kate/theory.htm]

Mitchell, J. (1974) *Psychoanalysis and Feminism*. Harmondsworth: Penguin. [This classic text re-examined the hostility of some feminists to psychoanalysis, and argued that the shift from biology to language in the work of Jacques Lacan opened the way to thinking about transformation of society instead of adaptation to it, a line explored in this online volume edited by Carol Owens: https://discourseunit.com/annual-review/7-2009/]

Mojab, S. (ed.) (2015) *Marxism and Feminism*. London: Zed Books. [This edited book includes chapters on intersectionality and standpoint and on other key issues that span the different keywords in this present book; a short introduction to connections between Marxism and feminism and a list of more resources is available here: http://www.feministezine.com /feminist/philosophy/Introduction-to-Marxist-Femin ism.html]

Nayak, S. (2014) *Race, Gender and the Activism of Black Feminist Theory: Working with Audre Lorde*. Abingdon/New York: Routledge. [This study is devoted to the work of Audre Lorde and to the connection between her theoretical writings and contemporary Black feminist political practice: Audre Lorde's 1980 text 'Age, Race, Class and Sex: Women Redefining Difference' is available here: www.clc.wvu.edu/r/down load/29781]

Puar, J. (2007) *Terrorist Assemblages: Homonationalism in Queer Times*. Durham, NC: Duke University Press. [Jasbir Puar shows how gay culture becomes harnessed to capitalist state practices and to imperialism as a segregated niche category of identity that then functions ideologically; the ideas are explored in the specific context of Islamophobia and Zionism here: http://www.nopinkwashing.org.uk/background-read ing/]

Raymond, J. (1980) *The Transsexual Empire*. London: The Women's Press. [Janice Raymond's book gives a clear and polemical account of the radical feminist objection to 'trans', the way that gender binaries risk being reinforced as particular bodies transition from one gender to the other; some problems in Raymond's account are outlined in Jacqueline Rose's 2016 essay 'Who do you think you are?' here: http://www.lrb.co.uk/v38/n09/jacqueline-rose/who-do-you-think-you-are]

Reed, E. (1975) *Women's Evolution: From Matriarchal Clan to Patriarchal Family*. New York: Pathfinder Press. [This book takes forward Engels' anthropological claims in his classic 1884 text 'The Origin of the Family, Private Property, and the State'. The specific consequences for an analysis of women's oppression are spelled out in Evelyn Reed's 1970 article 'Women: Caste, Class or Oppressed Sex' available here: http://www.marxists.org/archive/reed-evelyn/1970/caste-class-sex.htm]

Rowbotham, S., Segal, L. and Wainwright, H. (2013) *Beyond the Fragments: Feminism and the Making of Socialism (3rd Edn)*. Pontypool, Wales: Merlin. [The first edition of 'Beyond the Fragments' was published as a pamphlet in 1979, bringing together feminist activists from three different far-left groups in Britain; reflections by Johanna Brenner on this third edition, published during a time of crisis in the British left over questions of sexual violence, are available here: http://www.internationalviewpoint.org/spip.php?article4162]

Said, E. (2003) *Orientalism: Western Conceptions of the Orient*. Harmondsworth: Penguin. [First published in 1978, Edward Said's book on 'orientalism' took up work by Michel Foucault and focused on the production and functions of representations of the exoticised and feared 'other'; Said opened the way to further analysis of orientalism and feminisation, explored here: http://www.europe-solidaire.org/spip.php?article27016]

Spender, D. (1980) *Man Made Language*. London: Routledge & Kegan Paul. [Dale Spender shows how the English language is skewed against women to render them as less than human, and this provides a feminist context to the argument Jean-François Lyotard made about 'language games' as defining interaction in his 1979 book *The Postmodern Condition*; the introduction to the English translation of Lyotard's book by

Fredric Jameson links postmodernism with Mandel's diagnosis of 'late capitalism', and is available here: https://www.marxists.org/reference/subject/philosophy/works/us/jameson.htm]

Spivak, GC (1990) *The Post-Colonial Critic*. London and New York: Routledge. [Gayatri Chakravorty Spivak translated and introduced writings of Jacques Derrida into English, reframing 'deconstruction' as something compatible with Marxism and feminism; her argument about a tactical use of identity categories in the notion of 'strategic essentialism' is explored here: http://www.dawn.com/news/1152482]

Tiqqun (2012) *Preliminary Materials For a Theory of the Young-Girl*. Los Angeles: Semiotext(e). [The Tiqqun collective provide a diagnosis of the way feminised imagery functions ideologically, but also tend to repeat this imagery in their own critique, as is made clear in this critical appraisal and review of their work: https://www.radicalphilosophy.com/reviews/individual-reviews/rp177-shes-just-not-that-into-you]

Trotsky, LD (1938) *The Death Agony of Capitalism and the Tasks of the Fourth International*, https://www.marxists.org/archive/trotsky/1938/tp/ [This document, written as a founding text for the Fourth International, is usually known as the 'Transitional Programme', and the updating of 'transitional demands' for the present day has often been debated, as in this example linking it with ecological questions: http://www.socialist.net/a-transitional-programme-for-the-environment.htm]

Tuhiwai Smith, L. (1999) *Decolonizing Methodologies: Research and Indigenous Peoples*. London: Zed Books. [This is an academic book for researchers that brings them out of their comfort zone and insists that any radical research worth the name must be rooted in the experiences and forms of knowledge of the oppressed. The ideas are worked through in the open-access online journal *Disability and the Global South* which can be accessed here: https://dgsjournal.org/]

Wilkinson, R. and Pickett, K. (2010) *The Spirit Level: Why Equality is Better for Everyone*. Harmondsworth: Penguin. [This book, with the argument that gross inequalities lead to greater unhappiness, has been influential on new generations of community and environmental activists, and the link with 'gender equality' has also been taken up by feminists like Carol Gilligan: http://www.port-magazine.com/commentary/the-world-after-men-carol-gilligan/]

Williams, R. (1976) *Keywords: A Vocabulary of Culture and Society*. London: Fontana. [Raymond Williams aimed to provide an overview of the keywords that have come to make up contemporary progressive culture, but although Williams himself was a 'cultural Marxist', he rather overlooked feminism and other new social movements; the analysis needs to also address a range of other links to radical critique, as it is here: https://www.vocabulary.com/lists/40460]

Zero Books
CULTURE, SOCIETY & POLITICS

Contemporary culture has eliminated the concept and public figure of the intellectual. A cretinous anti-intellectualism presides, cheer-led by hacks in the pay of multinational corporations who reassure their bored readers that there is no need to rouse themselves from their stupor. Zer0 Books knows that another kind of discourse - intellectual without being academic, popular without being populist - is not only possible: it is already flourishing. Zer0 is convinced that in the unthinking, blandly consensual culture in which we live, critical and engaged theoretical reflection is more important than ever before.

If you have enjoyed this book, why not tell other readers by posting a review on your preferred book site.

Malign Velocities
Accelerationism and Capitalism
Benjamin Noys
Longlisted for the Bread and Roses Prize 2015, *Malign Velocities*
argues against the need for speed, tracking acceleration as the
symptom of the ongoing crises of capitalism.
Paperback: 978-1-78279-300-7 ebook: 978-1-78279-299-4

Meat Market
Female flesh under Capitalism
Laurie Penny
A feminist dissection of women's bodies as the fleshy fulcrum of
capitalist cannibalism, whereby women are both consumers and
consumed.
Paperback: 978-1-84694-521-2 ebook: 978-1-84694-782-7

Poor but Sexy
Culture Clashes in Europe East and West
Agata Pyzik
How the East stayed East and the West stayed West.
Paperback: 978-1-78099-394-2 ebook: 978-1-78099-395-9

Romeo and Juliet in Palestine
Teaching Under Occupation
Tom Sperlinger
Life in the West Bank, the nature of pedagogy and the role of a
university under occupation.
Paperback: 978-1-78279-637-4 ebook: 978-1-78279-636-7

Sweetening the Pill
or How We Got Hooked on Hormonal Birth Control
Holly Grigg-Spall
Has contraception liberated or oppressed women? *Sweetening the Pill* breaks the silence on the dark side of hormonal contraception.
Paperback: 978-1-78099-607-3 ebook: 978-1-78099-608-0

Why Are We The Good Guys?
Reclaiming Your Mind from the Delusions of Propaganda
David Cromwell
A provocative challenge to the standard ideology that Western power is a benevolent force in the world.
Paperback: 978-1-78099-365-2 ebook: 978-1-78099-366-9

Readers of ebooks can buy or view any of these bestsellers by clicking on the live link in the title. Most titles are published in paperback and as an ebook. Paperbacks are available in traditional bookshops. Both print and ebook formats are available online.

Find more titles and sign up to our readers' newsletter at
http://www.johnhuntpublishing.com/culture-and-politics
Follow us on Facebook at https://www.facebook.com/ZeroBooks
and Twitter at https://twitter.com/Zer0Books